CLIFFS

Computer-Adaptive

Graduate Management

Admission Test

PREPARATION GUIDE

Jerry Bobrow, Ph.D.

CONTRIBUTING AUTHORS
William A. Covino, Ph.D.
Peter Z Orton, Ph.D.
Harold Nathan, Ph.D.
David A. Kay, M.S.
Dale Johnson, M.A.

INCORPORATED
LINCOLN, NEBRASKA 68501

I would like to thank Michele Spence of Cliffs Notes for final editing and careful attention to the production process and Dr. Albert Upton for the use of excerpts from his outstanding book Design for Thinking. *I would also like to thank my wife, Susan, daughter, Jennifer, and sons, Adam and Jonathan, for their patience, moral support, and comic relief.*

JERRY BOBROW

ISBN 0-8220-2062-9

SEVENTH EDITION

Contents

Part III: Full-Length GMAT CAT Practice Test

Preface

Many students are needlessly afraid of the computer-adaptive GMAT. Although the delivery system and format are different from those of the paper-and-pencil test, the types of questions are still the same. So don't be concerned about the computer-adaptive GMAT; be prepared.

Better scores result from thorough preparation. Because this new-format exam adapts to your ability level, you must use your study time more effectively than ever before to get that thorough preparation and raise that level. You need the most comprehensive test preparation guide that you can realistically complete in a reasonable time. It must be complete, direct, precise, and easy to use, giving you all the information you need to do your best on the computer-adaptive GMAT.

In keeping with the fine tradition of Cliffs Notes, this guide was developed by leading experts in the field of test preparation as a part of a series to specifically meet these standards. The testing strategies, techniques, and materials have been researched, tested, and evaluated and are presently used at GMAT CAT preparation programs at many leading colleges and universities. This guide features the Bobrow Test Preparation Services approach, which focuses on a careful **analysis of each exam area** followed by **strategies, techniques,** and **practice problems** categorized by level of difficulty to help you maximize your score. Taking, reviewing, charting, and analyzing a specially designed **simulation computer-adaptive type GMAT** will give you **invaluable insight** into the GMAT CAT as well as outstanding testing practice. All test and practice problems have answers and complete explanations.

Special introductory sections, including an **overview of the computerized test-taking process** and a **Patterned Plan of Attack** for each type of question, are also included.

This guide was written to give you the edge in doing your best by maximizing your effort in a minimum amount of time. If you take the time to follow the **Study Guide Checklist** in this book, you will get the best preparation possible.

Study Guide Checklist

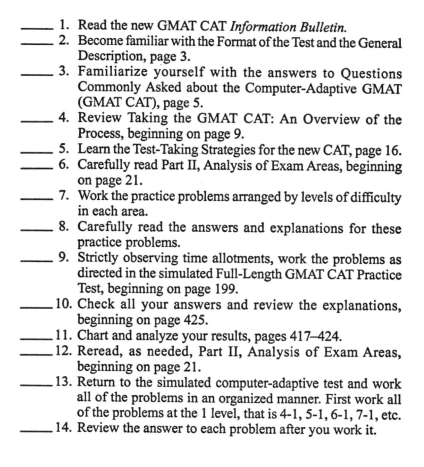

_____ 1. Read the new GMAT CAT *Information Bulletin*.

_____ 2. Become familiar with the Format of the Test and the General Description, page 3.

_____ 3. Familiarize yourself with the answers to Questions Commonly Asked about the Computer-Adaptive GMAT (GMAT CAT), page 5.

_____ 4. Review Taking the GMAT CAT: An Overview of the Process, beginning on page 9.

_____ 5. Learn the Test-Taking Strategies for the new CAT, page 16.

_____ 6. Carefully read Part II, Analysis of Exam Areas, beginning on page 21.

_____ 7. Work the practice problems arranged by levels of difficulty in each area.

_____ 8. Carefully read the answers and explanations for these practice problems.

_____ 9. Strictly observing time allotments, work the problems as directed in the simulated Full-Length GMAT CAT Practice Test, beginning on page 199.

_____ 10. Check all your answers and review the explanations, beginning on page 425.

_____ 11. Chart and analyze your results, pages 417–424.

_____ 12. Reread, as needed, Part II, Analysis of Exam Areas, beginning on page 21.

_____ 13. Return to the simulated computer-adaptive test and work all of the problems in an organized manner. First work all of the problems at the 1 level, that is 4-1, 5-1, 6-1, 7-1, etc.

_____ 14. Review the answer to each problem after you work it.

_____ 15. After attempting and reviewing the simpler problems, work all of the level 2 problems, that is 4-2, 5-2, 6-2, 7-2, etc.

_____ 16. Review the answer to each problem after you work it.

_____ 17. In the same manner, work and review the answers to the level 3 problems, then the level 4 problems, and then the level 5 problems.

_____ 18. Carefully reread Part II, Analysis of Exam Areas, beginning on page 21.

_____ 19. Review Taking the GMAT CAT: An Overview of the Process, beginning on page 9.

_____ 20. Go over Final Preparations on page 482.

PART I

Introduction

Introduction to the GMAT CAT
The Computer-Adaptive Graduate
Management Admission Test

FORMAT OF THE TEST

Test	Minutes	Number of Questions
Analytical Writing Assessment		
(not adaptive, but typed-in responses)		
Analysis of an Issue	30	1
Analysis of an Argument	30	1
(optional five-minute break)		
Quantitative Section (computer adaptive)	75	37
Problem Solving and Data Sufficiency questions are intermingled		
(optional five-minute break)		
Verbal Section (computer adaptive)	75	41
Sentence Correction, Reading Comprehension, and Critical Reasoning questions are intermingled		

Tutorials for simple word processing for the Analytical Writing Assessment and for quantitative and verbal sections will be available for review before test sections are administered.

Note: Format and scoring are subject to change.

GENERAL DESCRIPTION

The new GMAT CAT lasts approximately three and a half hours and is composed of two 30-minute analytical writing responses, a 75-minute (37 multiple-choice questions) quantitative section, and a 75-minute (41 multiple-choice questions) verbal section. The analytical writing responses are scored from 0 to 6, while the multiple-choice questions are scored from 200 to 800, with an average score of about 480. Two subscores are also generated: quantitative, scored 0 to 60 (average score approximately 28), and verbal, scored 0 to 60 (average score approximately 27).

The test is composed of the following sections:

Analytical Writing Assessment. You will type two essays (responses) on topics provided. One response will be an analysis of an issue, and the other will be an analysis of an argument.

Quantitative. (Data Sufficiency and Problem Solving questions are intermingled.)

Data Sufficiency—For each item you will decide how much of the mathematical data you are given is sufficient for answering a question.

Problem Solving—You will solve general math and word-type problems.

Verbal. (Sentence Correction, Reading Comprehension, and Critical Reasoning questions are intermingled.)

Sentence Correction—You will demonstrate your knowledge of correct and effective English expression.

Reading Comprehension—You will answer questions about reading passages from a variety of subjects.

Critical Reasoning—You will derive logical conclusions and relationships from a variety of situations and passages.

General college background is measured by these sections, not specific knowledge from any specialized course or courses. No formal background in business or management is required.

QUESTIONS COMMONLY ASKED ABOUT THE COMPUTER-ADAPTIVE GMAT (GMAT CAT)

Q: Who administers the GMAT CAT?

A: The GMAT CAT is written and administered by Educational Testing Service (ETS). The Graduate Management Admission Council (GMAC), made up of representatives from 113 graduate schools of management, works with ETS in an advisory capacity.

Q: When is the computer-adaptive GMAT given?

A: The computer-adaptive GMAT will be offered six days each week for three weeks each month. Testing center hours may vary.

Q: How do I schedule my GMAT CAT appointment?

A: You can schedule your appointment, or reschedule your appointment if necessary, by calling your local testing center or an 800 number. Phone numbers and a complete list of testing centers are in your information bulletin and on the GMAT Web site.

Q: When should I schedule my appointment?

A: Carefully check your admission deadlines to guide you in scheduling your appointment. You may schedule your appointment just a few days before taking the test, but you should schedule early to get preferred dates, times, and locations.

Q: Where do I take the GMAT CAT?

A: There are approximately 400 computer-based testing centers in North America and other selected cities. Testing centers will be located at Sylvan Technology Centers, at colleges and universities, and at ETS field service offices.

Q: Can I take the GMAT CAT more than once?

A: Yes. You may retake the exam the next month following your first exam. That is, if you take your first GMAT anytime in January, then the next time you can take the test is anytime in February or later.

Q: What is a computer-adaptive GMAT?

A: On the computer-adaptive GMAT, the screen will display one multiple-choice question at a time. The first question will be of medium difficulty. Each subsequent question will vary in difficulty based on responses to all previous questions. The questions that you will be responding to will be chosen from a large pool of questions that have been categorized by level of difficulty and content. As the level of questions adjusts to your ability level, you will get more questions that are within your range. This "adaptive" system will ultimately determine your level of ability. On this exam, you may not return to an earlier question, and you must answer each question.

Q: What will the test center be like?
A: The conditions at the test center should be quiet and private, since the tests are administered individually at separate testing stations.

Q: Can I use scratch paper on the test?
A: You will be given scratch paper at the testing site. Use the scratch paper to your advantage to brainstorm, outline, sketch diagrams, do calculations, and so on.

Q: Will there be any breaks during the test?
A: Yes, two. After the essay section and between the quantitative and verbal sections, you will have the opportunity to take a break.

Q: Can I repeat the test?
A: Yes. You may retake the GMAT once per calendar month. Understand that your latest score and your two most recent test scores since October 1992 will also be on your score report.

Q: Should I guess on the GMAT CAT?
A: Yes. If you get stuck on a question or simply don't know the answer, guess.

Q: What should I bring to the test center?
A: A valid photo-bearing ID, your score recipient information, your authorization voucher (if you requested one from ETS), and some sharpened pencils for scratch work on the scratch paper provided.

Q: How long does it take to get my scores?
A: For the multiple-choice sections (quantitative and verbal), you will be able to see your scores upon completion of the exam. Your official score report, including the Analytical Writing Assessment scores, will be mailed about two weeks after your test date. At the testing site you can also designate the schools that are to receive your scores.

Q: Are the scores for the computer-based GMAT comparable to those of the paper-based GMAT?

A: GMAC and ETS research indicates that the scores are comparable.

Q: Will accommodations be made for test-takers with disabilities?

A: Yes, accommodations similar to those for previous exams will be available. All centers should be equipped with appropriate devices to aid test-takers with disabilities, such as wheelchair access and screen magnification. Check with your center to make sure that the proper accommodations are available.

Q: What computer skills are necessary for the GMAT CAT?

A: Since the GMAT CAT is preceded by a tutorial program that starts at the very basics, minimal computer skills are required. The tutorials will include using the simple word-processing program, using a mouse, entering and confirming a response, changing a response, accessing the "help" function, and moving to the next question. A "help" function will be available throughout the test.

Q: How should I prepare for the GMAT CAT?

A: Preparing well for the GMAT CAT requires following a careful plan: (1) You should make sure that you are familiar with and understand each question type. (2) You should understand and become comfortable with the format of the new exam and the computer delivery system (learn to use a simple word processor, a mouse, etc.). (3) You should review subject matter—math and grammar—and analytical writing skills. (4) You should practice, practice, practice.

Q: How is my GMAT score used?

A: The GMAT is used as part of an assessment of your probable success in graduate business school. Other factors, such as undergraduate grades, interviews, and letters of recommendation, also figure into this assessment. The importance of GMAT scores varies from institution to institution, so you are wise to contact the graduate schools to which you are applying for further information.

Q: Can I get more information?
A: Yes. Contact ETS by phone, fax, e-mail, or mail at:

GMAT
Educational Testing Service
P.O. Box 6103
Princeton, New Jersey 08541-6103
Phone: (609) 771-7330.
FAX: (609) 883-4349
E-mail: gmat@ets.org
Internet: http://www.gmat.org

TAKING THE GMAT CAT:
AN OVERVIEW OF THE PROCESS

TEST CENTER PROCEDURE

- Be sure to arrive at the test center at least 30 minutes before your scheduled time. Don't be late! When you arrive at the test center, you will be checked in. Be sure to have
    a valid photo-bearing ID
    your score recipient information
    your authorization voucher (if you requested one from ETS)
- After you have checked in, you will be assigned a seat. You will be given scratch paper and may request more during the test. Following general instructions and preliminary procedures, you will be given time to work through the interactive tutorials. After the tutorials, you will begin the actual GMAT.
- The first section (two 30-minute responses) will be the Analytical Writing Assessment. You will be given 30 minutes to respond to the first topic by entering your response on the computer through the word-processing program. You will then be given 30 minutes to respond to the second topic in the same manner. Following this hour of testing, you will have the opportunity to take a 5-minute break.
- You will then have 75 minutes for a multiple-choice section. All answers will be entered on the computer using a mouse. Following this 75 minutes of testing, you will be given the opportunity to take a 5-minute break.
- You will then have 75 minutes for another multiple-choice section. All answers will be entered on the computer using a mouse.
- During the exam, if you are having a problem with the computer, need additional scratch paper, or wish to speak to an administrator for any reason, raise your hand to get his or her attention.

USING THE INTERACTIVE TUTORIALS

Many test takers are needlessly afraid of a computerized exam. You should understand that the testing company has gone to great lengths to make sure that the computerized test is easy to use, even for the computer novice. The test makers have included very basic tutorials to make sure that you are comfortable working with the computer. Take advantage of these tutorials; work through them slowly.

The interactive tutorials explain and let you try the simple word-processing program you'll use for the two essay questions and the basic functions for the multiple-choice questions. You'll have plenty of time to become familiar with the computer.

The Answer-Selection and Word-Processing Tutorial

One tutorial explains and reviews the simple word-processing program you will use for the two essay questions and the method by which you select answers in the multiple-choice sections. This tutorial carefully explains and lets you try the various word-processing functions and selecting an answer oval and changing answers on multiple-choice questions. The basic typing keyboard is used for the essays and the functions include

Movement arrows move the cursor left, right, up, or down.

left   right   up   down

Movement keys

moves cursor to beginning of the line you are on

moves cursor to the end of the line you are on

moves cursor up one "page"

moves cursor down one "page"

moves cursor to beginning of next line

removes text to the left of the cursor

removes text to the right of the cursor

 does not work—no tabs can be used

Simple editing (these icons appear on the right of the screen)

 removes a block of text (highlighted with the mouse) and keeps it in the computer's memory—saved text will remain in memory until you replace it by text from another cut

 inserts the block of text you cut into a place you designate with your cursor

Undo reverses your *last* action

Reviewing and practicing each of the above functions on a basic word-processing program before you go to take the test will be helpful.

The screen for the essays is similar to this:

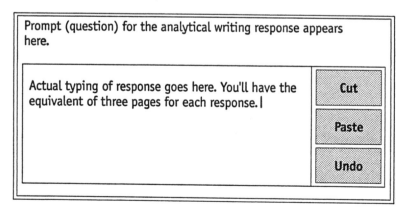

Selecting an Answer

You will use your mouse to select your answer choice in the multiple-choice sections simply by moving the arrow to the oval in front of your answer choice and clicking. At that time, the oval will become blackened, showing your choice. For example,

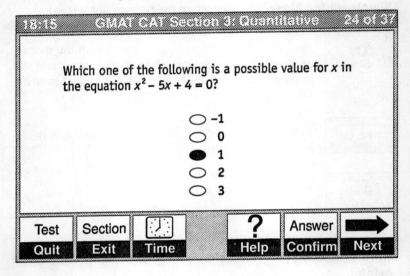

Notice the time display in the upper left-hand corner of the screen and the problem you are on and the total number of problems in the section in the upper right.

The Functions Tutorials

These tutorials review using a mouse, using the testing tools, and scrolling through long passages or graphs.

Using a Mouse

You will use a mouse to enter your answer choice or input other information. Simply move the arrow to your selection by moving the mouse to the appropriate position and clicking (pressing) a button on the mouse. Remember that the tail (cord) of the mouse should always be pointing away from you and that your fingers should be close to the buttons.

Using the Screen Tools

The illustration below shows the bottom part of the screen, on which the various tools are displayed.

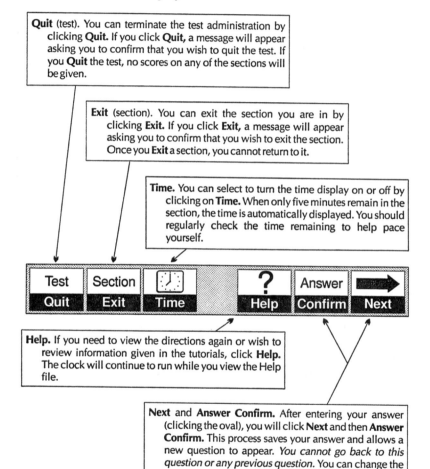

Quit (test). You can terminate the test administration by clicking **Quit**. If you click **Quit,** a message will appear asking you to confirm that you wish to quit the test. If you **Quit** the test, no scores on any of the sections will be given.

Exit (section). You can exit the section you are in by clicking **Exit**. If you click **Exit,** a message will appear asking you to confirm that you wish to exit the section. Once you **Exit** a section, you cannot return to it.

Time. You can select to turn the time display on or off by clicking on **Time.** When only five minutes remain in the section, the time is automatically displayed. You should regularly check the time remaining to help pace yourself.

Test	Section	🕐		?	Answer	➡
Quit	Exit	Time		Help	Confirm	Next

Help. If you need to view the directions again or wish to review information given in the tutorials, click **Help**. The clock will continue to run while you view the Help file.

Next and **Answer Confirm.** After entering your answer (clicking the oval), you will click **Next** and then **Answer Confirm.** This process saves your answer and allows a new question to appear. *You cannot go back to this question or any previous question.* You can change the answer as often as you want **until** you have finally confirmed it by clicking **Answer Confirm.**

Note: If a tool is gray (not dark), it will not work. Only dark tools can be clicked on to work.

Using the Scroll Bar

If a passage is too long to fit on the screen or there is too much information in a graph or chart to fit on the screen, a **scroll bar** will appear alongside the passage or graph that is contained in the left portion of the screen. The scrolling portion of the screen is called a scrolling pane. The **scroll bar** is used to vertically move (scroll) the nonvisible information onto the scrolling pane. The information will not move horizontally. In the screen below, you will notice the **scroll bar, the arrows in the scroll bar,** and the **status bar** (the gray area with white letters) at the top of the scrolling pane.

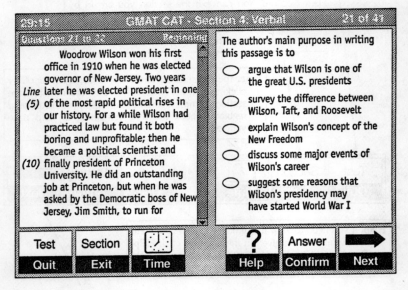

By clicking the arrows in the scroll bar, you can move the information up or down by line. By clicking between an arrow and the box, you can move the information up or down the page in larger increments. Holding the mouse button down on an arrow makes the lines scroll very quickly.

The status bar indicates if you are at the **Beginning** or **End** of a passage or if there is **More Available.** These messages will assist you in keeping track of where you are when you are scrolling.

If you are even slightly familiar with a Macintosh or PC Windows system, you should be very comfortable with the GMAT computerized format.

SCRATCH PAPER

Before you start the exam, you will be given scratch paper. It is important that you use this scratch paper to its maximum benefit. Doing mathematical computations, listing wrong answers, taking notes, and redrawing diagrams are some of the ways to take advantage of the scratch paper. These and other strategies are discussed in the following sections.

TEST-TAKING STRATEGIES: THE APPROACH

DON'T GET STUCK

Many who take standardized exams don't get the score they are entitled to because they spend too much time dwelling on a single question, leaving insufficient time to answer other questions they could get right. Don't let this happen to you. Never spend more than a minute and a half to two minutes on any one question. With sufficient practice, you will almost automatically know when a problem is taking too long. If this happens, try to eliminate some choices, and then take a guess. *The key is not to get stuck!*

ELIMINATE WRONG ANSWERS

Eliminate answer choices from consideration when possible. Since you can't mark on the computer screen, use your scratch paper to help you keep track of choices you've eliminated. You may wish to simply list answer choices and mark them out as follows. (**Note that you would use markings A, B, C, D, and E only to signify the *order* of the choices, since no letters are used for choices on the screen.**)

or you may wish to be a little more sophisticated and use question marks to signify possible answers as follows:

$$\begin{array}{l}\cancel{A}\\ ?B\\ \cancel{C}\\ ?D\\ \cancel{E}\end{array}$$

Either of these methods will help you avoid reconsidering those choices already eliminated and will help you narrow down your possible answers. Remember to keep this marking system very simple.

WORKING FROM MULTIPLE-MULTIPLE CHOICE ANSWERS

You may encounter a few questions of the multiple-multiple choice type. This question gives you answers marked with roman numerals (I, II, III) and then asks you if one, two, or possibly all three of the choices are correct answers. This type of question can appear as a Problem Solving, Reading Comprehension, or Critical Reasoning question. Here's an example in the form of a Problem Solving question:

Which of the following are equations with the only solution $x = 6$?

   I. $x^2 - 36 = 0$
  II. $x^2 - 7x + 6 = 0$
 III. $x + 5 = 3x - 7$

  Ⓐ I only
  Ⓑ II only
  Ⓒ III only
  Ⓓ I and III only
  Ⓔ I, II, and III

A good strategy for this question type is to try to answer one of the roman numeral choices quickly. On your scratch paper, write

I
II
III
A
B
C
D
E

Then place a "T" or "F" by the numeral (for true or false) and go to the choices and eliminate possibilities. In the example, since I, $x^2 - 36 = 0$, gives you an answer of 6 and –6 ($x^2 = 36$ gives $x = 6$ or $x = -6$), it is false. Immediately place an "F" by roman numeral I and eliminate any answer choices that include I

F I
~~I~~
II
III
~~A~~
B
C
~~D~~
~~E~~

So now you know that the answer must be Ⓑ II or Ⓒ III, since you've eliminated choices Ⓐ, Ⓓ, and Ⓔ because they contain I. You can now work either answer II or answer III, since only one of them can be true. Working II gives

$$x^2 - 7x + 6 = 0$$
$$(x - 1)(x - 6) = 0$$
$$x - 1 = 0; x - 6 = 0$$
$$x = 1; x = 6$$

So II is not true. Therefore, the answer must be Ⓒ, III only. To finish the example, working III gives the following (although remember that there's no need to work it in the exam because you've eliminated all the other answers).

$$x + 5 = 3x - 7$$
$$x + 5 = 3x - 7$$
$$\underline{\quad -5 \qquad\quad -5\quad}$$
$$x \quad = 3x - 12$$
$$\underline{-3x \qquad -3x\quad}$$
$$-2x \quad = \qquad -12$$
$$\frac{-2x}{-2} = \frac{-12}{-2}$$
$$x = 6$$

So $x = 6$, and III and Ⓒ are true.

PART II

Analysis of Exam Areas

This section is designed to introduce you to each GMAT CAT area by carefully reviewing the

1. Ability Tested
2. Basic Skills Necessary
3. Directions
4. Analysis of Directions
5. Suggested Approach with Samples

This section features the patterned plan of attack for each subject area and emphasizes important test-taking techniques and strategies and how to apply them to a variety of problem types.

Note: On the actual GMAT CAT, the letters Ⓐ, Ⓑ, Ⓒ, Ⓓ, **and** Ⓔ **do NOT appear with the answer choices, and the questions do not have numbers next to them.** To select an answer, you will select the appropriate oval on the computer screen. Even though the actual test does not label the answer choices with letters, or the questions with numbers, letters and numbers are used in this book to assist you in following answers and explanations.

Introduction to the Analytical Writing Assessment

The Analytical Writing Assessment section requires you to write two prose responses with a time limit of 30 minutes for each. You will be given two types of questions: (1) an analysis of an issue, which presents an issue to be discussed, and (2) an analysis of an argument, which presents an argument to be analyzed.

Since the GMAT is now computerized, you will enter your response to each of the analytical writing questions into the computer through a very simple word-processing system. Prior to starting the test, you will be walked through a tutorial that carefully explains how to use the word processor. This word processing includes the basic typing keyboard including movement arrows, cut, paste, undo functions, and Home, End, Backspace, Delete, Page Up, Page Down, and Enter keys. No tabs can be used.

You will have the equivalent of three pages to type each response and scratch paper for prewriting, outlining, notes, etc. The prompt (question) for each type of response will appear at the top of the page, and the response will be typed in the writing box below.

The screen is similar to this:

Prompt (question) for the analytical writing response appears here.

Actual typing of response goes here. You'll have the equivalent of three pages for each response. |

Cut

Paste

Undo

A list of possible analytical writing prompts will be prepublished in the information bulletin and on the GMAT Web site, so it is important that you check this information carefully. You should take advantage of the information given and write practice responses to some of the prepublished essay prompts.

ABILITY TESTED

This section tests your ability to think critically, to analyze issues and features of arguments, and to communicate complex ideas.

BASIC SKILLS NECESSARY

You should possess good college-level writing, reading, and reasoning skills. You should be able to express your ideas in correct, clear, concise, and persuasive language.

DIRECTIONS

Analysis of an issue: This section will require you to analyze and explain your views on the issue given. Consider many points of view as you develop your own position on the issue. There is no right or wrong answer to the question.

Read the statement and directions carefully. Make any notes or do any prewriting (clustering, outline, etc.) on your scratch paper. Then type your response into the computer.

Analysis of an argument: This section will require you to critique the argument given. Questioning underlying assumptions, finding alternative explanations or counterexamples, and delineating evidence to strengthen or weaken an argument are some possible approaches.

Read the argument and directions carefully. Make any notes or do any prewriting (clustering, outlining, etc.) on your scratch paper. Then type your response into the computer.

ANALYSIS

This section presents an analysis of an issue topic and an analysis of an argument topic, usually in about three or four sentences each. The topics are followed by questions and/or directions that set forth the tasks you must accomplish in your responses. Here is a typical set of such questions (notice the difference):

Analysis of an issue: Do you agree with this statement? Explain your position with specific supporting details from your own experience, observations, or readings.

Analysis of an argument: Write a critique of this argument. Consider what questionable assumptions underlie it and what other explanations or examples might weaken its conclusion. What other evidence could strengthen or weaken this argument?

SCORING THE ANALYTICAL WRITING SECTION

The two responses are scored holistically by teachers skilled in the evaluation of writing. Their concern will be with the overall quality of the responses—the command of logic, clarity, and cogency—and not with minor errors of spelling or grammar.

The scoring guides for each section (which follow) were developed by categorizing responses written during the development of this section of the GMAT, rather than from a preconceived notion of what responses should be like. Each of the two responses is given a score ranging from 0 (lowest) to 6 (highest) by two readers who are not aware of the other's score. If the two scores differ by more than two points, the response is graded by a third reader. If the third reader's score is the same as that of one of the other readers, that score is assigned. If the score is between the two differing scores, the three grades are averaged. The scores of the issue analysis response and the argument analysis response are averaged, and the result is the final Analytical Writing Assessment score (a single grade ranging from 0 to 6).

Again, response scores are determined by the quality of thought and the writing skill. In the scoring of the analysis of an issue, a well-written, thoughtful response will receive a high score regardless of what side of the issue the writer chooses. A minor spelling error or a small error in grammar will not affect the final score. In the scoring of the analysis of an argument, the content of the response is more important than the quality of the writing. The readers are instructed to reward students for what they do well. Readers are chosen for their competence and experience (and to balance the group with regard to gender, ethnicity, and geography).

ANALYZING THE SCORES

Grading the Analysis of an Issue Response

Because the responses must be written in a limited period of time, minor errors of grammar or mechanics will not affect the scores. The responses scored at 6 will not be errorless, but they will be superior to the others.

Score of 6: Excellent

These responses are characterized by all of the following:

- coverage of all the tasks required by the exam question
- an understanding of the complexity of the issue
- cogent reasoning and logical development of a position
- relevant persuasive supporting details
- superior organization
- superior command of standard written English

Score of 5: Good

These responses are characterized by the following:

- coverage of all the tasks required by the exam question
- clear reasoning and development of a position
- use of well-chosen supporting evidence
- good organization
- good handling of standard written English

Score of 4: Competent

These responses are characterized by the following:

- coverage of all the tasks
- development of a position
- adequately reasoned and supported arguments
- competent organization
- adequate handling of standard written English

Score of 3: Limited

These responses are characterized by the following:

- failure to fully understand the issue and develop a position
- failure to respond to all the assigned tasks
- failure to use supporting details
- numerous minor errors in grammar or mechanics
- less than adequate use of standard written English

Score of 2: Weak

These responses compound the deficiencies of responses in the 3 range. They are likely to fail in presenting a position on the issue or fail in employing supporting detail. The organization, grammar, diction, and mechanics are likely to be incompetent.

Score of 1: Poor

These responses compound the deficiencies of the responses in the 2 range. They display an inability to deal with the topic and write standard English prose. They are often unacceptably brief.

Score of 0

A score of zero is given to responses that are wholly off-topic.

Score of NR

If there is no response, the score is NR.

Grading the Analysis of an Argument Response

Because the responses must be written in a limited period of time, minor errors of grammar or mechanics will not affect the scores. The responses scored at 6 will not be errorless, but they will be superior to the others.

Score of 6: Excellent

These responses are characterized by all of the following:

- thorough coverage of all the tasks required by the exam question
- careful analysis of the important features of the argument
- cogent reasoning and logical development
- relevant supporting details of the critique
- superior organization
- superior command of standard written English

Score of 5: Good

These responses are characterized by the following:

- good coverage of all the tasks required by the exam question
- good analysis of the important features of the argument
- clear reasoning and development
- use of supporting evidence of the critique
- good organization
- good handling of standard written English

Score of 4: Competent

These responses are characterized by the following:

- some coverage of the tasks required by the exam question
- competent analysis of the important features of the argument
- adequately reasoned and supported points of the critique
- competent organization
- adequate handling of standard written English

Score of 3: Limited

These responses are characterized by one or more of the following weaknesses:

- failure to respond to all of the assigned tasks
- failure to understand or to analyze the important features of the argument
- failure to use supporting details of the critique
- numerous minor errors in grammar or mechanics
- less than adequate use of standard written English

Score of 2: Weak

Most 2 responses fail to analyze the argument and instead present, in place of critique, the writer's ideas about the topic. These papers are often well written but wholly lacking in analysis of an argument.

Other of these responses compound the deficiencies of responses in the 3 range. They are likely to misunderstand the main features of the argument, fail to present an analysis, and fail to employ supporting detail. The organization, grammar, diction, and mechanics are likely to be incompetent.

Score of 1: Poor

These responses compound the deficiencies in the 2 range. They display an inability to respond to the topic and write standard English prose. They are often unacceptably brief.

Score of 0

A score of zero is given to responses that are wholly off-topic.

Score of NR

If there is no response, the score is NR.

SUGGESTED APPROACH WITH SAMPLES

Again, two distinct tasks are given in the Analytical Writing Assessment: (1) analyze an issue and (2) analyze an argument. To analyze an issue you are asked to take a position on the issue presented and support your position with relevant details or examples. To analyze an argument you are asked the weaknesses of an argument that is presented. In explaining your point of view you must analyze failures of the reasoning in the argument itself and in its use of evidence or support.

ANALYSIS OF AN ISSUE

For any timed writing task, you should envision three steps leading to the finished product:

1. Preparing to write (prewriting)
2. Writing
3. Proofreading (editing)

Preparing to Write

• Note time and space constraints.

   Before you begin analyzing the topic itself, you should be aware of the amount of time allotted for the assignment as well as the space available. For the Analytical Writing Assessment, you have thirty minutes to write each response. You will have the equivalent of three pages to complete your response. Use the scratch paper provided to organize your writing before you begin inputting your response.

• Carefully read the topic.

   Next, read and understand the topic. A major mistake is to give too little time and attention to this task. Remember that if you address the topic incorrectly, or even partially, your score is significantly lowered, no matter how well the response is organized, supported, and written. Therefore, you must spend adequate time carefully reading and understanding the topic and its exact requirements.

Pay special attention to key words in the directions, like *describe, compare, explain,* and *contrast.* Be aware that *or* requires a choice. For example, "Present your opinions for or against . . ." means take one point of view, not both. Be careful to assess completely all the tasks required. You may find it helpful to read the topic several times, focusing on the key words or tasks.

Be sure to discriminate between tasks that are required and ones that are optional. If the instructions use the word *may,* you may omit that task or a part of it.

• Plan by brainstorming and organizing.

Remembering, inventing, and organizing information at short notice can be difficult unless you are prepared with an effective technique. Writing your response immediately after reading the topic often results in a poorly organized, haphazard response. Take time to organize your thoughts on paper before writing.

Brainstorming

The process of creating and accumulating ideas, examples, and illustrations is called "brainstorming." Brainstorming is simply jotting down on scratch paper as many thoughts, ideas, and possibilities as you can remember, invent, or otherwise bring to mind in order to address the topic. Neatness, order, and spelling are unimportant at this point.

Organizing

After generating as many illustrations as you can within the time allotted, assess these ideas. Remembering that development relies on specific examples, decide which examples best enable you to support your points. Eliminate (cross out) those you don't wish to use, and number those you'll want to address in your response. Add any notes regarding more specific details or new thoughts that come to mind. However, don't worry about developing everything completely, since these planning notes are for your use. Your time will be better spent developing these points in your writing and not in your notes.

Writing

Opening Paragraph

A strong opening paragraph is essential. One type of introduction, easy to master and very effective, is a GENERALIZE-FOCUS-SURVEY structure. This is a three- to four-sentence paragraph in which the first sentence generalizes about the given topic, the second sentence focuses on what you have chosen to discuss, and the last one or two sentences survey the particulars you intend to present.

An effective first paragraph tells your reader what to expect in the body of the response. The GENERALIZE-FOCUS-SURVEY paragraph points toward the specifics you will discuss and suggests the order in which you will discuss them.

Body

Writing the body of the response involves presenting specific details and examples that are related to the aspects you have introduced. The body may consist of one longer paragraph or several shorter paragraphs. If you choose to break your discussion into several paragraphs, make sure that each paragraph consists of at least three sentences. Very short paragraphs may make your response appear to be insubstantial and scattered.

Be realistic about how much you will be able to write. Your readers do not give more credit for longer responses. Although they want you to support your points adequately, they understand that you must write concisely in order to finish in time.

It is important to provide at least one substantial example, or "for instance," for each aspect you discuss in the body of your response.

Conclusion

As you prepare to write the conclusion, you should be paying special attention to time. It is not necessary to have a formal conclusion to your response, but a conclusion may function to (1) complete your response to the question, (2) add information that was not introduced earlier, or (3) point toward the future.

Proofreading

Always allow a few minutes to proofread your response for errors in grammar, usage, and spelling.

One Approach: The "Why" Format

One good way to approach a question that asks you to explain, analyze, or evaluate is to use a "why" format. A "why" response is built around a thesis sentence. The thesis sentence begins with your opinion, followed by the word *because* and then a list of the most important reasons the opinion is valid, reasonable, or well founded.

The "why" format could look like this:

Paragraph	"Why" Response Format
1	Introduction—Thesis Sentence
2	Reason 1
3	Reason 2
4	Reason 3
5	Conclusion

Each paragraph should contain at least three to five sentences. The introduction invites the reader to read on. Your reasons (three are often sufficient) that follow should give examples or evidence to support each reason. Your concluding paragraph summarizes your reasons and restates the thesis statement.

Sample: Analysis of an Issue

More than half of the Americans recently surveyed expressed approval of the use of flogging to punish young offenders guilty of crimes such as vandalism. Opponents of flogging argue that the punishment is cruel and barbaric and that it leaves both physical and psychological scars.

Do you believe that flogging should be used in this country? Explain your position with support from your observations, readings, and/or experience.

Sample Analysis of an Issue Response

In light of the disturbing increase in crime in our cities and suburbs in recent years, many Americans have expressed an interest in the use of flogging to punish young offenders guilty of crimes such as vandalism. I am opposed to the use of flogging as punishment based on humanitarian, psychological, and moral grounds.

While I share the frustration of other law-abiding citizens who are trying to stem the tide of senseless destruction of personal property, I believe that flogging is a cruel and uncivilized form of punishment that has no place in our country. The public infliction of painful physical punishment was banished from civilized countries years ago with the disappearance of the stocks, pillories, and public whippings. As witnessed in the case of the American teenager who was sentenced to a caning for vandalism in Singapore, most civilized countries around the world objected vehemently to the severity and barbarism of this form of punishment for a nonviolent crime.

On psychological grounds, inflicting physical punishment to teach a lesson has been frowned upon for years by child psychologists and behavioral experts. Spankings, beltings, and beatings are all considered forms of abuse and have been proved to have only very negative affects on behavior. Studies have also supported the conclusion that violence begets violence, and it would seem very probable that the use of flogging to punish a young person who committed vandalism may well lead to a more violent expression of anger next time. The troubled individual whose antisocial behavior was directed toward property may well be incited to take his anger out in a physically violent way against people after being subjected to such treatment.

Finally, on moral grounds, we need to make the distinction between crimes against persons and crimes against property. In terms of the Biblical injunction of "an eye for an eye, a tooth for a tooth," inflicting physical injury on an offender who committed damage to property is hardly equitable. What is the lesson we are trying to teach? In the 1970s, the movie "A Clockwork Orange" dealt with the issue of violent crime in a futuristic setting and society's increasingly cruel methods of "rehabilitation." It left the viewer questioning which was more barbaric, the crime or the punishment?

In conclusion, we must continue to search for ways to reduce the incidence of crimes against property as well as persons, but we must above all keep sight of our humanity. Flogging is not the answer.

Evaluation of Analysis of an Issue Response

This excellent analysis would probably be an example of a score of 6. The writer takes a stand and develops it with apt examples, referring to current events, a psychological film, and personal attitudes. Though it is *not* necessary to write a five-paragraph response, this one shows well how easily and effectively such a response can be organized. This first, introductory paragraph lists three grounds of opposition (humanitarian, psychological, and moral), and each of the next three paragraphs develops one of these. The final paragraph is a summing up. The response is gracefully written and syntactically varied (the last paragraph, for example, plays a long sentence against a short one). Though its mechanics are not perfect (*affects* in the third paragraph should be *effects*), the writer's command of standard written English is first-rate.

A PATTERNED PLAN OF ATTACK
Analysis of an Issue

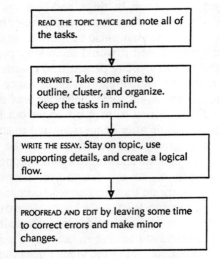

READ THE TOPIC TWICE and note all of the tasks.

PREWRITE. Take some time to outline, cluster, and organize. Keep the tasks in mind.

WRITE THE ESSAY. Stay on topic, use supporting details, and create a logical flow.

PROOFREAD AND EDIT by leaving some time to correct errors and make minor changes.

ANALYSIS OF AN ARGUMENT

In the analysis of an argument section, your analysis is more important than your style. You may, in fact, use the "bullet format" —you might use asterisks (*) or dashes (--) preceding each of your points— and still score in the upper half of the scale if your analysis is cogent. You will score even better if you use the "bullet format" in combination with conventional prose paragraphs.

The argument you will be asked to analyze is never going to be strong. Do not waste your time trying to find something good to say about it. Common errors in its line of reasoning are likely to be one or more of the following:

- Assuming because *x* happened after *y,* that *x* was the cause of *y* (*post hoc, ergo propter hoc—after that, therefore because of that*). *Last night there was a full moon, and this morning my cat was sick. Therefore, a full moon makes my cat sick.*

- Drawing a conclusion from a failure to respond or act—assuming, for example, that because there was no hostile response, the response was favorable.

- Assuming that a survey can be trusted without full information about the people questioned and the questions asked.

The weakest responses are usually those in which students write about the subject of the quotation (how a restaurant should be run, why television advertising is a good idea, why student fees should be reduced) but never analyze the weakness in the reasoning of the argument. Even very well-written responses that fail to analyze the argument will receive low scores, while an essay in broken but understandable English with twice as many errors in grammar and spelling will, if it explains the flaws in reasoning, receive a score in the upper half of the six-point scale.

Sample: Analysis of an Argument

Read the following sample question and the two student responses. Then decide which is the better of the two.

1. The following announcement appeared in an East-West Bus Line company memorandum:

> "Beginning on June 1, the East-West Bus Company will no longer run buses on any of its interstate routes on Saturdays and Sundays. A survey of the riders on the Boston-New York route taken over a ten-day period in November showed that more than 95% of the passengers do not use the buses on weekends. This reduction in the schedule will allow the company to continue to increase its return to stockholders with a minimum of inconvenience to the bus-riding public."

Write a critique of the argument. You should consider what doubtful assumptions underlie the reasoning, what other explanations might apply and weaken the conclusions, and/or what other evidence would strengthen or weaken the argument. Do NOT write a response on your views of the issue.

Sample Analysis of an Argument Response 1

The revealing phrase in this announcement is "increase its return to stockholders." Just where does the bus company think its real primary responsibility lies? To the stockholders or to the bus-riding public? The stockholders are probably well-heeled men who are used to flying first-class to their travel destinations, or riding in their BMWs and Cadillacs. Meanwhile, the people who cannot afford to fly and take the bus because it is less costly and expensive, who have to take buses to get to work or to see their families and loved ones, will have to find a new way to travel or be unable to travel at all.

Too many firms see only "the bottom line," and forget their responsibility to the general public at large. Did it ever occur to them that there are several airlines that run shuttle services between Boston and New York, so if the buses stop running, there is still no problem getting from one city to the other? But what bothers them is that the weekend bus service is not a big money-maker. What the argument needs is more concern with the public who ride on buses and less worry about the profits of the "fat cats."

Sample Analysis of an Argument Response 2

The argument is weak for several reasons.

--we don't know when the ten days in November were. Over Thanksgiving weekend?

--where else are routes of bus company?

--how does number of riders on Boston-New York compare with other routes?

--how many riders didn't read or take survey?

--how much profit and loss are made in company on weekend?

The announcement is weak argument because it doesn't tell enough about the survey. If the the survey was taken on Thanksgiving week there were probably no riders on Thursday. Anyway, we don't know if more people ride in November or in July. And we don't know other routs of this company. Maybe some of them are in hard to get to places like Montana or Oregon unlike Boston-New York.

Before we can judge argument, we should know what the survey asked and who on the bus took the survey. Did all people on the bus take the survey. Or did just some of them? What if more peole didn't take the survey than did take it? Without knowing more about the survey, we cant accept the argument. The evidence is to uncertain to trust.

Evaluation of Analysis of an Argument Responses

The first of these two responses would be scored a 2, rescued from the lowest possible grade by its competent prose and the glimmer of recognition that the Boston-New York route may not be representative. The second response would be scored a 5, in recognition of its perception of a number of the weaknesses in the argument. The flaws in the writing would prevent its receiving the highest score.

A PATTERNED PLAN OF ATTACK
Analysis of an Argument

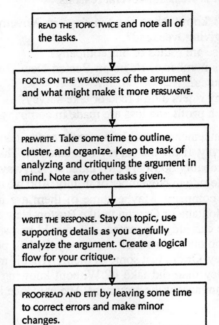

READ THE TOPIC TWICE and note all of the tasks.

↓

FOCUS ON THE WEAKNESSES of the argument and what might make it more PERSUASIVE.

↓

PREWRITE. Take some time to outline, cluster, and organize. Keep the task of analyzing and critiquing the argument in mind. Note any other tasks given.

↓

WRITE THE RESPONSE. Stay on topic, use supporting details as you carefully analyze the argument. Create a logical flow for your critique.

↓

PROOFREAD AND ETIT by leaving some time to correct errors and make minor changes.

EXTRA PRACTICE TOPICS

In addition to the topics and questions provided in the practice test, here are sample topics for practicing Analytical Writing Assessment responses. Limit your time on each to thirty minutes to simulate the actual examination. Find someone skilled in writing to evaluate your responses using the checklist and grading scale following these extra practice topics. Remember, because the responses must be written in a limited time period, minor errors of grammar or mechanics will not affect your scores.

Analysis of an Issue Questions

1. "Some environmentalists believe that wood-burning stoves are among the best ways to conserve natural resources and protect the environment. But in many parts of the world, wood is in short supply, some wooded areas house animals, and wood smoke may be more harmful to air quality than emissions from fossil fuels like coal or oil."

   Which of these positions do you prefer? Explain your choice with support from your personal experience or knowledge of the issues.

2. "Violence is the unavoidable consequence of the Western idea of manhood: winning at all costs, physical supremacy, the primacy of work, the suppression of sensitivity."

   Do you agree with this position? Support your view from your reading and/or your observations.

3. "The result of tuition raises in state colleges is a better education. Classes are no longer overcrowded, and a far higher percentage of the entering first-year students complete their degrees in four years or fewer."

   Do you believe the benefits of higher tuition in state colleges outweigh the disadvantages? Make your opinion clear with specific support drawn from your observations or readings.

4. "The government should enable parents to pay tuition at either a public or private school. If fewer children attend public schools, the state will save money and healthy competition for students will inevitably lead to an improvement of all schools."

Do you disagree with this statement? Write a response supporting or opposing a voucher system to support education. Use your readings or personal experience to develop your argument.

5. "Experience should teach us to be most on our guard to protect liberty when the government's purposes are beneficent. The greatest dangers to liberty lurk in insidious encroachment by men of zeal, well-meaning but without understanding."

Are "men of zeal" a threat to liberty? Write an response in which you explain your position for or against this position. Support your case with information from your reading or experience.

Analysis of an Argument Questions

1. The following appeared in the editorial pages of a national news magazine:

"A nationwide survey conducted in 1990 found that fifty percent of high school seniors had experimented with drugs at least once, while a survey in 1992 found that the number had increased to fifty-five percent. The results of the 1994 survey are unavailable, but we can infer that by 1995, at least sixty percent of the teen-age population had experimented with drugs at least once."

Discuss how convincing you find this argument. Analyze its line of reasoning and its use of evidence. You may, if you wish, discuss what might make the argument more persuasive.

2. The following appeared as part of an editorial in a local newspaper:

"The notion that American voters do not turn out on election day can be believed no longer. In the most recent state by-elections, a contest in which no important national office was at stake, over sixty percent of the registered voters cast ballots on the referenda and bond measures. The participation by the electorate is up almost twenty percent over last year's totals and makes clear that the days of the low election turnout are over for good."

Discuss how convincing you find this argument. Analyze its line of reasoning and its use of evidence. You may, if you wish, discuss what might make the argument more persuasive.

3. The following appeared in the minutes of a school board meeting:

"In the three months since metal detectors and random locker searches were introduced at Ben Franklin High School, no serious weapons incidents have been reported. Consequently, despite the high costs, all of the junior high and high schools in the city must have metal detectors at all entrances and random locker searches throughout the school term. To protect the safety of our students, no cost is too high."

Discuss how convincing you find this argument. Analyze its line of reasoning and its use of evidence. You may, if you wish, discuss what might make the argument more persuasive.

4. The following is part of a memorandum from a government sub-committee:

"In keeping with its concern for a more equitable distribution of the tax burden, the Subcommittee on Taxation has proposed the elimination of all taxes on capital gains and, to replace this revenue, a one half of one percent tax on all domestic electrical use charges to be collected by the local utility companies. The income from this tax will be almost the same as the income now generated by the twenty-eight percent tax on capital gains, but it will be distributed more fairly over a much wider population."

Write a critique of the argument. You should consider what doubtful assumptions underlie the reasoning, what other explanations might apply and weaken the conclusions, and/or what other evidence would strengthen or weaken the argument. Do NOT write an essay on your views of the issue.

5. The following announcement was made by the regents of a state university:

"Beginning in the fall of next year, the public colleges and universities in the state system will no longer offer remedial courses in mathematics and English. These courses should be unnecessary for students in the state university system. Few of the private colleges in the state offer remedial education classes. In any event, they are readily available at lower cost at junior colleges throughout the state. The savings in classroom space and instructors' wages will allow greater expenditure on the research programs that are central to the university's well-being."

Discuss how convincing you find this argument. Analyze its line of reasoning and its use of evidence. You may, if you wish, discuss what might make the argument more persuasive.

RESPONSE SCORING CHECKLIST

ANALYSIS OF AN ISSUE

Questions	Completely	Partially	No
1. Does the response focus on the assigned topic and cover all of the tasks?			
2. Does the response show an understanding of the complexity of the issue?			
3. Does the response show cogent reasoning and logical position development?			
4. Are there sufficient relevant persuasive supporting details?			
5. Is the response well organized?			
6. Does the response show a command of standard written English?			

ANALYSIS OF AN ARGUMENT

Questions	Completely	Partially	No
1. Does the response focus on the assigned topic and cover all of the tasks?			
2. Does the response carefully analyze the important weaknesses of the argument?			
3. Does the response show cogent reasoning and logical development?			
4. Are there sufficient relevant supporting details of the critique?			
5. Is the response well organized?			
6. Does the response show a command of standard written English?			

ANALYSIS OF AN ARGUMENT

Introduction to the Quantitative Section

Prior to starting the exam, you will be carefully walked through a very basic tutorial program explaining how to use the computer for this exam. The computer-adaptive GMAT gives you 75 minutes to answer 37 quantitative questions. These questions are composed of Problem Solving questions and Data Sufficiency questions, and the question types are intemingled. You will be given a medium difficulty question to start with, and then the computer will adapt the level of questions you receive based on your responses to all the previous questions. All of your work will be done on the scratch paper provided, and all of your answers will be recorded on the computer screen by using a mouse to fill in the appropriate ovals. You will not be allowed to go back to a previous question, so be sure to answer each question before you attempt to move to the next question.

In this book—to assist you in understanding explanations and to direct your attention to different questions and answer choices—each question is given a number, and letters have been placed inside the ovals of the answer choices. **Note that on the actual exam, questions will not have numbers next to them, and there will be no letters in the ovals.**

INTRODUCTION TO PROBLEM SOLVING

Problem Solving questions are mostly word problems. Occasionally, questions refer to a graph or chart.

ABILITY TESTED

Problem Solving questions test your ability to solve mathematical problems involving arithmetic, algebra, and geometry and word problems by using problem-solving insight, logic, and application of basic skills.

BASIC SKILLS NECESSARY

The basic skills necessary to do well on this section include high school arithmetic, algebra, and intuitive geometry—no formal trigonometry or calculus is necessary. These skills, along with logical insight into problem-solving situations, are covered by the examination.

DIRECTIONS

Solve each problem in this section by using the information given and your own mathematical calculations. Then select the correct answer of the five choices given. Use the scratch paper given for any necessary caculations.

Note: Some problems may be accompanied by figures or diagrams. These figures are drawn as accurately as possible except when it is stated in a specific problem that the figure is not drawn to scale. The figure is meant to provide information useful in solving the problem or problems.

Unless otherwise stated or indicated, all figures lie in a plane.

All numbers used are real numbers.

ANALYSIS

All scratchwork is to be done on the paper given at the test; get used to referring back to the screen as you do your calculations and drawings. You are looking for the *one* correct answer; therefore, although other answers may be close, there is never more than one right answer.

SUGGESTED APPROACH WITH SAMPLES

Always carefully focus on what you are looking for to ensure that you are answering the right question.

1. If $x + 6 = 9$ then $3x + 1 =$

    Ⓐ 3
    Ⓑ 9
    Ⓒ 10
    Ⓓ 34
    Ⓔ 46

You should first focus on $3x = 1$, because this is what you are solving for. Solving for x leaves $x = 3$, and then substituting into $3x + 1$ gives $3(3) + 1$, or 10. The most common mistake is to solve for x, which is 3, and *mistakenly choose* Ⓐ as your answer. But remember, you are solving for $3x + 1$, not just x. You should also notice that most of the other choices would all be possible answers if you made common or simple mistakes. The correct answer is Ⓒ. *Make sure that you are answering the right question.*

Substituting numbers for variables can often be an aid to understanding a problem. Remember to substitute simple numbers, since you have to do the work.

2. If $x > 1$, which of the following decreases as x decreases?

    I. $x + x^2$

    II. $2x^2 - x$

    III. $\dfrac{1}{x+1}$

    Ⓐ I only
    Ⓑ II only
    Ⓒ III only
    Ⓓ I and II only
    Ⓔ II and III only

This problem is most easily solved by taking each situation and substituting simple numbers.

However, in the first situation, I, $x + x^2$, you should recognize that this expression will decrease as x decreases.

Trying $x = 2$ gives $2 + (2)^2$, which equals 6.

Now trying $x = 3$ gives $3 + (3)^2 = 12$.

Notice that choices Ⓑ, Ⓒ, and Ⓔ are already eliminated because they do not contain I. You should also realize that now you need to try only the values in II; since III is not paired with I as a possible choice, III cannot be one of the answers.

Trying $x = 2$ in the expression $2x^2 - x$ gives $2(2)^2 - 2$, or $2(4) - 2$, which leaves 6.

Now trying $x = 3$ gives $2(3)^2 - 3$, or $2(9) - 3 = 18 - 3 = 15$. This expression also decreases as x decreases. Therefore, the correct answer is choice Ⓓ. Once again notice that III was not even attempted because it was not one of the possible choices.

Sometimes you will immediately recognize the proper formula or method to solve a problem. If this is not the situation, try a reasonable approach and then work from the answers.

3. Barney can mow the lawn in 5 hours, and Fred can mow the lawn in 4 hours. How long will it take them to mow the lawn together?

   Ⓐ 5 hours

   Ⓑ $4\frac{1}{2}$ hours

   Ⓒ 4 hours

   Ⓓ $2\frac{2}{9}$ hours

   Ⓔ 1 hour

Suppose that you are unfamiliar with the type of equation for this problem. Try the "reasonable" method. Since Fred can mow the lawn in 4 hours by himself, he will take less than 4 hours if Barney helps him. Therefore, choices Ⓐ, Ⓑ, and Ⓒ are not sensible. Taking this method a little farther, suppose that Barney could also mow the lawn in 4 hours. Then together it would take Barney and Fred 2 hours. But since Barney is a little slower than this, the total time should be more than 2 hours. The correct answer is Ⓓ, $2\frac{2}{9}$ hours.

Using the equation for this problem would give the following calculations:

$$\frac{1}{5} + \frac{1}{4} = \frac{1}{x}$$

In 1 hour, Barney could do $\frac{1}{5}$ of the job, and in 1 hour, Fred could do $\frac{1}{4}$ of the job; unknown $\frac{1}{x}$ is the part of the job they could do together in one hour. Now, solving, you calculate as follows:

$$\frac{4}{20} + \frac{5}{20} = \frac{1}{x}$$

$$\frac{9}{20} = \frac{1}{x}$$

Cross multiplying gives $9x = 20$; therefore, $x = \frac{20}{9}$, or $2\frac{2}{9}$.

"Pulling" information out of the word problem structure can often give you a better look at what you are working with, and therefore, you gain additional insight into the problem. Organize this information on your scratch paper.

4. If a mixture is $\frac{3}{7}$ alcohol by volume and $\frac{4}{7}$ water by volume, what is the ratio of the volume of alcohol to the volume of water in this mixture?

   Ⓐ $\frac{3}{7}$

   Ⓑ $\frac{4}{7}$

   Ⓒ $\frac{3}{4}$

   Ⓓ $\frac{4}{3}$

   Ⓔ $\frac{7}{4}$

The first bit of information that should be pulled out should be what you are looking for: "ratio of the volume of alcohol to the volume of water." Rewrite it as $A{:}W$ and then into its working form: A/W. Next, you should pull out the volumes of each; $A = \frac{3}{7}$ and $W = \frac{4}{7}$. Now the answer can be easily figured by inspection or substitution: using $\frac{3}{7}/\frac{4}{7}$, invert the bottom fraction and multiply to get $\frac{3}{7} \times \frac{7}{4} = \frac{3}{4}$. The ratio of the volume of alcohol to the volume of water is 3 to 4. The correct answer is ⓒ. When pulling out information, actually write out the numbers and/or letters on your scratch paper, putting them into some helpful form and eliminating some of the wording.

Sketching diagrams or simple pictures can also be very helpful in problem solving because the diagram may tip off either a simple solution or a method for solving the problem.

5. What is the maximum number of pieces of birthday cake of size 4" by 4" that can be cut from a cake 20" by 20"?

    Ⓐ 5
    Ⓑ 10
    ⓒ 16
    Ⓓ 20
    Ⓔ 25

Sketching the cake and marking in as follows makes this a fairly simple problem.

Notice that five pieces of cake will fit along each side; therefore, $5 \times 5 = 25$. The correct answer is Ⓔ. Finding the total area of the cake and dividing it by the area of one of the 4×4 pieces would also give you the correct answer, but beware of this method because it may not work if the pieces do not fit evenly into the original area.

Redrawing and marking in diagrams on your scratch paper as you read them can save you valuable time. Marking can also give you insight into how to solve a problem because you will have the complete picture clearly in front of you.

6. In the triangle, $\overline{CD}$ is an angle bisector, angle *ACD* is 30°, and angle *ABC* is a right angle. What is the measurement of angle *x* in degrees?

Ⓐ 80°
Ⓑ 75°
Ⓒ 60°
Ⓓ 45°
Ⓔ 30°

After redrawing the diagram on your scratch paper, you should read the problem and mark as follows:

In the triangle above, $\overline{CD}$ is an angle bisector (*stop and mark in the drawing*), angle *ACD* is 30° (*stop and mark in the drawing*), and angle *ABC* is a right angle (*stop and mark in the drawing*). What is the measurement of angle *x* in degrees? (*Stop and mark in or circle what you are looking for in the drawing.*)

Now with the drawing marked in, it is evident that since angle *ACD* is 30°, angle *BCD* is also 30° because they are formed by an angle bisector (divides an angle into two equal parts). Since angle *ABC* is 90° (right angle) and *BCD* is 30°, then angle *x* is 60° because there are 180° in a triangle; 180 − (90 + 30) = 60. The correct answer is Ⓒ. *After redrawing the diagrams on your scratch paper, always mark in the diagrams as you read their descriptions and information about them. This includes what you are looking for.*

If it appears that extensive calculations are going to be necessary to solve a problem, check to see how far apart the choices are, and then approximate. The reason for checking the answers first is to give you a guide for how freely you can approximate.

7. The value for $(0.889 \times 55)/9.97$ to the nearest tenth is

   Ⓐ   0.5

   Ⓑ   4.63

   Ⓒ   4.9

   Ⓓ   7.7

   Ⓔ 49.1

Before starting any computations, take a glance at the answers to see how far apart they are. Notice that the only close answers are choices Ⓑ and Ⓒ, but Ⓑ is not possible, since it is to the nearest hundredth, not tenth. Now, making some quick approximations, $0.889 \cong 1$ and $9.97 \cong 10$, leaves the problem in this form

$$\frac{1 \times 55}{10} = \frac{55}{10} = 5.5$$

The closest answer is Ⓒ; therefore, it is the correct answer. Notice that choices Ⓐ and Ⓔ are not reasonable.

In some instances, it will be easier to work from the answers. Do not disregard this method because it will at least eliminate some of the choices and could give you the correct answer. Since the answer choices are usually in ascending or descending order (lowest to highest or highest to lowest), it is usually a good idea to start with the middle choice and then work up or down as necessary.

8. Which of the following is a counting number that when divided by 3 has a remainder of 1 and when divided by 4 has a remainder of 2?

   Ⓐ 13

   Ⓑ 12

   Ⓒ 10

   Ⓓ   8

   Ⓔ   5

In this problem, if you start with choice Ⓒ you would immediately have the correct answer, since 10 leaves a remainder of 1 when divided by 3 and a remainder of 2 when divided by 4. Also notice that if you simply work from the answers, you would quickly eliminate some choices. Choices Ⓑ and Ⓓ can be immediately eliminated because they *are* divisible by 4, leaving no remainder. Choices Ⓐ and Ⓔ can also be eliminated because they leave a remainder of 1 when divided by 4. Therefore, the correct answer is choice Ⓒ, by process of elimination.

A PATTERNED PLAN OF ATTACK
Problem Solving

PRACTICE PROBLEM SOLVING QUESTIONS

EASY TO MODERATE

1. What percent of 60 is 80?

    (A) $133\frac{1}{3}$
    (B)   75
    (C)   60
    (D) $33\frac{1}{3}$
    (E)   25

2. On a map, 1 centimeter represents 35 kilometers. Two cities 245 kilometers apart would be separated on the map by how many centimeters?

    (A)   5
    (B)   7
    (C)   9
    (D) 210
    (E) 280

3. Harriet planned to complete a certain task on Wednesday, January 1, but because of illness the completion date was postponed 48 days. On which day of the week in February was the task completed?

    (A) Monday
    (B) Tuesday
    (C) Wednesday
    (D) Thursday
    (E) Friday

4. How many combinations are possible if a person has 4 sport jackets, 5 shirts, and 3 pairs of slacks?

    (A)   4
    (B)   5
    (C)   12
    (D)   60
    (E) 120

5. John received a 10% raise each month for three consecutive months. What was his salary after the three raises if his starting salary was $1,000 per month?

    Ⓐ $1,248
    Ⓑ $1,300
    Ⓒ $1,331
    Ⓓ $1,410
    Ⓔ $1,463

**Maximum Temperature Readings
July 10–16, 1995**

6. Based on the graph above, what was the percent increase in the maximum temperature from July 12 to July 14, 1995?

    Ⓐ 10%
    Ⓑ 10.6%
    Ⓒ 10.9%
    Ⓓ 11.9%
    Ⓔ 13.6%

**AVERAGE FAMILY'S
EXPENSES**

1990

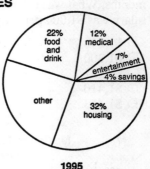

1995

7. Based on the graphs, what was the percent increase from 1990 to 1995 in the percentage spent on food and drink?

Ⓐ 4%
Ⓑ 18%
Ⓒ 22%
Ⓓ 40%
Ⓔ 50%

8. If $x = 6$ and $y = -2$, what is the value of $(x - 2y)^y$?

Ⓐ −100
Ⓑ   0.01
Ⓒ   0.25
Ⓓ   4
Ⓔ   8

9. If $x > 0$, which of the following is equal to $\sqrt{72x^5}$?

Ⓐ $36\sqrt{2x^5}$
Ⓑ $36x\sqrt{2x}$
Ⓒ $18x^2\sqrt{2x}$
Ⓓ $6x^2\sqrt{2x}$
Ⓔ $6x\sqrt{2x^2}$

Questions 10-11

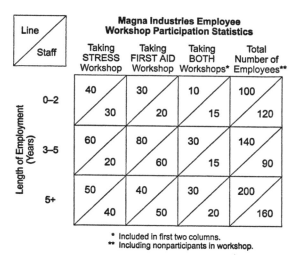

Magna Industries Employee
Workshop Participation Statistics

Line / Staff	Taking STRESS Workshop	Taking FIRST AID Workshop	Taking BOTH Workshops*	Total Number of Employees**
0–2	40 / 30	30 / 20	10 / 15	100 / 120
3–5	60 / 20	80 / 60	30 / 15	140 / 90
5+	50 / 40	40 / 50	30 / 20	200 / 160

Length of Employment (Years)

* Included in first two columns.
** Including nonparticipants in workshop.

10. What is the number of line employees with 3 to 5 years of employment NOT taking the First Aid workshop?

   © 20
   © 60
   © 80
   © 140
   © 190

   Ⓐ 20
   Ⓑ 60
   Ⓒ 80
   Ⓓ 140
   Ⓔ 190

11. Approximately what percent of the employees with 5 or more years of employment are NOT taking either workshop?

   Ⓐ 86%
   Ⓑ 64%
   Ⓒ 50%
   Ⓓ 14%
   Ⓔ 7%

12. A girl runs k miles in n hours. How many miles will she run in x hours at the same rate?

   Ⓐ knx

   Ⓑ $\dfrac{k}{n}$

   Ⓒ $\dfrac{kx}{n}$

   Ⓓ kx

   Ⓔ $\dfrac{kn}{x}$

13. If $ax + by = c$, then $b =$

   Ⓐ $\dfrac{c}{y} - ax$

   Ⓑ $c - ax - y$

   Ⓒ $\dfrac{c}{ax} - y$

   Ⓓ $\dfrac{c - ax}{y}$

   Ⓔ $\dfrac{ax - c}{y}$

14. What is the total surface area in square meters of a rectangular solid whose length is 7 meters, width is 6 meters, and depth is 3 meters?

   Ⓐ 32 m^2
   Ⓑ 81 m^2
   Ⓒ 126 m^2
   Ⓓ 162 m^2
   Ⓔ 252 m^2

15. If $1/3 + 1/2 + 1/x = 4$, then $x =$

   Ⓐ 18/5
   Ⓑ 19/6
   Ⓒ 24/11
   Ⓓ 6/19
   Ⓔ 5/18

16. If two numbers have only the number 1 as a common divisor, then they are called "relatively prime." Which of the following are NOT relatively prime?

   I.   3
   II. 4
   III. 7
   IV. 12

   Ⓐ I and II, I and III
   Ⓑ I and IV, II and IV
   Ⓒ II and III, II and IV
   Ⓓ II and IV, III and IV
   Ⓔ I and II, I and IV

AVERAGE

17. If 5 machines can produce 20 units in 10 hours, how long would it take 20 machines to produce 100 units?

   Ⓐ 50 hours
   Ⓑ 40 hours
   Ⓒ 12.5 hours
   Ⓓ 12 hours
   Ⓔ 8 hours

18. Pete has some apples. He sold 40% more than he ate. If he sold 70 apples, how many did he eat?

   Ⓐ 90
   Ⓑ 50
   Ⓒ 42
   Ⓓ 28
   Ⓔ 6

19. What is the perimeter of right triangle *PQR*?

    Ⓐ 8 cm
    Ⓑ 40 cm
    Ⓒ 41 cm
    Ⓓ 42 cm
    Ⓔ 64 cm

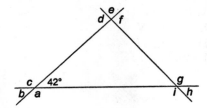

20. In the figure above, what is the sum of the nine angles labeled with letters?

    Ⓐ 138°
    Ⓑ 378°
    Ⓒ 678°
    Ⓓ 900°
    Ⓔ It cannot be determined from the information given.

21. Approximately how many cubic feet of water are needed to fill a circular swimming pool that is 50 feet across and 8 feet deep?

    Ⓐ   400
    Ⓑ 6,000
    Ⓒ 16,000
    Ⓓ 20,000
    Ⓔ 42,000

22. Dividing by $\frac{3}{8}$ and then multiplying by $\frac{5}{6}$ is the same as dividing by what number?

    Ⓐ $3\frac{1}{5}$

    Ⓑ $\frac{16}{5}$

    Ⓒ $\frac{20}{9}$

    Ⓓ $\frac{9}{20}$

    Ⓔ $\frac{5}{16}$

23. At an elementary school, 70% of the faculty members are women and 60% of the faculty members are married. If $\frac{2}{3}$ of the men are single, what fraction of the women are married?

    Ⓐ $\frac{5}{7}$

    Ⓑ $\frac{7}{10}$

    Ⓒ $\frac{1}{3}$

    Ⓓ $\frac{7}{30}$

    Ⓔ $\frac{5}{70}$

24. At a party, there were five times as many females as males. There were three times as many adults as children. Which of the following could NOT be the number of people at the party?

    Ⓐ 384
    Ⓑ 258
    Ⓒ 216
    Ⓓ 120
    Ⓔ 72

25. The Arnolds purchased 550 square feet of Kentucky Gem sod at $1.89 per square foot and 270 square feet of Zelzea Blue sod at $1.38 per square foot. What was the approximate average price per square foot paid for all the sod?

    Ⓐ $1.63
    Ⓑ $1.64
    Ⓒ $1.68
    Ⓓ $1.72
    Ⓔ $1.76

26. While traveling from city A to city B, Sharon and Andy average 50 miles per hour. For the return trip, they average 40 miles per hour. What was their average speed for the round trip?

    Ⓐ 45 mph
    Ⓑ More than 45 mph
    Ⓒ Less than 45 mph
    Ⓓ More than 50 mph
    Ⓔ It cannot be determined from the information given.

27. If $g < 0$ and $f \neq 0$, which of these four expressions must have a positive sign?

    I. gf
    II. g^2f
    III. gf^2
    IV. $(gf)^2$

    Ⓐ IV only
    Ⓑ I and III only
    Ⓒ I and IV only
    Ⓓ II and III only
    Ⓔ II and IV only

28. If $x = y + y^2$, and y is a negative integer, when y decreases in value, then x

    Ⓐ increases in value
    Ⓑ fluctuates
    Ⓒ decreases in value
    Ⓓ remains the same
    Ⓔ decreases in constant increments

29. If m and n are integers and $\sqrt{mn} = 10$, which of the following cannot be a value of $m + n$?

Ⓐ 25
Ⓑ 29
Ⓒ 50
Ⓓ 52
Ⓔ 101

30. The three digits of a number add up to 11. The number is divisible by 5. The leftmost digit is double the middle digit. What is the product of the three digits?

Ⓐ 40
Ⓑ 72
Ⓒ 78
Ⓓ 88
Ⓔ 125

31. Which is closest to 1?

Ⓐ $\dfrac{3}{3 + 0.03}$

Ⓑ $\dfrac{3}{(3 + 0.03)^2}$

Ⓒ $\dfrac{3}{3 + 0.3}$

Ⓓ $\dfrac{3}{3 + (0.03)^2}$

Ⓔ $\dfrac{3}{(3 + 0.3)^2}$

32. The smallest of three consecutive even integers is 40 less than three times the largest. What is the largest of these integers?

Ⓐ 14
Ⓑ 17
Ⓒ 18
Ⓓ 19
Ⓔ 20

ABOVE AVERAGE TO DIFFICULT

33. In ten years, David will be four times as old as Aaron. Twenty years ago, David was twice as old as Ellen. If David is seven years older than Ellen, how old is Aaron?

    Ⓐ 1–5
    Ⓑ 6–10
    Ⓒ 11–15
    Ⓓ 16–20
    Ⓔ 21–25

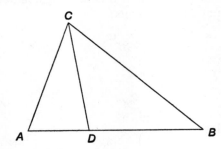

34. In the figure, *AB = BC, CD = BD,* and angle *CAD* = 70°. Therefore, what is the measure of angle *ADC*?

    Ⓐ 50
    Ⓑ 60
    Ⓒ 70
    Ⓓ 80
    Ⓔ 85

35. Two airplanes take off from one airfield at noon. One flies due east at 200 miles per hour while the other flies directly northeast at 283 miles per hour. Approximately how many miles apart are the airplanes at 2 P.M.?

    Ⓐ 166
    Ⓑ 332
    Ⓒ 400
    Ⓓ 483
    Ⓔ 566

36. A square, with perimeter 16, is inscribed in a circle. What is the area of the circle?

    (A) 4π
    (B) 8π
    (C) 12π
    (D) 16π
    (E) 32π

37. Approximately how many revolutions will be made by a car tire with a 14-inch diameter if the car travels $\frac{1}{2}$ mile?

    (A)   120
    (B)   180
    (C)   360
    (D)   720
    (E) 1,440

38. If a man travels f miles an hour for t hours and r miles an hour for s hours, what is his average rate in miles per hour for the entire distance traveled?

    (A) $ft + rs$

    (B) $\dfrac{ft + rs}{2}$

    (C) $\dfrac{f}{t} + \dfrac{r}{s}$

    (D) $\dfrac{ft + rs}{t + s}$

    (E) $\dfrac{ft + rs}{t - s}$

39. The greatest common factor of two positive integers is X. The least common multiple of these two integers is Y. If one of the integers is Z, what is the other?

Ⓐ $\dfrac{XY}{Z}$

Ⓑ $XZ + YZ$

Ⓒ $\dfrac{X}{Z} + Y$

Ⓓ $X + \dfrac{Y}{Z}$

Ⓔ $X + \dfrac{Z}{Y}$

40. Given the exponential quantities $m = 8^5$ and $n = 2^{12}$, what is the quotient m/n?

Ⓐ 6^{-7}
Ⓑ 7^{-6}
Ⓒ 6
Ⓓ 8
Ⓔ 16

41. What is the area of a square that has a diagonal of length $\sqrt{10}$?

Ⓐ 5
Ⓑ 10
Ⓒ 20
Ⓓ 40
Ⓔ 45

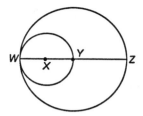

42. In the figure, X and Y are the centers of the two circles. If the area of the larger circle is 144π, what is the area of the smaller circle?

    Ⓐ 72π
    Ⓑ 36π
    Ⓒ 24π
    Ⓓ 12π
    Ⓔ It cannot be determined from the information given.

43. The length of a rectangle is decreased by 15% and its width is increased by 40%. Does the area of the rectangle decrease or increase and by what percent?

    Ⓐ Decreases by 19%
    Ⓑ Decreases by 25%
    Ⓒ Increases by 6%
    Ⓓ Increases by 19%
    Ⓔ Increases by 25%

44. A prize of $600 is to be distributed among 20 winners, each of whom must be awarded at least $20. If $\frac{2}{5}$ of the prize will be distributed to $\frac{3}{5}$ of the winners, what is the greatest possible individual award?

    Ⓐ $20
    Ⓑ $25
    Ⓒ $200
    Ⓓ $220
    Ⓔ $300

45. If electricity costs x cents per kilowatt hour for the first 30 kilowatt hours and y cents per kilowatt hour for each additional kilowatt hour, what is the cost of z kilowatt hours $(z > 30)$?

   Ⓐ $30(x-y)+yz$
   Ⓑ $30y-30x+yz$
   Ⓒ $30(x-y+z)$
   Ⓓ $(z-30)x+30y$
   Ⓔ $30x+(y-30)z$

46. A right circular cylinder has a diameter of 20, as shown in the figure. If its height is 100, then its total surface area in square inches is approximately

   Ⓐ   600
   Ⓑ   3,000
   Ⓒ   6,000
   Ⓓ   6,600
   Ⓔ 30,000

47. If the @ of an integer is defined as the product of its cube root and its square root, then the @ of N equals 50% of N for which of the following?

   Ⓐ   1
   Ⓑ   64
   Ⓒ   100
   Ⓓ   144
   Ⓔ 1,000,000

48. Macey is three times as old as Mike. In eight years, she will be twice as old as Mike. How old was Macey three years ago?

    Ⓐ 5
    Ⓑ 8
    Ⓒ 21
    Ⓓ 24
    Ⓔ 30

49. If *a*, *b*, and *c* are consecutive positive odd integers, not necessarily in that order, which of the following must be true?

    I. $a + b > c$
    II. $bc > a$
    III. $(a + c)^2 > b$

    Ⓐ I only
    Ⓑ II only
    Ⓒ III only
    Ⓓ I and II only
    Ⓔ II and III only

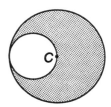

50. In the figure above, point C is the center of the larger circle. What is the ratio of the area of the shaded crescent to the area of the small circle?

    Ⓐ 2
    Ⓑ 2.4
    Ⓒ 3
    Ⓓ 3.25
    Ⓔ 4

51. If x, y, and z are consecutive positive integers greater than 1, not necessarily in that order, then which of the following is (are) true?

   I. $x > z$
   II. $x + y > z$
   III. $yz > xz$
   IV. $xy > y + z$

  Ⓐ I only
  Ⓑ II only
  Ⓒ II and III only
  Ⓓ II and IV only
  Ⓔ III and IV only

52. An empty fuel tank is filled with brand Z gasoline. When the tank is half empty, it is filled with brand Y gasoline. When the tank is half empty again, it is filled with brand Z gasoline. When the tank is half empty again, it is filled with brand Y gasoline. At this time, what percent of the gasoline in the tank is brand Z?

  Ⓐ 50%
  Ⓑ 40%
  Ⓒ 37.5%
  Ⓓ $33\frac{1}{3}\%$
  Ⓔ 25%

53. Forty percent of the employees of Company A are females, and 60% of Company B are females. If 30 female employees move from Company B to Company A, making the percent of female employees of each of the two companies equal, and if the total number of employees in each company are equal, how many total male employees are there in Companies A and B together?

  Ⓐ 400
  Ⓑ 300
  Ⓒ 200
  Ⓓ 100
  Ⓔ 50

ANSWERS AND EXPLANATIONS FOR THE PRACTICE PROBLEM SOLVING QUESTIONS

EASY TO MODERATE

1. Ⓐ One method is

$$\frac{\text{is number}}{\text{of number}} = \frac{\text{percent}}{100}$$

$$\frac{80}{60} = \frac{x}{100}$$

Cross-multiplying gives $60x = 8{,}000$

Divide by 60 $x = \dfrac{8{,}000}{60}$

Then $x = 133\tfrac{1}{3}\%$

Another method is making an equation by replacing "what percent" with $x/100$, "of" by times ($\cdot$) and "is" by equals ($=$) giving the equation

$$\frac{x}{100} \cdot 60 = 80$$

Simplifying gives $\dfrac{3}{5}x = 80$

Multiplying by $\dfrac{5}{3}$ $\left(\dfrac{5}{3}\right)\left(\dfrac{3}{5}\right)x = 80\left(\dfrac{5}{3}\right)$

$$x = \frac{400}{3}$$

Then $x = 133\tfrac{1}{3}\%$

2. Ⓑ Solve by setting up a proportion.

If 1 cm = 35 km
then x cm = 245 km

and
$$\frac{1}{x} = \frac{35}{245}$$
$$35x = 245$$
$$\frac{35x}{35} = \frac{245}{35}$$
$$x = 7$$

3. Ⓑ Forty-eight days late is one day shy of exactly 7 weeks (7 weeks × 7 days/week = 49 days). If the job were finished in 49 days, then it would have been complete on the same day, Wednesday. But since 48 is one day less than 7 weeks, it was completed one day earlier than Wednesday: Tuesday.

4. Ⓓ Since each of the 4 sport jackets may be worn with 5 different shirts, we have 20 possible combinations. These may be worn with each of the 3 pairs of slacks for a total of 60 possible combinations. Stated simply, 5 × 4 × 3 = 60 possible combinations. Notice that answers Ⓐ and Ⓑ are not reasonable.

5. Ⓒ We have

10% of 1,000 is 100. (1,000 + 100) = 1,100
10% of 1,100 is 110. (1,100 + 110) = 1,210
10% of 1,210 is 121. (1,210 + 121) = 1,331

6. Ⓓ The increase was 94 − 84 = 10. The percent increase is found by dividing the increase by the *original* or *from* amount. Thus 10/84 = 11.9%.

7. Ⓒ There was an increase from 18% to 22%. That is a 4% increase. Therefore, a 4% increase from 18% is a 22% increase in the percent spent on food and drink.

8. Ⓑ Substituting for x and y, the expression is
$$(6-2(-2))^{-2}$$
$$=(6+4)^{-2}=(10)^{-2}$$
$$=\frac{1}{(10)^2}=\frac{1}{100}=0.01$$

9. Ⓓ Simplify the problem as follows:
$$\sqrt{72x^5}=\sqrt{36\cdot 2\cdot x^4\cdot x}$$
Since the $\sqrt{36}$ is 6, and $\sqrt{x^4}$ is x^2, then
$$\sqrt{36\cdot 2\cdot x^4\cdot x}=6x^2\sqrt{2x}$$

You could also work from the answers.

10. Ⓑ There are 140 line employees with 3 to 5 years of employment. There are 80 of them taking the First Aid workshop. Thus $140-80=60$.

11. Ⓑ For the line employees, there are 30 taking both workshops, 20 taking only the Stress workshop, and 10 taking only the First Aid workshop. For the staff employees, there are 20 taking both, 20 taking only the Stress workshop, and 30 taking only the First Aid workshop. Thus 130 are taking at least one workshop. Therefore, 230 out of 360 are not taking a workshop, or 64%.

12. Ⓒ Distance = rate × time
$$d=rt$$
$$k=rn$$
$$r=\frac{k}{n}\text{ miles per hour}$$
$$d=\frac{k}{n}\cdot(x)=\frac{kx}{n}$$

13. ⓓ
$$ax + by = c$$
$$\underline{-ax \qquad\qquad -ax}$$
$$by = c - ax$$
$$\frac{by}{y} = \frac{c - ax}{y}$$
$$b = \frac{c - ax}{y}$$

14. ⓓ A rectangular solid consists of six rectangular faces. This one in particular has two 7 × 6, two 6 × 3, and two 7 × 3 rectangles with areas of 42, 18, and 21, respectively. Hence the total surface area will be 2(42) + 2(18) + 2(21) = 84 + 36 + 42 = 162 square meters.

15. ⓓ Multiplying the equation 1/3 + 1/2 + 1/x = 4 by common denominator 6x, we get $6x/3 + 6x/2 + 6x/x = 4(6x)$. Reducing, we get

$$2x + 3x + 6 = 24x$$
$$5x + 6 = 24x$$
$$6 = 19x$$
$$\frac{6}{19} = x$$

16. ⓑ Checking each possible pair of numbers for common divisions:

    I.   3 ⎫ Only common divisor 1
    II. 4 ⎬ These are relatively prime
    I.   3 ⎫ Only common divisor 1
   III. 7 ⎬ These are relatively prime

I. 3⎫ Common divisors are 1 and 3
IV. 12⎭ These are *not* relatively prime

Since I and IV are *not* relatively prime, check the choices to see which include I and IV. Notice that I and II are only in choices Ⓑ and Ⓔ; therefore, those are the two possible choices. A closer look eliminates choice Ⓔ because I and II have numbers that are relatively prime. For good measure, check II and IV:

II. 4⎫ Common divisors are 1 and 4
IV. 12⎭ These are *not* relatively prime

Therefore I and IV, and II and IV are *not* relatively prime, giving the correct answer of Ⓑ.

AVERAGE

17. Ⓒ If 5 machines can produce 20 units in 10 hours, then 20 machines can produce 80 units in 10 hours. Since 100 is 25% more than 80, the correct answer is 25% more than 10, or 12.5 hours.

18. Ⓑ Let x = number of apples Peter ate. Thus $x + 0.4x = 1.4x$ is the number of apples Peter sold. Thus $1.4x = 70$; $x = 70/1.4$, or 50. Notice that answers Ⓐ, Ⓓ, and Ⓔ are not reasonable.

19. Ⓑ The third side of the right triangle can be found using the Pythagorean theorem.

$$a^2 + b^2 = c^2$$
$$a^2 + (15)^2 = (17)^2$$
$$a^2 + 225 = 289$$
$$a^2 = 64$$
$$a = 8$$

The perimeter is the sum of the three sides of the triangle.

$$18 + 15 + 17 = 40 \text{ cm}$$

20. Ⓓ The four angles around each point of intersection sum to 360°, a complete revolution. The twelve angles in the figure must sum to $3 \times 360° = 1,080°$. Three of the angles are the interior angles of a triangle, so the nine lettered angles equal $1,080° - 180° = 900°$. The 42° angle is merely a distraction.

21. Ⓒ The volume of the swimming pool equals its area times its depth. The circular area has a radius of 25 feet.

$$V = \pi r^2 h = 3.14(25)^2(8) = 15,700$$

That volume is closest to choice Ⓒ.

22. Ⓓ Dividing by a number is the same as multiplying by its inverse, and vice versa. Thus multiplying by $\frac{5}{6}$ is the same as dividing by $\frac{6}{5}$. Thus the answer is $(\frac{3}{8})(\frac{6}{5}) = \frac{18}{40} = \frac{9}{20}$.

23. Ⓐ Suppose that there are 100 faculty members at the school. If 70% are women, then 30% are men. We then have 70 women and 30 men. If $\frac{2}{3}$ of the men are single, then $\frac{1}{3}$ of 30 = 10 men who are married. 60% or 60 teachers are married. If 10 are men, then 50 are women. Therefore, the fraction of women who are married is $\frac{50}{70}$, or $\frac{5}{7}$.

24. Ⓑ From the first sentence, we see that the total number of persons at the party must be divisible by 6 (5:1). From the second sentence, the total must be divisible by 4 (3:1). Thus the total must be a number divisible by both 6 and 4; such a number would be divisible by 12. The only number given that is not divisible by 12 is 258.

25. Ⓓ Notice that approximately 2 square feet of Kentucky Gem sod was purchased for every 1 square foot of Zelzea Blue. Therefore, the problem may be simplified by using a simple 2 to 1 ratio. The average of

$$\begin{array}{ll} 2 \text{ square feet @ } \$1.89 = & \$3.78 \\ \underline{1 \text{ square foot @ } \$1.38 =} & \underline{1.38} \\ 3 \text{ square feet} & \$5.16 \end{array}$$

Dividing $5.16 by 3 = $1.72 per square foot.

26. Ⓒ Since more time was spent traveling at 40 mph, the average will be closer to 40 than to 50.

27. Ⓐ Since g is negative and f may be negative, it is necessary to square each of the two parameters to be assured of obtaining a positive expression. Note that $(gf)^2 = g^2f^2$.

28. Ⓐ Substituting small negative integers is the most effective method for this problem.

$$\text{Let} \quad y = -1$$
$$\text{then} \quad x = -1 + (-1)^2$$
$$x = -1 + 1$$
$$x = 0$$

$$\text{Now let } y = -2$$
$$\text{then} \quad x = -2 + (-2)^2$$
$$x = -2 + 4$$
$$x = 2$$

Therefore, x increases in value.

29. Ⓒ Since $\sqrt{mn} = 10$, $mn = 100$, and the possible values for m and n would be as follows: 1 and 100, 2 and 50, 4 and 25, 5 and 20, 10 and 10. Since none of these combinations yield $m + n = 50$, choice Ⓒ is correct.

30. Ⓐ Since the number is divisible by 5, it must end with a 0 or a 5. Because the first digit is double the second, the first two digits of the number must be 21, 42, 63, or 84. The only combination that adds to 11 is 425. The product of those digits is $4 \times 2 \times 5 = 40$.

31. Ⓓ Note that choices Ⓑ and Ⓔ are approximately equal to $3/(3)^2$ or $1/3$. For the remaining choices, the fraction closest to 1 will be the fraction whose denominator has the *least* value added to 3. Choice Ⓓ has the smallest value, 0.0009, added to 3. Note: $(0.03)^2 = 0.0009$.

32. Ⓒ Set the three consecutive even integers equal to x, $x + 2$, and $x + 4$. The equation: $x = 3(x + 4) - 40$, $x = 3x + 12 - 40$, $-2x = -28$. Thus $x = 14$. But that is the smallest of the three integers. Thus 18 is the largest.

ABOVE AVERAGE TO DIFFICULT

33. Ⓐ The solution to this problem can be seen through the following grid. The sequence of the solution is indicated by the arrows.

	20 years ago	now	in 10 years
David	$4x - 30$	$4x - 10$	$4x$
Ellen	$2x - 15$	$2x + 5$	
Aaron		$x - 10$	x

$$4x - 10 = (2x + 5) + 7$$
$$4x - 10 = 2x + 12$$
$$2x = 22$$
$$x = 11$$

Therefore, Aaron is now $x - 10 = 1$.

34. Ⓓ Since $AB = BC$, angle CAD is equal to angle ACB (isoceles triangle ABC). Thus angle ACB is also 70°. This makes angle B equal to 40° (180° in a triangle). Also, angle BCD equals 40° (same reason as above). Thus angle ADC equals 80° (external angle theorem: external angle of a triangle is equal to the sum of the opposite two angles).

35. Ⓒ It is helpful to sketch a map of the positions, as shown following. You should know that the northeast direction is 45° north of east, bisecting the north and east directions. After two hours the airplanes are at the arrowheads on the map. Since $566 \cong 400\sqrt{2}$, they are at two corners of a 45° right triangle. At that time, the airplanes are approximately 400 miles apart.

36. Ⓑ In the square $ABCD$, each side is 4, since the perimeter is 16. Then by the Pythagorean theorem, $d = 4\sqrt{2}$.

$$4^2 + 4^2 = d^2$$
$$16 + 16 = d^2$$
$$32 = d^2$$
$$\sqrt{32} = d$$

Simplifying

$$d = \sqrt{32}$$
$$= \sqrt{16 \times 2}$$
$$= \sqrt{16} \times \sqrt{2}$$
$$= 4\sqrt{2}$$

The radius is

$$r = \frac{d}{2}$$
$$= \frac{4\sqrt{2}}{2}$$
$$= 2\sqrt{2}$$

The area of the circle

$$= \pi r^2$$
$$= \pi (2\sqrt{2})^2$$
$$= \pi \times 4 \times 2$$
$$= 8\pi$$

Thus ⒷⒷ is correct. If you recognize DBC as a 45°-45°-90° triangle with side ratios $1:1:1\sqrt{2}$, you can quickly find d by $4:4:4\sqrt{2}$.

37. ⒹⒹ First calculate the circumference of the circle using the equation $C = \pi d$ (or $C = 2\pi r$). $C = (\frac{22}{7})14 = 44$. The circumference is 44 inches. Now change $\frac{1}{2}$ mile to feet (2,640) to inches, $2,640 \times 12 = 31,680$. Dividing 31,680 by 44 = 720 revolutions.

38. ⒹⒹ Average rate is total distance (found by multiplying rate times time and adding $ft + rs$) divided by total time ($t + s$); therefore, the average rate is

$$\frac{ft + rs}{t + s}$$

39. ⒶⒶ The product of the LCM and GCF of two numbers is the same as the product of the two original numbers. Thus the answer is XY/Z.

40. ⒹⒹ Exponential quantities can be readily divided (or multiplied) if they have the same base. To convert m from base-8 to base-2, consider that $8 = 2^3$. Therefore, $m = 8^5 = (2^3)^5 = 2^{15}$.

$$\frac{m}{n} = \frac{2^{15}}{2^{12}} = 2^3 = 8$$

If two exponential quantities have the same base, they may be divided by subtracting the exponent of the denominator from the exponent of the numerator.

41. ⒶⒶ From the relationship that exists in a right triangle, we see that the sides of the square must equal the square root of 5. Thus the area of the square is 5.

42. ⒷⒷ Area of the larger circle = 144π

Since area = πr^2, then

$$\pi r^2 = 144\pi$$
$$r^2 = 144$$
$$r = 12$$

Radius of larger circle = 12
Diameter of smaller circle = 12
Radius of smaller circle = 6
Area of smaller circle = πr^2
$$= \pi(6)^2$$
$$= 36\pi$$

43. Ⓓ Let 85%L represent a 15% decrease in length. Then 140%W represents a 40% increase in width. The new rectangle will have

$$\text{area} = (\text{new length})(\text{new width})$$
$$= (85\%L)(140\%W)$$
$$= \frac{\overset{17}{\cancel{85}}}{\underset{20}{\cancel{100}}}L \cdot \frac{\overset{7}{\cancel{140}}}{\underset{5}{\cancel{100}}}W$$
$$= \frac{119}{100}LW$$
$$= 119\%LW$$

The old rectangle has area 100%LW. Thus, the new rectangle has area 19% *greater* than the original 100%.

44. Ⓓ If $\frac{2}{5}$ of the prize ($\frac{2}{5}$ of $600 = $240) is distributed to $\frac{3}{5}$ of the winners ($\frac{3}{5}$ of 20 is 12 winners), this indicates that each of those 12 winners will receive the minimum of $20. That leaves $360 to be divided among 8 remaining winners. If 7 of those winners receive the minimum $20 (total $140), then the eighth winner would receive all the remaining prize money, $360−$140 = $220.

45. Ⓐ From the given information, it costs 30x for the first 30 kilowatt hours. Thus $z - 30$ kilowatt hours remain at y cents per kilowatt hour. Thus $30x + (z - 30)y = (30x) - (30y) + yz = 30(x - y) + yz$.

46. ⓓ To find the total surface area of a right circular cylinder, you must find not only the area of the "barrel" portion but also the area of the top and bottom circles. The area of the "barrel" portion equals the circumference of either the top or bottom circle times the height. $C = \pi d \cong 3 \times 20 = 60$. Thus the area of the "barrel" $= C \times h = 60 \times 100 = 6,000$. Now to find the *total* surface area, add the areas of both top and bottom circles, or $2 \times \pi r^2 \cong 2 \times 3 \times 10^2 = 600$. Therefore, the total surface area $\cong 6,000 + 600 = 6,600$.

47. ⓑ Working from the answer choices, the @ of $64 = 4 \times 8 = 32$, which is 50% of 64.

48. ⓒ Let x be Mike's age. Thus $3x$ is Macey's age. Thus $3x + 8 = 2(x + 8)$, $3x + 8 = 2x + 16$. Thus $x = 8$. Therefore, $3x = 24$. Thus Macey is 24 and 3 years ago was 21.

Notice you could also work from the answers.

49. ⓒ The positive odd integers a, b, and c could be 1, 3, and 5. Option I is not necessarily true: $1 + 3$ is not greater than 5. Option II is not necessarily true: 1×3 is not greater than 5. Only option III must be true: the square of the sum of any two of the integers will be greater than the third integer.

50. ⓒ The radius of the large circle equals the diameter of the small circle, so the radius of the large circle is twice the radius of the small circle. Area is proportional to the square of the radius, so the large circle has an area $2^2 = 4$ times that of the small circle. If the small circle is $\frac{1}{4}$ of the large circle, then the crescent area is $\frac{3}{4}$ of the large circle. The crescent and small circle are in the ratio $(\frac{3}{4})/(\frac{1}{4}) = 3$.

51. ⓑ Adding any two of three consecutive positive integers greater than 1 will always be greater than the other integer; therefore, II is true. The others cannot be determined, as they depend on the values and/or the order of x, y, and z.

52. © We can tabulate the data:

	part of tank brand Z	part of tank brand Y
after first fill up	1	0
before second fill up	$\frac{1}{2}$	0
after second fill up	$\frac{1}{2}$	$\frac{1}{2}$
before third fill up	$\frac{1}{4}$	$\frac{1}{4}$
after third fill up	$\frac{3}{4}$	$\frac{1}{4}$
before fourth fill up	$\frac{3}{8}$	$\frac{1}{8}$
after fourth fill up	$\frac{3}{8}$	$\frac{5}{8}$

Since the tank is now full, $\frac{3}{8}$, or 37.5%, is brand Z.

53. ⑧ Try a simple number of total employees and see what happens. If the total employees for Company A is 100, then 40 are female and 60 are male. Then Company B has 60 females and 40 males. If 30 female employees move from Company B to A, then there are 70 in A and 30 in B. They are not equal. Next try 200. Then Company A has 80 females and 120 males, while Company B has 120 females and 80 males. Try 300. If A has 300, then 120 are female, and 180 are male, and B has 180 female and 120 male. If 30 females from Company B join Company A, then each company has 150 females, so each company must have 150 males for a total of 300.

INTRODUCTION TO DATA SUFFICIENCY

Data Sufficiency questions do not require you to answer the question necessarily, but only to recognize if it could be answered. These problems usually take less time then Problem Solving questions.

ABILITY TESTED

Data Sufficiency questions test your ability to analyze a problem, to recognize relevant or irrelevant information in determining the solution of that problem, and to determine when you have sufficient information to solve that problem.

BASIC SKILLS NECESSARY

Correctly answering these questions requires competence in high school arithmetic, algebra, and intuitive geometry. Mathematical insight and problem-solving skills are also necessary. No advanced mathematics is required.

DIRECTIONS

Each of the problems below consists of a question and two statements, labeled (1) and (2), in which certain data are given. You must decide whether the data given in the statements are *sufficient* to answer the question. Using the data given in the statements plus your knowledge of mathematics and everyday facts (such as the number of days in July or the meaning of *counterclockwise*), you are to choose oval

-   (A) if statement (1) ALONE is sufficient, but statement (2) alone is not sufficient to answer the question asked;
-   (B) if statement (2) ALONE is sufficient, but statement (1) alone is not sufficient to answer the question asked;
-   (C) if both statements (1) and (2) TOGETHER are sufficient to answer the question asked, but NEITHER statement ALONE is sufficient;

Ⓓ if EACH statement ALONE is sufficient to answer the question asked;

Ⓔ if statements (1) and (2) TOGETHER are NOT sufficient to answer the question asked, and additional data specific to the problem are needed.

Remember that on the actual exam the statements will not be lettered. You will simply choose the oval of the correct statement.

ANALYSIS

The purpose here is to determine whether information given is sufficient to answer the question; therefore, do not solve the problem unless it is absolutely necessary.

The memory aid 12TEN will simplify the directions, making it easier to avoid reading them again for every question. 12TEN stands for:

1 *First* statement alone is sufficient, not the second. CHOOSE Ⓐ.

2 *Second* statement alone is sufficient, not the first. CHOOSE Ⓑ.

T *Together* is the only way they are sufficient. CHOOSE Ⓒ.

E *Either* statement alone is sufficient. CHOOSE Ⓓ.

N *Neither* statement, together or alone, is sufficient, CHOOSE Ⓔ.

REMEMBER: ONE, TWO, TOGETHER, EITHER, NEITHER, or 12TEN. (*Note: Either* means choose answer Ⓓ *not* Ⓔ.)

Because of the structure of this type of question, you should always be able to eliminate some of the choices. If statement (1) ALONE is sufficient to answer the question, then the answer *must* be Ⓐ or Ⓓ. If statement (1) ALONE is *not* sufficient to answer the question, then the answer *must* be Ⓑ, Ⓒ, or Ⓔ. If statements (1) and (2) ALONE are not sufficient, then the answer *must* be Ⓒ or Ⓔ.

If statements (1) or (2) ALONE *are* sufficient, then you *never* try them TOGETHER.

Sometimes geometric figures are included; they should be used only for positional value. They are not to be measured as they are not necessarily drawn to scale.

SUGGESTED APPROACH WITH SAMPLES

Note that on the exam the answer choices will appear at the bottom of the screen for each question.

Quickly decide what is the necessary basic information to answer the question. Then see if the data supplies that information.

1. What is the area of circle *O*?

   (1) The circumference is 12π.

   (2) The diameter is 12.

   Ⓐ Statement (1) ALONE is sufficient, but statement (2) alone is not sufficient.

   Ⓑ Statement (2) ALONE is sufficient, but statement (1) alone is not sufficient.

   Ⓒ BOTH statements (1) and (2) TOGETHER are sufficient, but NEITHER statement ALONE is sufficient.

   Ⓓ EACH statement ALONE is sufficient.

   Ⓔ Statements (1) and (2) TOGETHER are NOT sufficient.

To find the area of a circle, it is necessary to have the radius. (1) gives enough information to find the radius by substituting into the circumference formula, $C = 2\pi r$, and getting $12\pi = 2\pi r$. Then simply solve for *r*, which is 6. Thus this area is 36π. None of this solving is necessary, only knowing that you need the radius and can find it from the information given. (2) also gives enough information to find the radius; therefore, the answer is Ⓓ, either will be sufficient.

Don't solve unless it is absolutely necessary.

2. What is the value of *x*?

   (1) $3x + 12 = 36$

   (2) $5x + 3y = 16$

This problem is most easily solved by inspecting the first bit of data and quickly noticing that (1) is enough to answer the question (one variable, one equation, solvable). (2) does not answer the question.

This can also be determined by inspection (two variables, one equation, not solvable for a single value). The correct answer is Ⓐ, yet no actual solving needs to be done.

Use a simple marking system on your scratch paper to assist you in making your decision.

3. What is the average height of Tom, Bob, and Luke?

   (1) Bob is 4 inches shorter than Luke, and Tom is 4 inches taller than Luke.

   (2) Luke is 5 feet 6 inches tall.

Write a (1) and (2) on your scratch paper to represent the data given. (1) is not sufficient, since no actual height is given; therefore mark a slash through (1). Note that the answer is immediately narrowed to Ⓑ, Ⓒ, or Ⓔ. (2) by itself is also not sufficient, as the other two, Tom and Bob, aren't mentioned; therefore, a slash should be made through (2). Notice that the answer is now narrowed to Ⓒ or Ⓔ. The markings on your paper should look as follows:

Now trying them together, they are sufficient. The answer is Ⓒ. In marking the data, if you are in doubt whether it is sufficient or not, put a question mark by the data and try the next bit of data. Don't waste time trying one bit of data for more than about 30 seconds.

Don't read in specialized knowledge; use only the information given and general or common knowledge.

4. What is the runner's average speed in running around the track?

   (1) One lap took 49 seconds.

   (2) He ran 5 seconds faster than his previous best time.

Someone familiar with track and field would quickly assume that one lap is the standard 440 yards and would then *incorrectly answer* Ⓐ. This sort of assumption cannot be made because it is from specialized knowledge in the area and therefore is not general knowledge. The correct answer is Ⓔ, as the distance around the track is not given in either bit of data.

If a geometric figure is involved in the question, redraw the figure on your scratch paper, mark the figure with the information given, and circle what you are looking for.

5. In the equilateral triangle above, what is the measure of angle *x*?

   (1) $\overline{BD}$ is a median.

   (2) Angle *BDE* is 90°.

After redrawing the figure, notice the markings from the information given:

Mark in information given in data (1) as you read it, but *remember to erase that information before you try data* (2). (1) If $\overline{BD}$ is a median in an equilateral triangle, then it is also an angle bisector, making angle *x* equal to 30°. (Once again, the answer is not necessary, just the knowledge that it could be found.) (2) also gives enough information because if angle *BDE* is 90°, then angle *BDC* is 90°, and angle *x* is 30°, as there are 180° in a triangle. Redrawing and marking the diagram makes the problem easier to solve.

If a geometric diagram is discussed, but no figure is given, draw a simple diagram on your scratch paper.

6. If the legs of a trapezoid are equal, what is the area?

    (1) The smaller base is 8 inches and the legs are 6 inches.

    (2) The height is 5 inches.

Drawing the diagram helps give important insight into what is needed to answer the question.

base

base

Now consider what is needed to find the area—the length of each base and the height, since the area formula is $\frac{1}{2}h(b_1 + b_2)$ or $h(b_1 + b_2)/2$.

(1) does not give sufficient information to find the larger base or the height. (2), by itself, does not give enough information to find the bases. (1) and (2) together give enough information to find the bases and the height. The answer is ©. The Pythagorean theorem would be necessary to find the length of the difference between the smaller and larger bases. Adding this difference to the length of the shorter base would give the longer base. You now have the necessary information. Notice the markings on the diagram below, to assist you in deciding what you have to work with.

8

8

A PATTERNED PLAN OF ATTACK
Data Sufficiency

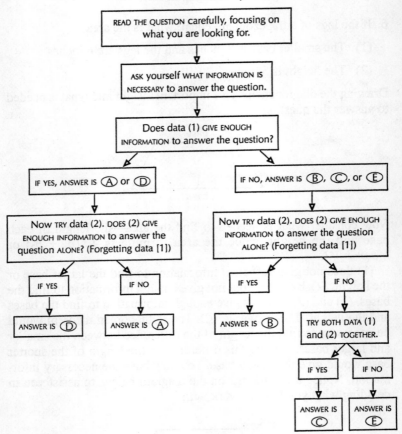

READ THE QUESTION carefully, focusing on what you are looking for.

ASK yourself WHAT INFORMATION IS NECESSARY to answer the question.

Does data (1) GIVE ENOUGH INFORMATION to answer the question?

IF YES, ANSWER IS (A) or (D)

IF NO, ANSWER IS (B), (C), or (E)

Now TRY data (2). DOES (2) GIVE ENOUGH INFORMATION to answer the question ALONE? (Forgetting data [1])

IF YES → ANSWER IS (D)

IF NO → ANSWER IS (A)

Now TRY data (2). DOES (2) GIVE ENOUGH INFORMATION to answer the question ALONE? (Forgetting data [1])

IF YES → ANSWER IS (B)

IF NO → TRY BOTH DATA (1) and (2) TOGETHER.

IF YES → ANSWER IS (C)

IF NO → ANSWER IS (E)

KEEP THE FOLLOWING TIPS IN MIND.
1. Don't solve unless it is absolutely necessary.
2. Use a simple marking system (slashes, question marks, etc.).
3. Don't read in specialized knowledge. Use only common information.
4. Redraw or draw and mark in geometric figures when appropriate.

PRACTICE DATA SUFFICIENCY QUESTIONS

EASY TO MODERATE

1. Who is the tallest of four men?

    (1) Jim is shorter than Steve.

    (2) Mark and Steve are shorter than Walter.

    Ⓐ Statement (1) ALONE is sufficient, but statement (2) alone is not sufficient.

    Ⓑ Statement (2) ALONE is sufficient, but statement (1) alone is not sufficient.

    Ⓒ BOTH statements (1) and (2) TOGETHER are sufficient, but NEITHER statement ALONE is sufficient.

    Ⓓ EACH statement ALONE is sufficient.

    Ⓔ Statements (1) and (2) TOGETHER are NOT sufficient.

2. Does $A = C$?

    (1) $A \neq B$

    (2) $B \neq C$

    Ⓐ Statement (1) ALONE is sufficient, but statement (2) alone is not sufficient.

    Ⓑ Statement (2) ALONE is sufficient, but statement (1) alone is not sufficient.

    Ⓒ BOTH statements (1) and (2) TOGETHER are sufficient, but NEITHER statement ALONE is sufficient.

    Ⓓ EACH statement ALONE is sufficient.

    Ⓔ Statements (1) and (2) TOGETHER are NOT sufficient.

3. Which is more expensive, a peach or a plum?

   (1) A dozen plums cost $1.79.

   (2) Peaches are 69¢ a pound.

   Ⓐ Statement (1) ALONE is sufficient, but statement (2) alone is not sufficient.

   Ⓑ Statement (2) ALONE is sufficient, but statement (1) alone is not sufficient.

   Ⓒ BOTH statements (1) and (2) TOGETHER are sufficient, but NEITHER statement ALONE is sufficient.

   Ⓓ EACH statement ALONE is sufficient.

   Ⓔ Statements (1) and (2) TOGETHER are NOT sufficient.

4. What is the distance from Chicago to Miami?

   (1) A 550 mph turbojet takes $3\frac{1}{4}$ hours for the flight.

   (2) The jet consumes 3 gallons of fuel per mile.

   Ⓐ Statement (1) ALONE is sufficient, but statement (2) alone is not sufficient.

   Ⓑ Statement (2) ALONE is sufficient, but statement (1) alone is not sufficient.

   Ⓒ BOTH statements (1) and (2) TOGETHER are sufficient, but NEITHER statement ALONE is sufficient.

   Ⓓ EACH statement ALONE is sufficient.

   Ⓔ Statements (1) and (2) TOGETHER are NOT sufficient.

5. In the equation $3a - 7b + 14 = 0$, what is the value of b?

   (1) $a = b$

   (2) $a = 3$

   Ⓐ Statement (1) ALONE is sufficient, but statement (2) alone is not sufficient.

   Ⓑ Statement (2) ALONE is sufficient, but statement (1) alone is not sufficient.

   Ⓒ BOTH statements (1) and (2) TOGETHER are sufficient, but NEITHER statement ALONE is sufficient.

   Ⓓ EACH statement ALONE is sufficient.

   Ⓔ Statements (1) and (2) TOGETHER are NOT sufficient.

6. What is the area of a circular garden?

   (1) The circumference is 314 feet.

   (2) The radius is 50 feet.

   Ⓐ Statement (1) ALONE is sufficient, but statement (2) alone is not sufficient.
   Ⓑ Statement (2) ALONE is sufficient, but statement (1) alone is not sufficient.
   Ⓒ BOTH statements (1) and (2) TOGETHER are sufficient, but NEITHER statement ALONE is sufficient.
   Ⓓ EACH statement ALONE is sufficient.
   Ⓔ Statements (1) and (2) TOGETHER are NOT sufficient.

7. How far is Sacramento from Los Angeles?

   (1) A car that obtains 28 miles per gallon drove the distance on exactly one tank of gasoline.

   (2) Another car averaged 50 miles per hour and arrived in 8 hours.

   Ⓐ Statement (1) ALONE is sufficient, but statement (2) alone is not sufficient.
   Ⓑ Statement (2) ALONE is sufficient, but statement (1) alone is not sufficient.
   Ⓒ BOTH statements (1) and (2) TOGETHER are sufficient, but NEITHER statement ALONE is sufficient.
   Ⓓ EACH statement ALONE is sufficient.
   Ⓔ Statements (1) and (2) TOGETHER are NOT sufficient.

AVERAGE

8. What was the percentage increase of Mr. Doolittle's rent?

    (1) His rent was raised $45.

    (2) He now pays $315 per month.

    Ⓐ Statement (1) ALONE is sufficient, but statement (2) alone is not sufficient.
    Ⓑ Statement (2) ALONE is sufficient, but statement (1) alone is not sufficient.
    Ⓒ BOTH statements (1) and (2) TOGETHER are sufficient, but NEITHER statement ALONE is sufficient.
    Ⓓ EACH statement ALONE is sufficient.
    Ⓔ Statements (1) and (2) TOGETHER are NOT sufficient.

9. What is the numerical value of the ratio n/m?

    (1) $mn = 14$

    (2) $m = 6n$

    Ⓐ Statement (1) ALONE is sufficient, but statement (2) alone is not sufficient.
    Ⓑ Statement (2) ALONE is sufficient, but statement (1) alone is not sufficient.
    Ⓒ BOTH statements (1) and (2) TOGETHER are sufficient, but NEITHER statement ALONE is sufficient.
    Ⓓ EACH statement ALONE is sufficient.
    Ⓔ Statements (1) and (2) TOGETHER are NOT sufficient.

10. How many brothers does David have?

    (1) His parents have seven surviving children.

    (2) He has twice as many sisters as brothers.

    Ⓐ Statement (1) ALONE is sufficient, but statement (2) alone is not sufficient.
    Ⓑ Statement (2) ALONE is sufficient, but statement (1) alone is not sufficient.
    Ⓒ BOTH statements (1) and (2) TOGETHER are sufficient, but NEITHER statement ALONE is sufficient.
    Ⓓ EACH statement ALONE is sufficient.
    Ⓔ Statements (1) and (2) TOGETHER are NOT sufficient.

11. Is x greater than y?

    (1) $(x - y) > 0$

    (2) $x^2 < y^2$

    Ⓐ Statement (1) ALONE is sufficient, but statement (2) alone is not sufficient.
    Ⓑ Statement (2) ALONE is sufficient, but statement (1) alone is not sufficient.
    Ⓒ BOTH statements (1) and (2) TOGETHER are sufficient, but NEITHER statement ALONE is sufficient.
    Ⓓ EACH statement ALONE is sufficient.
    Ⓔ Statements (1) and (2) TOGETHER are NOT sufficient.

12. What was the interest rate on a savings account?

    (1) The saver collected $42 in simple interest over several months.

    (2) There was $1,680 in the account initially.

    Ⓐ Statement (1) ALONE is sufficient, but statement (2) alone is not sufficient.
    Ⓑ Statement (2) ALONE is sufficient, but statement (1) alone is not sufficient.
    Ⓒ BOTH statements (1) and (2) TOGETHER are sufficient, but NEITHER statement ALONE is sufficient.
    Ⓓ EACH statement ALONE is sufficient.
    Ⓔ Statements (1) and (2) TOGETHER are NOT sufficient.

13. Which is the smallest of three numbers that average 7?

    (1) One of the numbers is 4.

    (2) One of the numbers is 6.

    Ⓐ Statement (1) ALONE is sufficient, but statement (2) alone is not sufficient.
    Ⓑ Statement (2) ALONE is sufficient, but statement (1) alone is not sufficient.
    Ⓒ BOTH statements (1) and (2) TOGETHER are sufficient, but NEITHER statement ALONE is sufficient.
    Ⓓ EACH statement ALONE is sufficient.
    Ⓔ Statements (1) and (2) TOGETHER are NOT sufficient.

14. How many Mondays are in December of a particular year?

    (1) There are four Tuesdays that December.

    (2) There are four Saturdays that December.

    Ⓐ Statement (1) ALONE is sufficient, but statement (2) alone is not sufficient.

    Ⓑ Statement (2) ALONE is sufficient, but statement (1) alone is not sufficient.

    Ⓒ BOTH statements (1) and (2) TOGETHER are sufficient, but NEITHER statement ALONE is sufficient.

    Ⓓ EACH statement ALONE is sufficient.

    Ⓔ Statements (1) and (2) TOGETHER are NOT sufficient.

15. Students took a test and received either A's, B's, C's, D's, or F's. If 30% of the class got A's or B's, and 50% got C's or D's, how many students got F's?

    (1) 10 students received B's.

    (2) There was a total of 40 students in the class.

    Ⓐ Statement (1) ALONE is sufficient, but statement (2) alone is not sufficient.

    Ⓑ Statement (2) ALONE is sufficient, but statement (1) alone is not sufficient.

    Ⓒ BOTH statements (1) and (2) TOGETHER are sufficient, but NEITHER statement ALONE is sufficient.

    Ⓓ EACH statement ALONE is sufficient.

    Ⓔ Statements (1) and (2) TOGETHER are NOT sufficient.

16. Were more new sports cars or new sedans purchased in Wichita during the years 1985 through 1995?

   (1) In the years 1985 through 1995, one fourth of the population of Wichita purchased new sedans.

   (2) In the years 1985 through 1995, one third of the population of Wichita purchased new sports cars.

   Ⓐ Statement (1) ALONE is sufficient, but statement (2) alone is not sufficient.

   Ⓑ Statement (2) ALONE is sufficient, but statement (1) alone is not sufficient.

   Ⓒ BOTH statements (1) and (2) TOGETHER are sufficient, but NEITHER statement ALONE is sufficient.

   Ⓓ EACH statement ALONE is sufficient.

   Ⓔ Statements (1) and (2) TOGETHER are NOT sufficient.

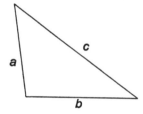

17. What is the length of side c?

   (1) $a = 6$

   (2) $b = 7$

   Ⓐ Statement (1) ALONE is sufficient, but statement (2) alone is not sufficient.

   Ⓑ Statement (2) ALONE is sufficient, but statement (1) alone is not sufficient.

   Ⓒ BOTH statements (1) and (2) TOGETHER are sufficient, but NEITHER statement ALONE is sufficient.

   Ⓓ EACH statement ALONE is sufficient.

   Ⓔ Statements (1) and (2) TOGETHER are NOT sufficient.

18. Is x greater than y?

   (1) $x = \sqrt{3}$

   (2) y is a prime number.

   Ⓐ Statement (1) ALONE is sufficient, but statement (2) alone is not sufficient.
   Ⓑ Statement (2) ALONE is sufficient, but statement (1) alone is not sufficient.
   Ⓒ BOTH statements (1) and (2) TOGETHER are sufficient, but NEITHER statement ALONE is sufficient.
   Ⓓ EACH statement ALONE is sufficient.
   Ⓔ Statements (1) and (2) TOGETHER are NOT sufficient.

ABOVE AVERAGE TO DIFFICULT

19. What is the value of j if h is $k\%$ of j?

   (1) h is 25% of 40.

   (2) $k = 20$

   Ⓐ Statement (1) ALONE is sufficient, but statement (2) alone is not sufficient.
   Ⓑ Statement (2) ALONE is sufficient, but statement (1) alone is not sufficient.
   Ⓒ BOTH statements (1) and (2) TOGETHER are sufficient, but NEITHER statement ALONE is sufficient.
   Ⓓ EACH statement ALONE is sufficient.
   Ⓔ Statements (1) and (2) TOGETHER are NOT sufficient.

20. Eloise's aquarium contains six tropical fish. If the largest fish is 4 ounces heavier than the smallest fish, how heavy is the smallest fish?

(1) If the largest fish were 6 ounces heavier, it would weigh twice as much as the smallest fish.

(2) The six fish average 14 ounces in weight.

Ⓐ Statement (1) ALONE is sufficient, but statement (2) alone is not sufficient.

Ⓑ Statement (2) ALONE is sufficient, but statement (1) alone is not sufficient.

Ⓒ BOTH statements (1) and (2) TOGETHER are sufficient, but NEITHER statement ALONE is sufficient.

Ⓓ EACH statement ALONE is sufficient.

Ⓔ Statements (1) and (2) TOGETHER are NOT sufficient.

21. Otto and his wife, Anna, leave home at 1 P.M. and bicycle in different directions. How far apart are they at 4 P.M.?

(1) Otto rides at 12 mph westward for two hours and then stops.

(2) Anna rides at 10 mph southward for one hour and then rides westward at the same speed for three hours.

Ⓐ Statement (1) ALONE is sufficient, but statement (2) alone is not sufficient.

Ⓑ Statement (2) ALONE is sufficient, but statement (1) alone is not sufficient.

Ⓒ BOTH statements (1) and (2) TOGETHER are sufficient, but NEITHER statement ALONE is sufficient.

Ⓓ EACH statement ALONE is sufficient.

Ⓔ Statements (1) and (2) TOGETHER are NOT sufficient.

22. How long is the diagonal through the center of a particular cube?

    (1) A diagonal across one face is 4.24 centimeters.

    (2) The surface area of the cube is 54 square centimeters.

    Ⓐ Statement (1) ALONE is sufficient, but statement (2) alone is not sufficient.

    Ⓑ Statement (2) ALONE is sufficient, but statement (1) alone is not sufficient.

    Ⓒ BOTH statements (1) and (2) TOGETHER are sufficient, but NEITHER statement ALONE is sufficient.

    Ⓓ EACH statement ALONE is sufficient.

    Ⓔ Statements (1) and (2) TOGETHER are NOT sufficient.

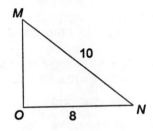

23. What is the perimeter of triangle *MNO*?

    (1) The area of triangle *MNO* is 24.

    (2) Angle *MON* equals 90°.

    Ⓐ Statement (1) ALONE is sufficient, but statement (2) alone is not sufficient.

    Ⓑ Statement (2) ALONE is sufficient, but statement (1) alone is not sufficient.

    Ⓒ BOTH statements (1) and (2) TOGETHER are sufficient, but NEITHER statement ALONE is sufficient.

    Ⓓ EACH statement ALONE is sufficient.

    Ⓔ Statements (1) and (2) TOGETHER are NOT sufficient.

24. A hexagonal playing field is composed of six equilateral triangles, each the same size. If one player controls each triangle, how much area is controlled by all six players?

    (1) One edge of one triangle equals 15 feet.

    (2) The perimeter of one triangular region equals 45 feet.

    ⒜ Statement (1) ALONE is sufficient, but statement (2) alone is not sufficient.

    ⒝ Statement (2) ALONE is sufficient, but statement (1) alone is not sufficient.

    ⒞ BOTH statements (1) and (2) TOGETHER are sufficient, but NEITHER statement ALONE is sufficient.

    ⒟ EACH statement ALONE is sufficient.

    ⒠ Statements (1) and (2) TOGETHER are NOT sufficient.

25. What is the value of $(u + v)$?

    (1) $2w - 7 = 0$

    (2) $u + v - 3w = 11$

    ⒜ Statement (1) ALONE is sufficient, but statement (2) alone is not sufficient.

    ⒝ Statement (2) ALONE is sufficient, but statement (1) alone is not sufficient.

    ⒞ BOTH statements (1) and (2) TOGETHER are sufficient, but NEITHER statement ALONE is sufficient.

    ⒟ EACH statement ALONE is sufficient.

    ⒠ Statements (1) and (2) TOGETHER are NOT sufficient.

ANSWERS AND EXPLANATIONS FOR THE PRACTICE DATA SUFFICIENCY QUESTIONS

EASY TO MODERATE

1. ⓒ From both statements, Jim must also be shorter than Walter, who is taller than any of the other men.

2. ⓔ The relationship between two quantities is uncertain given merely that each is unequal to a third quantity.

3. ⓔ The first statement enables us to find the cost of one plum. But without the weight of one peach, we cannot use (2) to find the cost of a peach.

4. ⓐ Distance equals rate times time. Statement (1) tells us the rate and time. Multiplying 550 by $3\frac{1}{4}$ yields a distance of 1,788 miles.

5. ⓓ Either statement transforms the equation so there is only one unknown, which therefore could be found:

$$(1) \quad 3b - 7b + 14 = 0$$
$$(2) \quad 9 - 7b + 14 = 0$$

6. ⓓ The area can be calculated from $A = \pi r^2$ if we know the radius, which is given in the second statement. The first statement gives the circumference, from which the radius may be found by $r = C/2\pi$.

7. ⓑ Statement (1) lacks the capacity of the tank. But from (2) and the formula $d = rt$, you can compute the distance to be 400 miles.

AVERAGE

8. ⓒ His initial rent was $315 − $45 = $270, so the increase was 45 divided by 270 equals 16.7%.

9. ⓑ Statement (1) reveals a product, not a quotient. However, dividing both sides of equation (2) by $6/m$ demonstrates that $n/m = 1/6$.

10. Ⓒ From the first statement, David has six sisters and brothers (he is the seventh child). Combining that piece of data with the second statement, he must have four sisters and two brothers.

11. Ⓐ Inequality (1) informs us that x exceeds y, whether positive, zero, or negative. Inequality (2) does not tell us so much, for the sign of the numbers is masked by the squaring.

12. Ⓔ Simple interest equals principal times rate times time. We are not told the length of time the money was in the account.

13. Ⓒ With both statements, we know that the third number must exceed 7, so the smallest number is 4. But with the first statement alone, all we know is $4 + x + y = 3 \times 7$, and one of the unknown numbers could be less than 4.

14. Ⓒ You must know that December has 31 days. (For the GMAT, you should know the number of days in each month of the year.) Therefore, December has 4 weeks and 3 extra days. For the 7 days of the week, 4 occur 4 times and the other 3 occur 5 times. Since there are only 2 days between Saturday (statement 2) and Tuesday (statement 1), there must be 4 Sundays and Mondays that month.

15. Ⓑ Since a total of 80% received A's, B's, C's, and D's, then 20% received F's. 20% of 40 (the total given in statement 2) = 8 students. The first statement does not help because we don't know how many students received A's.

16. Ⓔ Neither of the statements gives definitive information about the *number* of new sedans or the *number* of the new sports cars purchased. For example, although one fourth of the population may have purchased new sedans, the members of that fraction of the population may have each purchased *several* new sedans, bringing the number of new sedans purchased above the number of new sports cars purchased.

17. Ⓔ The Pythagorean theorem, $a^2 + b^2 = c^2$, can be employed only for a triangle known to have a right angle.

18. © The smallest prime is 2, which exceeds $\sqrt{3}$ (approximately 1.73). Consequently, x is less than y.

ABOVE AVERAGE TO DIFFICULT

19. © From statement (1), we find $h = 10$. From (2), $k = 20$. Then the question translates to the number 10 is 20% of what number j? Therefore, $10 = 0.2j$, and $j = 10/0.2 = 50$.

20. Ⓐ From statement (1), the following equation may be derived:

$$L + 6 = 2S$$

From the information given in the question, the following equation may be derived:

$$L = S + 4$$

Using simultaneous equations, we may solve for both S and L.

Notice that statement (2) tells nothing about the individual weight of any fish.

21. © Since the compass directions are at right angles, the distance can be computed fromt the Pythagorean theorem, providing Otto's and Anna's positions at 4 P.M. are known. Otto will be 24 miles west of the origin. Anna will be 10 miles south and 20 miles west of the origin. Relative to Otto, Anna is 10 miles south and 4 miles east at 4 P.M. It is helpful to sketch a map in a problem involving positions.

22. Ⓓ The diagonal through the center of a cube, from one corner to the opposite corner, may be found with the Pythagorean theorem providing that the length of the cube's edge is known. Statement (1) implies that the edge is $4.24/\sqrt{2}$ centimeters. Moreover, since the surface area (2) has 6 faces, each face has an area of $54/6 = 9$ cm^2, and so the edge is $\sqrt{9} = 3$ cm.

23. ⒟ Since statement (1) tells us the area of triangle *MNO* is 24, its height must be 6. Note that side *MO* will be the height because 6-8-10 is a Pythagorean triple. Thus we can find the perimeter. Using statement (2) we know $\triangle MON$ is a right triangle and can use the Pythagorean theorem to find the third side.

24. ⒟ Given the edge (*N*) of an equilateral triangle, one can determine its height ($N\sqrt{3}/2$) and therefore its area. So one can determine the area of all six equilateral triangular regions, each of the same size.

25. ⒞ From the first statement, $w = 3\frac{1}{2}$. Substituting that into (2) yields $u + v - 3 \cdot 3\frac{1}{2} = 11$, which can be solved for $(u + v) = 21\frac{1}{2}$.

INTRODUCTION TO GRAPHS AND CHARTS

Graphs and charts can appear in the quantitative section of the exam.

ABILITY TESTED

You will need to understand and to derive information from graphs, charts, and tables. Many of the problems require brief calculations based on the data, so your mathematical ability is also tested.

BASIC SKILLS NECESSARY

The mathematics associated with diagrammatic interpretation does not go beyond high-school level. Your familiarity with a wide range of chart and graph types will help you feel comfortable with these problems and read the data accurately.

DIRECTIONS

You are given data represented in chart or graph form. Following each set of data are questions based on that data. Select the best answer to each question by referring to the appropriate chart or graph and mark your choice on the screen. Use only the given or implied information to determine your answer.

ANALYSIS

Remember that you are looking for the best answer, not necessarily the perfect answer. Often, graph questions ask you for an approximate answer; if this happens, don't forget to round off numbers to make your work easier.

Use only the information given; never "read into" the information on a graph.

SUGGESTED APPROACH WITH SAMPLES

Here are some helpful strategies for extracting accurate information followed by some sample graph questions.

Skim the question and quickly examine the whole graph before starting to work the problem; this sort of prereading will tell you what to look for.

Sometimes the answer to a question is available in supplementary information given with a graph (headings, scale factors, legends, etc.); be sure to read this information.

Look for the obvious: dramatic trends, high points, low points, etc. Obvious information often leads directly to an answer.

You may need to scroll the graph to see all of the information it contains.

Questions 1–3

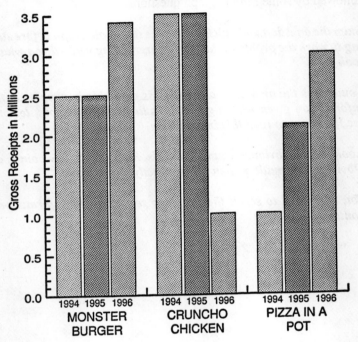

Gross Receipts of Several Fast-Food Restaurants 1994-1996

1. The 1994–96 gross receipts of Monster Burger exceeded those of Pizza In A Pot by approximately how much?

   Ⓐ 0.2 million
   Ⓑ 2 million
   Ⓒ 8.2 million
   Ⓓ 8.4 million
   Ⓔ 17 million

2. From 1995 to 1996, the percent increase in receipts for Pizza In A Pot exceeded the percent increase for Monster Burger by approximately how much?

    Ⓐ 0%
    Ⓑ 2%
    Ⓒ 10%
    Ⓓ 15%
    Ⓔ 43%

3. The 1996 decline in Cruncho Chicken's receipts may be attributed to

    Ⓐ an increase in the popularity of burgers
    Ⓑ an increase in the popularity of pizza
    Ⓒ a decrease in the demand for chicken
    Ⓓ a predictable slump attributable to the increase in terrorist activity
    Ⓔ It cannot be determined from the information given.

ANSWERS AND EXPLANATIONS

This is a bar graph. Typically, this type of graph has a number scale along one edge and individual categories along another edge. Here we have multiple bars representing each fast-food category; each single bar stands for the receipts from a single year.

You may be tempted to write out the numbers as you do your arithmetic (3.5 million = 3,500,000). This is unnecessary, as it often is on graphs that use large numbers. Since all measurements are in millions, adding zeros does not add precision to the numbers.

1. Ⓑ Referring to the Monster Burger bars, we see that gross receipts are as follows: 1994 = 2.5, 1995 = 2.5, 1996 = 3.4 (if you have trouble seeing how the bars line up with the numbers, you might want to use a piece of scratch paper against the screen as a straightedge to determine a number such as this last one). Totaling the receipts for all three years, we get 8.4.

Referring to the Pizza In A Pot bars, we see that gross receipts are as follows: 1994 = 1, 1995 = 2.1, 1996 = 3 (don't designate numbers beyond the nearest tenth, since the graph numbers and the answer choices prescribe no greater accuracy than this). Totaling the receipts for all three years, we get 6.1.

So Monster Burger exceeds Pizza In A Pot by 2.3 million. The answer that best approximates this figure is Ⓑ.

2. Ⓒ Graph questions on the GMAT may ask you to calculate percent increase or percent decrease. The formula for figuring either of these is the same:

$$\frac{\text{amount of the change}}{\text{"starting" amount (follows the word } from)}$$

In this case, we may first calculate the percent increase for Monster Burger.

Gross receipts in 1995 = 2.5
Gross receipts in 1996 = 3.4
Amount of the change = 0.9

The 1995 amount is the "starting" or "from" amount.

$$\frac{\text{amount of the change}}{\text{"starting" amount}} = \frac{0.9}{2.5} = 0.36 = 36\%$$

Percent increase for Pizza In A Pot:

Gross receipts in 1995 = 2.1
Gross receipts in 1996 = 3
Amount of the change = 0.9

$$\frac{\text{amount of the change}}{\text{"starting" amount}} = \frac{0.9}{2.1} \cong 0.428 \cong 43\%$$

So, Pizza In A Pot exceeds Monster Burger by 7% (43% − 36%). The answer that best approximates this figure is Ⓒ.

3. Ⓔ Never use information that you know is not given. In this case, the multiple factors which could cause a decline in receipts are not represented by the graph. All choices except Ⓔ require you to speculate beyond the information given.

Questions 4–6

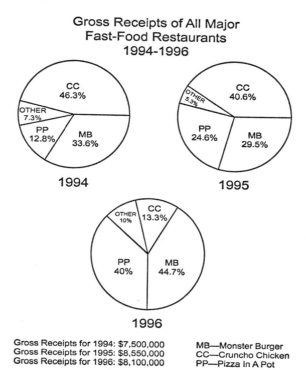

Gross Receipts of All Major
Fast-Food Restaurants
1994-1996

1994

1995

1996

Gross Receipts for 1994: $7,500,000
Gross Receipts for 1995: $8,550,000
Gross Receipts for 1996: $8,100,000

MB—Monster Burger
CC—Cruncho Chicken
PP—Pizza In A Pot

4. The gross receipts for 1994 are approximately what percentage of the gross receipts for all three years?

Ⓐ 30%
Ⓑ 46.3%
Ⓒ 46.7%
Ⓓ 50%
Ⓔ It cannot be determined from the information given.

5. Over all three years, the average percentage of gross receipts for Cruncho Chicken exceeds the average percentage of gross receipts for Pizza In A Pot by approximately how much?

    Ⓐ 53%
    Ⓑ 30%
    Ⓒ 23%
    Ⓓ 8%
    Ⓔ 4%

6. The gross receipts earned by other restaurants in 1996 amount to precisely how much?

    Ⓐ $1,810,650
    Ⓑ $810,000
    Ⓒ $547,500
    Ⓓ $453,150
    Ⓔ $405,000

ANSWERS AND EXPLANATIONS

These are circle graphs, or pie charts. One hundred percent is represented by the whole circle, and the various "slices" represent portions of that 100 percent. The larger the slice, the higher the percentage.

4. Ⓐ You can solve this problem without referring to the graphs; the necessary information is available in the list of gross receipts below the graphs. Don't write out all the zeros when calculating with these large figures; brief figures are easier to work with.

Gross receipts for 1994 = 7.5 million.
Gross receipts for all three years = 7.5 + 8.6 + 8.1 = 24.2 million.

$$\frac{7.5}{24.2} = 31\%$$

The answer that best approximates 31% is 30%, Ⓐ. Notice that even without doing the calculations, you may approximate 30% by realizing that the gross receipts for any one year are about a third of the total.

5. ⒟ To calculate the average percentage for Cruncho Chicken, add the percentages for each year and divide by 3.

$$46.3 + 40.6 + 13.3 = 100.2 \div 3 = 33.4\%$$

Do the same for Pizza In A Pot.

$$12.8 + 24.6 + 40 = 77.4 \div 3 = 25.8\%$$

Cruncho Chicken exceeds Pizza In A Pot by $33.4 - 25.8 = 7.6\%$. ⒟, 8%, best approximates this figure.

6. ⒝ In 1996, other restaurants earned precisely 10%. 10% of $8,100,000 = $810,000, ⒝.

A PATTERNED PLAN OF ATTACK
Graphs and Charts

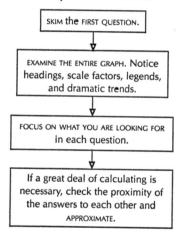

Introduction to the Verbal Section

Prior to starting the exam, you will be carefully walked through a very basic tutorial program explaining how to use the computer for this exam. The computer-adaptive GMAT gives you 75 minutes to answer 41 verbal questions. These questions are composed of Reading Comprehension, Sentence Correction, and Critical Reasoning questions, with the question types intermingled throughout the section. You will be given a medium difficulty question to start with, and then the computer will adapt the level of questions you receive based on your responses to all the previous questions. Any work or notes you take will be done on the scratch paper provided, and all of your answers will be recorded on the computer screen by using a mouse to click on the appropriate ovals. You will not be allowed to go back to a previous question, but you will be allowed to review a passage for each question. Always fill in an answer choice before attempting to move to the next question.

In this book—to assist you in understanding explanations and to direct your attention to different questions and answer choices—each question is given a number, and letters have been placed inside the ovals of the answer choices. **Note that on the actual exam, questions will not have numbers next to them, and there will be no letters in the ovals.**

INTRODUCTION TO READING COMPREHENSION

Reading Comprehension typically consists of a passage of about 350 words followed by three or four questions.

ABILITY TESTED

This question type tests your ability to understand, interpret, and analyze reading passages on a variety of topics. Passages are generally taken from the following categories:

- **Narrative**—passages from novels, short stories, essays, and biographies
- **Argumentative**—passages presenting different points of view
- **Biological science**—passages about botany, medicine, or zoology
- **Physical science**—passages about chemistry, physics, or astronomy
- **Humanities**—passages about art, literature, music, folklore, or philosophy
- **Social studies**—passages about history, government, economics, or sociology

The questions will frequently ask you

- about the **main idea, main point,** or **possible title** of the passage
- about **information** that is **directly stated** in the passage
- about **information** that is **implied, suggested,** or **can be inferred**
- to recognize **applications** of the author's **opinions** or **ideas**
- to evaluate how the author **develops** and **presents** the passage
- to recognize the **style** or **tone** of the passage

BASIC SKILLS NECESSARY

Students who have read widely and know how to read, analyze, and interpret stated and implied information efficiently tend to do well on this section.

DIRECTIONS

This passage is followed by questions based on its content. After reading a passage, choose the best answer to each question and choose the corresponding oval on the screen. Answer all questions about the passage on the basis of what is *stated* or *implied* in that passage. You may refer back to the passage.

ANALYSIS

Use only the information given or implied in a passage. Do not consider outside information, even if it seems more accurate than the given information.

If you don't know the answer, try to eliminate some choices; then take an educated guess.

SUGGESTED APPROACH WITH SAMPLES

Skim the first question before you read the passage. This could give you a clue about what to look for when you read the passage. (You can't skim other questions because you can't return to a question.)

Read the passage, focusing on main points, important conclusions, names, definitions, places, and numbers. Notice the structure, tone, and purpose of the passage.

Passage

Woodrow Wilson won his first office in 1910 when he was elected governor of New Jersey. Two years later he was elected president in one of the most rapid political rises in our history. For a while
LINE Wilson had practiced law but found it both boring and unprofit-
(5) able; then he became a political scientist and finally president of Princeton University. He did an outstanding job at Princeton, but when he was asked by the Democratic boss of New Jersey, Jim Smith, to run for governor, Wilson readily accepted because his position at Princeton was becoming untenable.
(10) Until 1910, Wilson seemed to be a conservative Democrat in the Grover Cleveland tradition. He had denounced Bryan in 1896 and had voted for the National Democratic candidate who supported gold. In fact, when the Democratic machine first pushed Wilson's nomination in 1912, the young New Jersey progressives
(15) wanted no part of him. Wilson later assured them that he would champion the progressive cause, and so they decided to work for his election. It is easy to accuse Wilson of political expediency, but it is entirely possible that by 1912 he had changed his views as had countless other Americans. While governor of New Jersey, he car-
(20) ried out his election pledges by enacting an impressive list of reforms.
Wilson secured the Democratic nomination on the forty-sixth ballot. In the campaign, Wilson emerged as the middle-of-the-road candidate—between the conservative William H. Taft and the more
(25) radical Theodore Roosevelt. Wilson called his program the New Freedom, which he said was the restoration of free competition as it had existed before the growth of the trusts. In contrast, Theodore Roosevelt was advocating a New Nationalism, which seemed to

(30) call for massive federal intervention in the economic life of the nation. Wilson felt that the trusts should be destroyed, but he made a distinction between a trust and legitimately successful big business. Theodore Roosevelt, on the other hand, accepted the trusts as inevitable but said that the government should regulate them by establishing a new regulatory agency.

Questions

1. The author's main purpose in writing this passage is to

    Ⓐ argue that Wilson is one of the great U.S. presidents
    Ⓑ survey the difference between Wilson, Taft, and Roosevelt
    Ⓒ explain Wilson's concept of the New Freedom
    Ⓓ discuss some major events of Wilson's career
    Ⓔ suggest reasons that Wilson's presidency may have started World War I

2. The author implies which of the following about the New Jersey progressives?

    Ⓐ They did not support Wilson after he was governor.
    Ⓑ They were not conservative Democrats.
    Ⓒ They were more interested in political expediency than in political causes or reforms.
    Ⓓ Along with Wilson, they were supporters of Bryan in 1896.
    Ⓔ They particularly admired Wilson's experience as president of Princeton University.

3. The passage supports which of the following conclusions about the progress of Wilson's political career?

    Ⓐ Few politicians have progressed so rapidly toward the attainment of higher office.
    Ⓑ Failures late in his career caused him to be regarded as a president who regressed instead of progressed.
    Ⓒ Wilson encountered little opposition once he determined to seek the presidency.
    Ⓓ The League of Nations marked the end of Wilson's reputation as a strong leader.
    Ⓔ Wilson's political allies were Bryan and Taft.

4. In the statement "Wilson readily accepted because his position at Princeton was becoming untenable" (lines 8–9), the meaning of "untenable" is probably which of the following?

    Ⓐ Unlikely to last for years
    Ⓑ Filled with considerably less tension
    Ⓒ Difficult to maintain or continue
    Ⓓ Filled with achievements that would appeal to voters
    Ⓔ Something he did not have a tenacious desire to continue

5. According to the passage, which of the following was probably true about the presidential campaign of 1912?

    Ⓐ Woodrow Wilson won the election by an overwhelming majority.
    Ⓑ The inexperience of Theodore Roosevelt accounted for his radical position.
    Ⓒ Wilson was unable to attract two thirds of the votes but won anyway.
    Ⓓ There were three nominated candidates for the presidency.
    Ⓔ Wilson's New Freedom did not represent Democratic interests.

Answers and Explanations

1. Ⓓ Choices Ⓐ and Ⓔ are irrelevant to the information in the passage, and choices Ⓑ and Ⓒ mention secondary purposes rather than the primary one.

2. Ⓑ In the second paragraph, Wilson's decision to champion the progressive cause after 1912 is contrasted with his earlier career, when he seemed to be a conservative Democrat. Thus, we may conclude that the progressives, whom Wilson finally joined, were not conservative Democrats, as was Wilson earlier in his career. Choices Ⓐ and Ⓓ contradict information in the paragraph, while choices Ⓒ and Ⓔ are not suggested by any information given in the passage.

3. Ⓐ This choice is explicitly supported by the second sentence in paragraph one in which we are told that Wilson was *elected president in one of the most rapid political rises in our history.*

4. Ⓒ On any reading comprehension test, it is best to be alert to the positive and negative connotations of words and phrases in each passage as well as in the questions themselves. In the case of *untenable,* the prefix *un-* suggests that the word has a negative connotation. The context in which the word occurs does so as well. Wilson *left* his position at Princeton; therefore, we may conclude that the position was somehow unappealing. Only two of the answer choices, Ⓒ and Ⓔ, provide a negative definition. Although choice Ⓔ may attract your attention because *tenacious* looks similar to *tenable,* the correct choice is Ⓒ, which is the conventional definition of *untenable.*

5. Ⓓ Choices Ⓐ, Ⓑ, and Ⓒ contain information that is not addressed in the passage. We may eliminate them as irrelevant. Choice Ⓔ contradicts the fact that Wilson was a Democratic candidate. The discussion of Taft and Roosevelt as the candidates who finally ran against Wilson for the presidency supports choice Ⓓ.

A PATTERNED PLAN OF ATTACK
Reading Comprehension

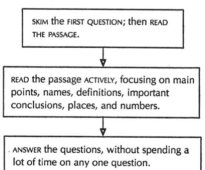

SKIM the FIRST QUESTION; then READ THE PASSAGE.

READ the passage ACTIVELY, focusing on main points, names, definitions, important conclusions, places, and numbers.

ANSWER the questions, without spending a lot of time on any one question.

PRACTICE READING COMPREHENSION PASSAGES AND QUESTIONS

Questions 1–8

The railroads played a key role in the settlement of the West. They provided relatively easy access to the region for the first time, and they also actively recruited farmers to settle there. The railroads are criticized for their part in settling the West too rapidly, with its resultant economic unrest. Of course there were abuses connected with building and operating the railroads, but it must be pointed out that they performed a useful service in extending the frontier and helping to achieve national unity.

The real tragedy of the rapid settlement of the Great Plains was the shameful way in which the American Indians were treated. Threatened with the destruction of their whole mode of life, the Indians fought back savagely. Justice was almost entirely on the Indians' side. The land was clearly theirs; frequently their title was legally certified by a treaty negotiated with the federal government. The Indians, however, lacked the military force and the political power to protect this right. Not only did white men encroach upon the Indians' hunting grounds, but they rapidly destroyed the Indians' principal means of subsistence—the buffalo. By 1869, the railroads had cut the herd in half, and by the middle of the 1880s, both the southern and northern herd were eliminated. The white man frequently killed the buffalo merely for sport, leaving the valuable carcass to rot in the sun.

The plains Indians were considered different from the Indians encountered by the English colonists on the Atlantic coast. Mounted on horses, typical plains Indians were fierce warriors who could shoot arrows with surprising accuracy while galloping at top speed. Although they quickly adapted themselves to the use of the rifle, the Indians were not equal to the firepower of the United States Army and thus were doomed to defeat.

Theoretically, at least, the government tried to be fair to the Indians, but all too often the Indian agents were either too indifferent or corrupt to carry out the government's promises conscientiously. The army frequently ignored the Indian Bureau and failed to coordinate its policies with the civilians who were nominally in charge of Indian affairs. The settlers hated and feared the Indians and wanted them exterminated. This barbaric attitude is certainly not excusable, but it is understandable in the context of the times.

1. The author's attitude toward the treatment of American Indians by whites is one of

   (A) qualified regret
   (B) violent anger
   (C) strong disapproval
   (D) objective indifference
   (E) unfair bias

2. The author implies which of the following about the forces at work during the settlement of the Great Plains?

   (A) The federal government represented the moral use of law.
   (B) Justice was overcome by military firepower.
   (C) Attempts by the government to be fair were rejected by the Indians.
   (D) The settlers' hatred and fear was offset by the Indians' attempts at kindness.
   (E) The Indians and the white settlers shared a sporting interest in the hunting of buffalo.

3. Which of the following is concrete evidence that the white settlers did not need the buffalo for their own subsistence, as did the Indians?

   (A) More than half of the great buffalo herd had disappeared by 1869.
   (B) Nearly fifteen million buffalo were killed within twenty years.
   (C) Buffalo carcasses were left rotting in the sun by whites.
   (D) The railroad brought necessary food and supplies to the white settlers from the East.
   (E) The white settlers had their own hunting grounds separate from the Indians'.

4. What is the point of the comparison between plains Indians and the Indians encountered on the Atlantic coast?

Ⓐ The Atlantic coast Indians were not as abused by white settlers.

Ⓑ Because they were considerably better warriors than the Atlantic coast Indians, the plains Indians were a match for the United States military.

Ⓒ If Indians such as those on the Atlantic coast had populated the plains, there would have been no bloodshed of the white settlement.

Ⓓ The Indians encountered by English colonists posed no violent threat to the colonists.

Ⓔ The Atlantic coast Indians were unfamiliar with horses.

5. Which of the following characteristics of the passage suggests that the abuse of the Indians is a more significant topic for the author than the beneficial role of the railroads?

Ⓐ The statement that the railroads "are criticized for their part in settling the West too rapidly" (lines 3–4)

Ⓑ The amount of discussion devoted to the abuse of the Indians

Ⓒ The reliance on statistical details in both the first and second paragraphs

Ⓓ The mention of the plains Indians' ability to fight

Ⓔ The perception that the achievement of national unity was one of the services that the railroad performed

6. The author of the passage would most likely disagree that

Ⓐ the United States government's policies toward the American Indians were shameful

Ⓑ the land that the Indians fought to retain belonged to them

Ⓒ numerous abuses were among the results of the railroads' rapid spread westward

Ⓓ some American Indian tribes used sophisticated weapons brought by settlers

Ⓔ the United States army could not be considered a friend of the American Indian

7. It can be inferred from the passage that the purpose of the Indian Bureau was to

   Ⓐ try Indians who violated the laws of the new territory
   Ⓑ establish reservations where the peaceful American Indians would live
   Ⓒ assist with Indian affairs and policies of the government regarding the American Indian
   Ⓓ bring to justice white settlers who treated the Indians in a savage or unlawful manner
   Ⓔ assist the Indians in learning a new method of procuring food to rely less on buffalo meat

8. All of the following are presented as overt enemies of the Indians EXCEPT the

   Ⓐ railroads
   Ⓑ white hunters
   Ⓒ army
   Ⓓ Indian agents
   Ⓔ western settlers

Questions 9–12

If you make a marked increase in the amount of light falling upon the normal eye, you observe an immediate adjustment of the iris to reduce the size of the pupil. This is called an unconditioned
LINE response, and the increased light is called an unconditioned stimu-
(5)   lus. Now, if you make numerous trials taking care to sound a buzzer whenever the light is increased, the iris can be "taught," that is to say, conditioned, to reduce the pupil at the sound of the buzzer alone. This learned response is called a conditioned response and the sound of the buzzer, a conditioned stimulus.
(10) Now symbols are our most important conditioned stimuli, and successful communication depends upon complementary conditioning, or complementary experience. Just as we find ourselves shouting at listeners who do not speak our language, so by a similar irrational impulse we assume that those with whom we attempt
(15) to communicate are equipped with complementary sets of conditioned responses to our own common stock of symbols. It is easy

to see the stupidity of expecting one who does not speak English to converse with you in English. It is not so easy to realize that one who does speak English may not have been conditioned to operate (20) with the same set of senses for the familiar terms common to your vocabulary and his.

9. The primary purpose of the passage is to

    Ⓐ define an aspect of a topic
    Ⓑ reconcile differing theories
    Ⓒ propose a topic for investigation
    Ⓓ solve a puzzle
    Ⓔ analyze a phenomenon

10. Which of the following may be best described as an unconditioned stimulus?

    Ⓐ An unanswered telephone ringing in an empty office
    Ⓑ A whistle that blows at five o'clock every week day
    Ⓒ A shoelace that breaks in two
    Ⓓ A match that burns the finger of a careless pipe smoker
    Ⓔ An alarm clock that rings at midnight

11. Applying information from the passage, we may conclude that a child who begins feeling hungry as the school lunch bell rings each day may be exhibiting

    Ⓐ an awareness of time
    Ⓑ a complementary structure
    Ⓒ a conditioned response
    Ⓓ an unconditioned stimulus
    Ⓔ a conditioned appetite

12. The passage suggests that those who speak English attempting to communicate with those who do not speak English are

    Ⓐ bound to fail completely
    Ⓑ still dependent upon complementary responses to common symbols
    Ⓒ likely to be more successful if they raise their voice
    Ⓓ likely to be able to communicate where there are familiar words common to both speakers' vocabularies
    Ⓔ subject to the limitations of third-party translations

Questions 13–16

Let us consider a hypothetical pair of communicants, utterer and interpreter, from the operation point of view. We shall assume that our utterer has six hats: red, blue, yellow, black, gray, and white. If the rods and cones (the tiny end organs packed together on what corresponds to the sensitive films in the stereoscopic or double-lens camera) of the retinae of his eyes are not defective, he will be able to see that the six hats differ even though they are of the same shape and material. If we reduce the light so that he can barely see, the white and the yellow will seem to be the same. But as the light grows stronger he will be able to see that the red, blue, and yellow affect him differently from black, gray, and white. He now has sufficient experience (remember, this is all grossly over-simplified) to conceive of color and shade. But he can also distinguish the red hat from the blue and yellow hats, the yellow from the blue and red, and so forth. He is thus ready for the concepts red, blue, and yellow if, for example, we provide him with a red feather, a blue feather, and a yellow feather. Indeed, he may have the human impulse to decorate the hat with the corresponding feather. And if the feathers seem to have more in common with the white hat than the other hats have in common with the white hat, he can see that his concept of shade will determine the difference between the two reds, the two blues, or the two yellows, and he will have need of the concepts of light and dark. And as we increase the number of shades he will require relation concepts like those expressed in the suffixes -er and -est. By repeating the conventional symbols "hat" and "red" with the red hat, he conditions the sound of the words to the sight of the hat. If he sees that the relation of each feather to its hat is similar to the other two, he has need of a relation concept like the one expressed by the preposition "in," and he is thus prepared to say to himself "light red feather in dark red hat." Now in the dark he is not able to tell one hat or one feather from another; but in the middle of a moonless night he is able to think "red feather in red hat" simply by uttering the appropriate symbols to himself. And with his human impulse to try new combinations, he can even think "yellow feather in blue hat" without ever having seen them thus combined.

13. By discussing the different effects of reduced and increased light, the author is

   I. pointing to a limitation in the dependence on perception by sight
   II. preparing to discuss the concepts of light and dark
   III. laying the ground for the distinction between what can be seen and what can be thought

   Ⓐ III only
   Ⓑ I and II only
   Ⓒ I and III only
   Ⓓ II and III only
   Ⓔ I, II, and III

14. Of the following, the most plausible criticism that could be directed at the "hats" example is that it is

   Ⓐ too difficult to follow
   Ⓑ irrelevant
   Ⓒ too hypothetical
   Ⓓ too dependent on the esoteric language
   Ⓔ unreasonable

15. According to the passage, the acquisition of symbols allows us not only to communicate, but also to

   Ⓐ argue logically
   Ⓑ imagine
   Ⓒ respond to unconditioned stimuli
   Ⓓ respond to conditioned stimuli
   Ⓔ decorate hats

16. The passage is most relevant to which of the following areas of study?

   Ⓐ Aesthetics of logic
   Ⓑ Literature and history
   Ⓒ Sociology
   Ⓓ Linguistics and psychology
   Ⓔ Anthropology

Questions 17–24

Many people seem to think that science fiction is typified by the covers of some of the old pulp magazines; the Bug-Eyed Monster, embodying every trait and feature that most people find repulsive, is about to grab, and presumably ravish, a sweet, blonde, curvaceous, scantily-clad Earth girl. This is unfortunate because it demeans and degrades a worthwhile and even important literary endeavor. In contrast to this unwarranted stereotype, science fiction rarely emphasizes sex, and when it does, it is more discreet than other contemporary fiction. Instead, the basic interest of science fiction lies in the relation between man and his technology and between man and the universe. Science fiction is a literature of change and a literature of the future, and while it would be foolish to claim that science fiction is a major literary genre at this time, the aspects of human life that it considers make it well worth reading and studying—for no other literary form does quite the same things.

What is science fiction? It is a literary sub-genre which postulates a change (for human beings) from conditions as we know them and follows the implications of these changes to a conclusion. That science fiction is a literary sub-genre is a point that is often overlooked. Specifically, science fiction is either a short story or a novel. There are only a few poems and plays which could be called science fiction, with Karel Capek's *RUR* being the only play that is well known. To say that science fiction is a sub-genre of prose fiction is to say that it has all the basic characteristics and serves the same basic functions in much the same way as prose fiction in general. Everything that can be said about prose fiction, in general, applies to science fiction. Every piece of science fiction, whether short story or novel, must have a narrator, a story, a plot, a setting, characters, language, and theme. And like any prose, the themes of science fiction are concerned with interpreting man's nature and experience in relation to the world around him. Themes in science fiction are constructed and presented in exactly the same ways that themes are dealt with in any other kind of fiction. They are the result of a particular combination of narrator, story, plot, character, setting, and language. In short, the reasons for reading and enjoying science fiction, and the ways of studying and analyzing it, are basically the same as they would be for any other story or novel.

17. Although few examples of science fiction written before 1900 exist, we can infer that it has been most popular in the twentieth century because

    Ⓐ with the growth of literacy, the size of the reading public has increased
    Ⓑ competition from television and film has created a demand for more exciting fiction
    Ⓒ science fiction is easier to understand than other kinds of fiction
    Ⓓ the increased importance of technology in our lives has given science fiction an increased relevance
    Ⓔ other media have captured the large audience that read novels in the nineteenth century

18. According to the definition in the passage, a fictional work that places human beings in a prehistoric world inhabited by dinosaurs

    Ⓐ cannot properly be called science fiction because it does not deal with the future
    Ⓑ cannot properly be called science fiction because it does not deal with technology
    Ⓒ can properly be called science fiction because it is prose fiction
    Ⓓ can properly be called science fiction because it places people in an environment different from the one we know
    Ⓔ can properly be called science fiction because it deals with humans' relation to the world around them

19. Science fiction is called a literary sub-genre because

    Ⓐ it is not important enough to be a literary genre
    Ⓑ it cannot be made into dramatic presentation
    Ⓒ it has its limits
    Ⓓ it shares characteristics with other types of prose fiction
    Ⓔ to call it a "genre" would subject it to literary jargon

20. From the passage, we can infer that science fiction films based upon ideas that have originally appeared in other media are chiefly adaptations of

    Ⓐ short stories
    Ⓑ plays
    Ⓒ novels
    Ⓓ poems
    Ⓔ folk tales

21. The author believes that, when compared to other literary genres, science fiction is

    Ⓐ deficient in its use of narrators
    Ⓑ unable to be adapted to drama
    Ⓒ a minor but worthwhile kind of fiction
    Ⓓ more concerned with plot than with theme
    Ⓔ in need of a unique literary approach if it is to be properly understood

22. The emphasis on theme in the second paragraph of the passage suggests that the author regards which of the following as an especially important reason for reading science fiction?

    Ⓐ The discovery of meaning
    Ⓑ The display of character
    Ⓒ The beauty of language
    Ⓓ The psychological complexity
    Ⓔ The interest of setting

23. One implication of the final sentence in the passage is that

    Ⓐ the reader should turn next to commentaries on general fiction
    Ⓑ there is no reason for any reader not to like science fiction
    Ⓒ the reader should compare other novels and stories to science fiction
    Ⓓ there are reasons for enjoying science fiction
    Ⓔ those who can appreciate other prose fiction can appreciate science fiction

24. An appropriate title for this passage would be

    Ⓐ On the Inaccuracies of Pulp Magazines
    Ⓑ Man and the Universe
    Ⓒ Toward a Definition of Science Fiction
    Ⓓ A Type of Prose Fiction
    Ⓔ Beyond the Bug-Eyed Monster

Questions 25–31

Let us take the terms "subjective" and "objective" and see if we can make up our minds what we mean by them in a statement like this: "Philosophers and artists are subjective; scientists, objective."
LINE First, the two terms make up a semantic pair. The one has no mean-
(5) ing without the other. We may define each by antonym with the other. We may define them by synonym by translating the last syllable and say that "subjective" pertains to a subject, and "objective" pertains to an object. By operation analysis we may say that subjects perceive or conceive objects in the process of knowing.
(10) The word "knowing" reminds us that we are talking about the central nervous system and should waste no time in examining our terms for their sensory, affective, and logical components. The terms are primarily logical. What, then, is the basic logical relation that establishes whatever meaning they have? What goes on in the world
(15) when a poet is being subjective, and how does it differ from what goes on when a scientist is being objective?

When the poet sings "Drink to me only with thine eyes," he is responding immediately or in retrospect to an object, his beloved, outside himself; but he is fundamentally concerned with the sen-
(20) sations and emotions which that object stimulates in him; and whether the object justifies his praise in the opinion of others, or indeed whether there actually is such an object, is quite irrelevant to his purpose, which is the weaving of a beautiful pattern of sound and imagery into a richly affective concept of feminine loveliness.
(25) This it is to be subjective.

Now the scientist is primarily concerned with the identity and continuity of the external object that stimulates his response. It need not seem absurd to locate the Eiffel Tower, or Everest, or the Grand Canyon, for that matter, in the mind because it is so per-
(30) fectly obvious that they can exist as the Eiffel Tower, Everest, or

the Grand Canyon nowhere else. Perhaps we can move a little closer
to our definition of "objective" by suggesting a distinction between
an object and thing. Let us define object as the external cause of a
thing. Whether objects "exist" is obviously not discussable, for
(35) the word "object" as used here must necessarily stand not for a
thing but for a hypothesis. There is, for example, no way of telling
whether objects are singular or plural, whether one should say the
stimulus of the Eiffel Tower experience or the stimuli of the Eiffel
Tower experience. If, then, it is impossible even for the scientist to
(40) escape the essential subjectivity of his sensations, generalizations,
and deductions, what do we mean by calling him objective?

25. Which of the following is NOT a semantic pair?

  (A) Chaos/order
  (B) Fact/fiction
  (C) Sitting/standing
  (D) Light/darkness
  (E) Virtue/vice

26. Which of the following pairs best exemplifies the subjective/ob-
jective opposition as defined by the passage?

  (A) Art/philosophy
  (B) Knower/known
  (C) Object/thing
  (D) Stimulus/stimuli
  (E) Emotion/sensation

27. The passage refers to "Drink to me only with thine eyes" (line
17) primarily in order to

  (A) suggest the affective powers of sound and imagery
  (B) exemplify the objective
  (C) exemplify the subjective
  (D) demonstrate how art can bestow universal significance on an
object
  (E) illustrate the difference between literal and metaphorical lan-
guage

28. Given the content of the first and second paragraphs, the reader expects that the third paragraph will

    Ⓐ explain how the scientist is objective
    Ⓑ define the identity and conformity of external objects
    Ⓒ analyze what it is to be subjective
    Ⓓ discriminate between an object and a thing
    Ⓔ explore the implications of objectivity

29. According to the passage, "objectivity" depends on the assumption that

    Ⓐ discrete objects exist external to the mind
    Ⓑ one's vocation in life should be logical
    Ⓒ subjectivity is a cognitive weakness
    Ⓓ science is a viable discipline
    Ⓔ the Eiffel Tower is a singular stimulus, not a diffuse experience

30. Faced with this statement, "What you see is just in your head," the author of the passage would be likely to

    Ⓐ strongly disagree
    Ⓑ agree that the statement is probably true
    Ⓒ argue against the appropriateness of the word "just"
    Ⓓ assume that the person making the statement is not a scientist
    Ⓔ argue that what is seen cannot be located outside or inside the mind

31. According to the definitions of the third paragraph, which of the following is (are) true of an object?

    I. The reality of an object is hypothetical.
    II. Whether objects are plural or singular is uncertain.
    III. An object is the external cause of a thing.

    Ⓐ III only
    Ⓑ I and II only
    Ⓒ I and III only
    Ⓓ II and III only
    Ⓔ I, II, and III

ANSWERS AND EXPLANATIONS FOR THE PRACTICE READING COMPREHENSION QUESTIONS

1. © Although the author does not express violent anger, the characterization of the treatment of the Indians as a *tragedy* and the pronouncement that the whites' behavior was *barbaric* certainly express strong disapproval.

2. Ⓑ Although justice was on the Indians' side (second paragraph), *the Indians were not equal to the firepower of the United States Army.* Each of the other choices contradicts information in the passage.

3. © This is evidence that the whites killed buffalo for sport rather than for subsistence. The disappearance of the buffalo herd is not, of itself, evidence that the buffalo did not provide subsistence to the whites.

4. Ⓓ The point of comparison is that the Atlantic coast Indians were not fierce warriors like the plains Indians. Thus they did not pose any kind of violent threat.

5. Ⓑ Three of the four paragraphs of the passage are devoted to discussing the abuse of the plains Indians. The "weight" the author gives to this topic suggests its significance.

6. Ⓐ The author states that the government itself *tried to be fair* but that the *agents'* indifference or corruption failed the American Indians.

7. © According to the final paragraph of the passage, *the Indian agents were either too indifferent or corrupt to carry out the government's promises conscientiously. The army frequently ignored the Indian Bureau and failed to coordinate its policies with the civilians who were nominally in charge of Indian affairs.* Choices Ⓑ and Ⓓ may be historically correct but cannot specifically be inferred from the passage.

8. Ⓐ Though the passage criticizes the railroads, it does not present them as overt enemies of the Indians, while the last paragraph cites the agents, the army, and the settlers.

9. Ⓐ Though Ⓒ is a possible response, the best option here is Ⓐ. The subject of the passage is the role of symbols in communication. Starting with that answer, choice Ⓐ is better than Ⓒ or the others.

10. Ⓓ An unconditioned stimulus is unprepared for and leads to an unconditioned response—in this case, no doubt, the holder's crying out and dropping the match.

11. Ⓒ The bell conditions the child's response, just as the buzzer conditions the eye's response in the example in the passage. That is, after many days of associating the bell with lunch, the child has been "taught" to feel hungry when the bell rings.

12. Ⓑ The passage suggests that complementary responses to common symbols are crucial in communication, even when there is no common language.

13. Ⓒ The discussion shows how perception by sight is determined by the availability of light and looks ahead to the conclusion that the imagination can work in darkness.

14. Ⓒ This answer might be arrived at by considering that the "hats" example is reasonable, relevant, pointed, and simply written; therefore, all choices except Ⓒ are eliminated. But it may also be argued that the example does not describe a "real" situation.

15. Ⓑ This is the passage's final point, that one can think *yellow feather in blue hat* without seeing or having seen the items together.

16. Ⓓ The passage is most clearly relevant to linguistics (the science of language) and to psychology (the science dealing with the mind and mental processes).

17. Ⓓ Choices Ⓐ, Ⓑ, and Ⓔ do not apply to science fiction as opposed to other fiction genres. Choice Ⓒ may or may not be true. Since science fiction is concerned with the *relation between man and his technology,* it follows that as technology becomes more important, the fiction of technology would become more popular.

18. Ⓓ Paragraph two defines science fiction as postulating a change from known to unknown conditions.

19. Ⓓ The sentence beginning at line 24 explains why science fiction is called a sub-genre of fiction.

20. Ⓒ Though short stories are a possible source, it is more probable that the longer novel is the source of science fiction films. The passage alludes to the scarcity of science fiction works in poetry or drama.

21. Ⓒ The first paragraph says science fiction is not *a major literary genre* but *well worth reading and studying.*

22. Ⓐ The theme is the controlling idea or meaning of a work of literature.

23. Ⓔ The final sentence presents a general comparison between *any other story or novel* and science fiction, emphasizing their similarities and thus suggesting that the sub-genre of science fiction should be read as one reads fiction in general.

24. Ⓒ The first paragraph leads up to the central question—*What is science fiction?* All of the passage is an attempt to answer that question. Choices Ⓐ and Ⓓ are too specific; Ⓑ is too general; and Ⓔ does not fit the tone of the passage.

25. Ⓒ Early in the passage we are told that in a semantic pair *the one* (term) *has no meaning without the other. We may define each by antonym with the other.* In short, semantic pairs are pairs of direct opposites. Only Ⓒ is not such a pair.

26. Ⓑ The first paragraph says *subjects perceive or conceive objects in the process of knowing.* The pair that may best be substituted in that is *knower* and *known.*

27. Ⓒ The passage uses *Drink to me only with thine eyes* to show that the poet is fundamentally concerned with sensations and emotions. The quotation is an example of the subjective. In fact, the author finishes the paragraph by saying *This it is to be subjective.*

28. Ⓐ Since the passage begins with the idea that the artist is subjective and the scientist objective, and the second paragraph deals with the subjectivity of the artist, we expect the third paragraph to be about the objectivity of the scientist.

29. Ⓐ The author tells us that scientists, whom he defines as *objective,* are *primarily concerned with the identity and continuity of the external object that stimulates* (their) *response.* That is, to be objective one must believe that the world is a collection of stable objects, each of which always looks the same. Ⓔ is a single example consistent with this assumption but is not itself broad enough to support the question of objectivity in general. Ⓓ is also too broad to be the best answer. Ⓒ is not an assumption allowed by the passage.

30. Ⓒ The author concludes by saying that *it is impossible even for the scientist to escape the essential subjectivity of his sensations, generalizations, and deductions.* Since everything is subjective, since different people each see the same thing a bit differently, one is seeming to devalue this case by saying that *what you say you see is just in your head. In your head* is not an unimportant place; according to the passage, it is the only place.

31. Ⓔ The third paragraph defines an *object* as the *external cause of a thing*—a *hypothesis,* with its singularity or plurality indeterminable. This is a definition peculiar to this passage.

INTRODUCTION TO SENTENCE CORRECTION

The Sentence Correction question type is composed of grammar-based questions and is very different from Reading Comprehension and Critical Reasoning.

ABILITY TESTED

This section tests your knowledge of correct and effective English expression.

BASIC SKILLS NECESSARY

Knowledge of basic rules of grammar and usage will help in this section.

DIRECTIONS

Some part of each sentence is underlined; sometimes the whole sentence is underlined. Five choices for rephrasing the underlined part follow each sentence; the first choice repeats the original, and the other four are different. If the first choice seems better than the alternatives, choose that answer; if not, choose one of the others.

For each sentence, consider the requirements of standard written English. Your choice should be a correct and effective expression, not awkward or ambiguous. Focus on grammar, word choice, sentence construction, and punctuation. If a choice changes the meaning of the original sentence, do not select it.

ANALYSIS

Several alternatives to an underlined portion may be correct; you are to pick the *best* (most clear and exact) one.

Any alternative that changes the meaning of the sentence should not be chosen, no matter how clear or correct it is.

SUGGESTED APPROACH WITH SAMPLES

Look for pronoun errors first. Focus on words like **he, him, she, her, we, us, they, them, who, whom, whoever, whomever, you, it, which,** *or* **that.**

There are two common pronoun errors. The first is confusing a subject **(I, he, she, we, they)** *and an object* **(me, him, her, us, them).**

1. The Rotary Club applauded Tom and I for our work helping the handicapped in town find secure jobs.

   Ⓐ The Rotary Club applauded Tom and I
   Ⓑ The Rotary club applauded Tom and I
   Ⓒ The Rotary Club applauded us both
   Ⓓ The Rotary Club applauded Tom and me
   Ⓔ The Rotary Club applauded both of us

Focus on *I* because it's a pronoun. To test whether *I* is correct, remove "Tom and." The result is "The Rotary Club applauded . . . I." *Me* would sound better, and in fact Ⓓ is the correct choice because the pronoun is the object of the verb *applauded.* Ⓒ and Ⓔ change the meaning of the sentence.

The second common pronoun error is confusing singulars **(I, he, she)** *and plurals* **(we, they).**

2. If either Mark or Jack is late again, the bus will leave without them.

   Ⓐ the bus will leave without them
   Ⓑ the bus will leave without him
   Ⓒ the bus will leave without their being on it
   Ⓓ they will miss the bus
   Ⓔ he will miss the bus

The problem here is the choice between the plural *them* and the singular *him.* Since the pronoun refers to *either Mark or Jack,* but not to both, the singular *him* in Ⓑ is the right choice. The other errors repeat the error or change the meaning.

If the sentence contains no pronouns or if the pronouns are correct, focus on the verb.

There are two common verb errors. The first is confusing singular and plural forms.

3. The trunk containing costumes, makeup, and props were left at the stage entrance of the theater.

   (A) costumes, makeup, and props were left
   (B) costumes, makeup, and props were all left
   (C) costumes, makeup, and props was left
   (D) costumes, makeup, and props to be left
   (E) costumes, makeup, and props left

The verb is *were left*. Since the subject is singular (*trunk*) the verb must be singular—*was* instead of *were*. Don't assume that the subject immediately precedes the verb; in this case, the subject and verb are some distance apart.

The second is an error of tense (present, past, future).

4. Tomorrow or the next day, I went to New York.

   (A) I went to New York
   (B) I have gone to New York
   (C) I will go to New York
   (D) I had gone to New York
   (E) I did go to New York

The word *tomorrow* tells us that the action is to take place in the future, so the correct answer must be (C), the future tense of the verb— "I will go."

Another common error is faulty parallelism. Look for a series of items separated by commas and make sure each item has the same form.

5. <u>To strive, to seek, to find, and not yielding</u> are the heroic goals of Ulysses in Tennyson's famous poem.

   Ⓐ To strive, to seek, to find, and not yielding
   Ⓑ To strive, to seek, to find, and to yield
   Ⓒ To strive, to seek, to find, and not to yield
   Ⓓ To strive, to seek, to find, and yet to yield
   Ⓔ Striving, seeking, finding, and yielding

Not yielding is incorrect; it should have the "to _____" form of the other items. Ⓒ is the best choice; Ⓑ, Ⓓ, and Ⓔ are correct, but they change the meaning of the sentence.

Sometimes a sentence contains an error in idiom; that is, it employs a word or phrase which is incorrect simply because it has not been established as standard usage. Such errors just don't "sound right."

6. <u>After waiting on the arrival of a washer repairman for hours,</u> the customer resigned himself to using the laundromat.

   Ⓐ After waiting on the arrival of a washer repairman for hours
   Ⓑ With no arrival of a washer repairman for hours
   Ⓒ After hours of waiting for the arrival of a washer repairman
   Ⓓ Waiting after hours for the arrival of a washer repairman
   Ⓔ In the face of hours of waiting for a washer repairman

Waiting on is not idiomatic; the correct expression is *waiting for.* Choices Ⓒ, Ⓓ, and Ⓔ employ this construction, but Ⓓ and Ⓔ significantly obscure and change the intended meaning of the original sentence.

Adjective or adverb misuse constitutes another type of error.

7. The tired mechanic, happily to be finished with a hard day's work, closed the hood over the newly tuned engine.

    Ⓐ The tired mechanic, happily to be finished with a hard day's work

    Ⓑ Happily, the tired mechanic being finished with a hard day's work

    Ⓒ Tired but happy with a hard day's work being done, the mechanic

    Ⓓ The tired mechanic, happy to be finished with a hard day's work

    Ⓔ With the pleasant fatigue of a job well done, the mechanic

Happily is used here to describe a person, the mechanic. The correct part of speech for describing a person or thing is an adjective, *happy.* Ⓓ is the correct choice—grammatically correct, logical, economical, and clear without unnecessarily changing the intended meaning of the original sentence.

When a word or phrase is not placed close to the word it modifies, the error is called a misplaced modifier. If the word that should be modified is missing, the error is called a dangling modifier.

8. Looking through the lens of a camera, Mount Rushmore seemed much smaller and farther away than it had only seconds before.

    Ⓐ Looking through the lens of a camera

    Ⓑ With camera in hand

    Ⓒ Through the effects of the lens of a camera she looked through

    Ⓓ When she looked through the camera lens

    Ⓔ Against the camera

The sentence seems to say that Mount Rushmore is looking through the camera lens (dangling modifier). Choice Ⓓ makes it clear that a person is looking through the lens and does so without the excessive wordiness of choice Ⓒ.

A sentence may contain a comparison error.

9. She wished that her career could be <u>as glamorous as the other</u> <u>women</u> but was not willing to work as hard as they had.

    Ⓐ as glamorous as the other women
    Ⓑ as glamorous as the other women's careers
    Ⓒ with the glamour of other women
    Ⓓ more glamorous than the careers of the other women
    Ⓔ glamorous

Here two very different *in*comparable things are being compared: her career is compared to the other women. Choice Ⓑ, the most clear, complete, and sensible construction, compares her career to the careers of other women.

Summary

Generally, watch out for pronouns, verbs, parallel constructions, and misplaced words or phrases. Other possible errors that have not been explained above are fully explained in the answer sections following the practice questions and test.

A PATTERNED PLAN OF ATTACK
Sentence Correction

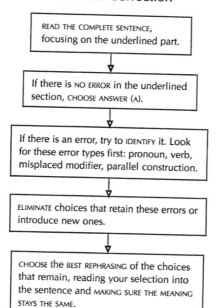

PRACTICE SENTENCE CORRECTION QUESTIONS

EASY TO MODERATE

1. Secretly determined to break up the drug dealer's ring, the undercover agent with the local pushers joined forces, without their realizing his identity.

   Ⓐ Secretly determined to break up the drug dealer's ring, the undercover agent with the local pushers joined forces
   Ⓑ Secretly determined to break up the drug dealer's ring, the undercover agent joined forces with the local pushers
   Ⓒ The undercover agent secretly joined forces with local pushers in order to destroy their ring
   Ⓓ The undercover agent joined forces with the local pushers and secretly determined to destroy their ring
   Ⓔ Secretly determined to destroy the rings, the local pushers and the undercover agent joined forces

2. In studying diabetes, many doctors have concluded that early detection of the disease can permit control through diet.

   Ⓐ In studying diabetes, many doctors have concluded
   Ⓑ Many doctors, by studying diabetes, have concluded
   Ⓒ Many doctors studying diabetes have concluded
   Ⓓ Diabetes studies have led many doctors to conclude
   Ⓔ The conclusion of those doctors who have studied diabetes is

3. Although he is liable to make political enemies with the decision, the President will propose severe tax cuts that may both stimulate business and reduce the availability of home loans.

   Ⓐ liable to
   Ⓑ liable from
   Ⓒ able to
   Ⓓ of a mind to
   Ⓔ acknowledging his liability to

4. To the behalf of many citizens who believe that some criminal statutes are unfair to the victims of crime, legislators in California drafted a "Victim's Bill of Rights" law, which passed handily in the election.

    Ⓐ To the behalf of many citizens who believe that some criminal statutes are unfair to the victims of crime

    Ⓑ Listening for many citizens' belief that criminal statutes are unfair to the victims of crime

    Ⓒ With the belief of their citizens that the victims of crime are unfairly served by some criminal statutes

    Ⓓ On the behalf of many citizens who believe that some criminal statutes are unfair to the victims of crime

    Ⓔ To believe on the behalf of many citizens about criminal statutes that are unfair to crime victims

5. The recent increase in the prime interest rate has encouraged some economists and worried others, who recall all too vividly the skyrocketing rates and consequent economic stagnation of the late 1970s.

    Ⓐ The recent increase in the prime interest rate

    Ⓑ Increasing recently, the prime interest rate

    Ⓒ The recent rate of increase in prime interest

    Ⓓ The prime interest rate, recently increased,

    Ⓔ The recently increasing prime interest rate

6. Whatever he aspired to achieve, they were thwarted by his jealous older brothers, who controlled the stock in the family companies.

    Ⓐ Whatever he aspired to achieve, they

    Ⓑ Whatever he had any aspirations to, they

    Ⓒ Whatever aspirations he had

    Ⓓ Whatever be his aspirations, they

    Ⓔ Many of his aspirations and goals

7. Irregardless of the "new modernism" in literature, which produces novels that often read like the diaries of madmen, most
readers still prefer a conventional plot and simple style.

Ⓐ Irregardless of the "new modernism" in literature, which
produces
Ⓑ Irregardless of the "new modernism" in literature, which
produced
Ⓒ Regardless, the "new modernism" in literature, which produces
Ⓓ Regardless of the "new modernism" in literature, which produces
Ⓔ Regardless of the "new modernism" in literature, which produce

8. If Swift's *Gulliver's Travels* attracts less of a readership than he
did in the eighteenth century, perhaps the reason is that modern
readers do not know enough political history to appreciate the
satire.

Ⓐ attracts less of a readership than he did in the eighteenth
century
Ⓑ attracts less readers than the eighteenth century did
Ⓒ attracts fewer readers than it did in the eighteenth century
Ⓓ attracts fewer readers than he did in the eighteenth century
Ⓔ attracts less reading than it did in the eighteenth century

9. Proposing that inordinate government spending was causative of the high deficit, the president presented a budget that maintained relatively high defense expenditures while it reduced funding for certain social programs which, the administration argued, were receiving sufficient support from the private sector.

Ⓐ Proposing that inordinate government spending was causative of the high deficit, the president presented a budget

Ⓑ Proposing that government spending causes deficits, the president presented a budget

Ⓒ With a proposal that inordinate government spending was causative of the high deficit, the president presented a budget

Ⓓ The president presented a budget proposal that inordinate government spending was causative of the high deficit

Ⓔ Proposing that inordinate government spending caused the high deficit, the president presented a budget

AVERAGE

10. Although the advisory commission on Central America has completed their report that address the political tensions in that area, no easing of tensions has resulted.

Ⓐ their report that address the political tensions in that area

Ⓑ their report that addresses the political tensions in that area

Ⓒ its report that address the political tensions for that area

Ⓓ its report that addresses the political tensions with that area in mind

Ⓔ its report that addresses the political tensions in that area

11. To enjoy exploring marine life in general, and so that they could learn in particular about the ways in which certain sea animals possess "human" traits, the university's school of oceanography offered supervised summer field trips for the elementary school children in the area.

   Ⓐ To enjoy exploring marine life in general, and so that they could learn in particular about the ways in which certain sea animals possess "human" traits
   Ⓑ To stress the enjoyment of marine life in general, and particularly the ways in which certain sea animals are "human"
   Ⓒ In order to teach young people about the "human" traits of certain sea animals, and to provide them an opportunity to enjoy marine exploration in general
   Ⓓ Because marine life in general shares certain "human" traits
   Ⓔ From general marine life to the specifically "human" possessions of sea animals

12. To bring to an end the 1984 Olympics, the festivities were highlighted by the arrival of an "alien" spaceship that hovered mysteriously over the Coliseum, to the amazement and delight of thousands of spectators.

   Ⓐ To bring to an end the 1984 Olympics, the festivities were highlighted
   Ⓑ The festivities to bring to an end to the 1984 Olympics were highlighted
   Ⓒ With the festivities that ended the 1984 Olympics highlighted
   Ⓓ Festive highlights brought an end to the 1984 Olympics
   Ⓔ The festive conclusion of the 1984 Olympics was highlighted

13. Many of us bemoan our lack of foresight <u>by complaining that if</u> <u>we would have bought property twenty years ago, we could have</u> <u>taken advantage of the recent real estate boom.</u>

Ⓐ by complaining that if we would have bought property twenty years ago, we could have taken advantage of the recent real estate boom

Ⓑ , looking backward to a potential property purchase twenty years ago and wishing we had done so for present purposes

Ⓒ : with real estate available so cheaply twenty years ago, the advantages of the recent boom would be ours for the asking

Ⓓ , complaining that if we had bought property twenty years ago, we could have taken advantage of the recent real estate boom

Ⓔ , the complaint being our lack of purchasing property twenty years ago and the consequent absence of profit in the recent real estate boom

14. Acting selfishly and impulsively, <u>the chairperson adapted the</u> <u>committee's recommendations to meet his own needs, without</u> <u>considering the negative affects of his changes.</u>

Ⓐ the chairperson adapted the committee's recommendations to meet his own needs, without considering the negative affects of his changes

Ⓑ without considering the negative affects of his changes, the chairperson adapted the committee's recommendations to meet his own needs

Ⓒ the chairperson adapted the committee's recommendations to meet his own needs, without considering the negative effects of his changes

Ⓓ necessarily, the chairperson adapted committee recommendations, despite negative effects

Ⓔ negative effects notwithstanding, the chairperson adapted the recommendations of the committee

15. The more the union stubbornly refused to budge from its original demand for a 20% across-the-board salary increase, <u>the more the district administration reiterated its original proposal of a mere 1% raise</u>.

Ⓐ the more the district administration reiterated its original proposal of a mere 1% raise

Ⓑ the district administration's original proposal for a mere 1% raise was reiterated all the more

Ⓒ proposing its original and mere 1% raise was the district administration's response, more and more

Ⓓ the district administration reiterated its proposal of a mere 1% raise

Ⓔ the more the district administration's original proposal of a mere 1% raise was reiterated

16. Homer's *Odyssey* is often dramatized as a series of hairbreadth escapes from terrible monsters and vengeful gods, <u>and while those episodes are exciting and important literary achievements</u>, they stand apart from the poem's extensive attention to domestic life, to domestic values, and to a hero whose most important achievement is the reestablishment of his home and family.

Ⓐ and while those episodes are exciting and important literary achievements

Ⓑ and although in fact these episodes are exciting, important achievements in literature

Ⓒ and while an exciting and important literary achievement

Ⓓ and those episodes are exciting and important literary achievements

Ⓔ and with those episodes as exciting and important literary achievements

17. Public enthusiasm that had been growing for airline travel, still in its infancy, when Amelia Earhart's plane disappeared in the 1930s, diminished for awhile; however, today fear of flying is rare.

 Ⓐ Public enthusiasm that had been growing for airline travel, still in its infancy, when Amelia Earhart's plane disappeared in the 1930s, diminished for awhile

 Ⓑ Public enthusiasm that had been growing for airline travel, still in its infancy when Amelia Earhart's plane disappeared in the 1930s, diminished for awhile

 Ⓒ Growing public enthusiasm for airline travel, still in its infancy, diminished for awhile after Amelia Earhart's plane disappeared in the 1930s

 Ⓓ When Amelia Earhart's plane disappeared in the 1930s, growing public enthusiasm for airline travel, still in its infancy, diminished for awhile

 Ⓔ After Amelia Earhart's plane disappeared in the 1930s, the enthusiasm that had been growing for airline travel in its infancy diminished for awhile

18. Golding's most famous novel concerns little boys, once a well-behaved and civilized group, whose resort to murder and savagery during their brief time on a tropical island without adult supervision.

 Ⓐ once a well-behaved and civilized group, whose
 Ⓑ once well-behaved and civilized, who
 Ⓒ once a well-behaved and civilized herd, who
 Ⓓ once civilized and well-behaved, whose
 Ⓔ behaved and civilized, who

19. When reading some of the most rich and beautiful speeches in Shakespeare's *Romeo and Juliet,* <u>when one stresses the singsong cadence of iambic pentameter, the lines take on an almost simpleminded, childish quality.</u>

   Ⓐ when one stresses the singsong cadence of iambic pentameter, the lines take on an almost simpleminded, childish quality

   Ⓑ stressing the singsong cadence of iambic pentameter gives the lines an almost simpleminded, childish quality

   Ⓒ if one stresses the singsong cadence of iambic pentameter, it gives the lines an almost simpleminded, childish quality

   Ⓓ the simpleminded, childish quality of some lines results from the singsong cadence of iambic pentameter

   Ⓔ the singsong cadence of iambic pentameter, sounds almost simpleminded and childish

20. During the French Revolution, especially the Reign of Terror, <u>citizens whom the government suspected of treasonous tendencies were eventually put to death</u> by Monsieur Sanson, the infamous executioner who supervised the killing of hundreds at the guillotine.

   Ⓐ citizens whom the government suspected of treasonous tendencies were eventually put to death

   Ⓑ citizens of which the government had suspicions were eventually put to death

   Ⓒ suspicious citizens were eventually killed

   Ⓓ citizens who the government suspected of treason were eventually put to death

   Ⓔ the citizenry under suspicion were eventually put to death

21. During the last century, whaling voyages departed regularly from the New England states, <u>and because each voyage normally extends for years,</u> the hold was packed with supplies before a whaling ship set sail.

   Ⓐ and because each voyage normally extends for years

   Ⓑ and because each trip was long

   Ⓒ and because each voyage normally extended for years

   Ⓓ and while these were long trips

   Ⓔ and because the voyage had lasted for years

22. <u>As he looked out on an expanse that seemed empty of gods or goddesses</u>, Odysseus must certainly have felt abandoned by the rulers on Olympus.

Ⓐ As he looked out on an expanse that seemed empty of gods or goddesses

Ⓑ As he looked out on an empty expanse of gods and goddesses

Ⓒ With no gods or goddesses as he looked out on the empty expanse

Ⓓ Facing the empty expanse of gods and goddesses

Ⓔ As he looked out on an expanse that seemed empty of either a god or a goddess

ABOVE AVERAGE TO DIFFICULT

23. <u>If the majority of your opponents have control, you may become defeated.</u>

Ⓐ If the majority of your opponents have control, you may become defeated.

Ⓑ If the majority of your opponents take control, you may lose.

Ⓒ If the majority of your opponents assumes control, you may see defeat.

Ⓓ If the majority of your opponents has control, you may lose.

Ⓔ Most of your opponents will have control, and you may lose.

24. <u>Focusing across several generations</u>, Alex Haley wrote *Roots,* a novel explaining both his family history and the history of American bigotry.

Ⓐ Focusing across several generations

Ⓑ Centering around several generations

Ⓒ Living through several generations

Ⓓ With an eye on several generations

Ⓔ Telling of several generations

25. In the early fourteenth century, almost 200 years before Colum-
bus reached the West Indies, and 250 years before the Reforma-
tion, Europe had been Catholic and the Church continued to
influence virtually every phase of human life.

   Ⓐ Europe had been Catholic and the Church continued to influence virtually every phase of human life

   Ⓑ the Catholic Church continued to influence every phase of
human life

   Ⓒ the Europe that had been Catholic was still influenced in
virtually every phase of human life by the Church

   Ⓓ Europe was Catholic and the Church influenced virtually
every phase of human life

   Ⓔ every phase of human life bore traces of the European influence of the Catholic Church

26. In the 1950s, toy stores sold thousands of play replicas of a gun
popularized by the *Wyatt Earp* television series, the "Buntline
Special," a long-barreled six-gun named after the legendary Ned
Buntline.

   Ⓐ In the 1950s, toy stores sold thousands of play replicas of a
gun popularized by the *Wyatt Earp* television series

   Ⓑ Popularized by the 1950s *Wyatt Earp* television series, toy
stores sold thousands of play replicas of a gun

   Ⓒ In the 1950s, the *Wyatt Earp* television series popularized
thousands of play replicas of a gun sold in toy stores

   Ⓓ A play replica of a gun popularized by the *Wyatt Earp* television series, which sold thousands in toy stores in the 1950s

   Ⓔ As toy stores sold thousands of the 1950s replicas of a gun
popularized by the *Wyatt Earp* television series

27. During the literary renaissance of the 1920s, a large number of new writers—William Faulkner, Ernest Hemingway, John Dos Passos, and F. Scott Fitzgerald—sought to record the inner life of Americans and to scrutinize the American dream, <u>the dream that anyone can earn his own fortune and live happily ever after through hard work, which had become tarnished.</u>

Ⓐ the dream that anyone can earn his own fortune and live happily ever after through hard work, which had become tarnished

Ⓑ the tarnished dream that anyone can make his own fortune and live happily ever after through hard work

Ⓒ the tarnished dream that anyone can, through hard work, make his own fortune and live happily ever after

Ⓓ the dream that anyone can earn his own fortune and live happily ever after, though tarnished, through hard work

Ⓔ that making one's own fortune and living happily ever after, through hard work, had become tarnished

28. Much like Macbeth when he interprets the witches' prophecies all too literally, <u>the mysterious harpooner who Ahab takes aboard the *Pequod* has the captain accepting his strange prophecies without questioning their hidden meaning.</u>

Ⓐ the mysterious harpooner who Ahab takes aboard the *Pequod* has the captain accepting his strange prophecies without questioning their hidden meaning

Ⓑ the strange prophecies of the mysterious harpooner he has taken aboard the *Pequod* are accepted by Ahab without questioning their hidden meaning

Ⓒ the mysterious harpooner whom Ahab takes aboard the *Pequod* has the captain accepting his strange prophecies without questioning their hidden meaning

Ⓓ Ahab accepts the strange prophecy of the mysterious harpooner whom he has taken aboard the *Pequod,* without questioning their hidden meaning

Ⓔ Ahab accepts the strange prophecies of the mysterious harpooner he has taken aboard the *Pequod,* without questioning their hidden meaning

29. The weather in San Diego, California, is temperate for most of the year, and although the air is not so clean as it used to be, it has remained virtually smog free through recent years of rapid industrial growth, <u>unlike most urban areas in southern California.</u>

   Ⓐ unlike most urban areas in southern California
   Ⓑ unlike the air in most southern California urban areas
   Ⓒ unlike other southern California air
   Ⓓ unlike southern California urban areas
   Ⓔ in contrast to the smog condition elsewhere in urban southern California

30. Brokers who offer foreign cars on the "gray market," thus bypassing the car dealer by shipping directly from the manufacturer to the waiting consumer at the dock, claim that their purpose is not to cheat dealerships out of a profit, but rather <u>to provide the consumer with the finest value for his or her dollar.</u>

   Ⓐ to provide the consumer with the finest value for his or her dollar
   Ⓑ the provision of the finest value for the dollar
   Ⓒ providing the finest values for consumer dollars
   Ⓓ that they have an obligation to give consumers value for their dollars
   Ⓔ to deliver value for the dollar

31. Two recent statements on the tenure of university professors offer conflicting points of view: <u>those that say that lifetime tenure ensures academic freedom and those that say that lifetime tenure encourages professional laziness and irresponsibility.</u>

Ⓐ those that say that lifetime tenure ensures academic freedom and those that say that lifetime tenure encourages professional laziness and irresponsibility

Ⓑ some declare that lifetime tenure ensures academic freedom, and others say that it encourages professional laziness and irresponsibility

Ⓒ saying that lifetime tenure either ensures academic freedom or encourages irresponsible laziness

Ⓓ one emphasizes the academic freedom that tenure ensures, and one stresses the professional laziness and irresponsibility it encourages

Ⓔ advocacies of academic freedom and warnings about professional laziness and irresponsibility

32. With an explosive capacity that can devastate life and property for a radius of hundreds of miles, proponents of peace from several Western bloc countries met to discuss the continuing manufacture and deployment of nuclear warheads.

Ⓐ With an explosive capacity that can devastate life and property for a radius of hundreds of miles, proponents of peace from several Western bloc countries met to discuss the continuing manufacture and deployment of nuclear warheads.

Ⓑ Proponents of peace from several Western bloc countries with an explosive capacity that can devastate life and property for a radius of hundreds of miles met to discuss the continuing manufacture and deployment of nuclear warheads.

Ⓒ Meeting to discuss the continuing manufacture and deployment of nuclear warheads with an explosive capacity that can devastate life and property for a radius of hundreds of miles were several Western bloc countries.

Ⓓ Proponents of peace from several Western bloc countries met to discuss the continuing manufacture and deployment of nuclear warheads that can devastate life and property with an explosive capacity for a radius of hundreds of miles.

Ⓔ Proponents of peace from several Western bloc countries met to discuss the continuing manufacture and deployment of nuclear warheads with an explosive capacity that can devastate life and property for a radius of hundreds of miles.

33. Arms talks <u>from Geneva between China, the United States, Russia, and other nations may be even more effecting than many world leaders think they would be.</u>

 Ⓐ from Geneva between China, the United States, Russia, and other nations may be even more effecting than many world leaders think they would be

 Ⓑ in Geneva between China, the United States, Russia, and other nations may be even more effective than many world leaders suppose

 Ⓒ in Geneva between China, the United States, Russia, and other nations may be even more affecting than many world leaders think they will be

 Ⓓ in Geneva among China, the United States, Russia, and other nations may be even more effective than many world leaders expect

 Ⓔ between China, the United States, Russia, and other nations in Geneva may be even more effective than many world leaders believe

34. <u>Acknowledging the volunteers' giving of a great deal of their time to canvass the neighborhood and collect donations from the neighbors, the chairman of the local United Way expressed his sincere gratitude.</u>

 Ⓐ Acknowledging the volunteers' giving of a great deal of their time to canvass the neighborhood and collect donations from the neighbors, the chairman of the local United Way expressed his sincere gratitude.

 Ⓑ Acknowledging the time spent by neighborhood volunteers to canvass and to collect neighborhood donations, the chairman of the local United Way expressed his sincere gratitude.

 Ⓒ With sincere gratitude, the chairman of the local United Way expressed his acknowledgment of the neighborhood donations canvassed and collected on the volunteers' time.

 Ⓓ The chairman of the local United Way offered sincere thanks to the volunteers who gave so much time to canvass the neighborhood to collect donations.

 Ⓔ The chairman of the local United Way thanked the neighborhood volunteers, sincerely.

35. A diagonal line connecting two corners of a rectangle is also the hypotenuse of each of two right triangles contained within the rectangle, <u>which is longer than any of the sides.</u>

    Ⓐ which is longer than any of the sides
    Ⓑ and the line is longer than any of the sides
    Ⓒ which is longer than the sides
    Ⓓ that is longer than any of the sides
    Ⓔ that is longer than any of the other sides

ANSWERS AND EXPLANATIONS FOR THE PRACTICE SENTENCE CORRECTION QUESTIONS

EASY TO MODERATE

1. Ⓑ Choice Ⓑ corrects the poor structure of the original wording. Choices Ⓒ, Ⓓ, and Ⓔ change the meaning of the original expression slightly—Ⓒ and Ⓓ suggesting that the ring belongs to the *pushers,* not to the *drug dealer,* and Ⓔ implying that the *pushers* were determined to destroy the ring.

2. Ⓒ All choices are grammatically correct; however, choice Ⓒ is the most direct expression of the original wording. Choices Ⓓ and Ⓔ change the meaning of the original, and choice Ⓑ is awkward.

3. Ⓐ The original is better than any of the alternatives.

4. Ⓓ *To the behalf* is not idiomatic. Choice Ⓓ corrects this error and does not make additional, unnecessary changes, as do the other choices.

5. Ⓐ None of the alternatives is more direct and clear than the original underlined portion. Since it is the *increase* that has encouraged some economists, not the *rate,* choices Ⓑ, Ⓒ, Ⓓ, and Ⓔ all change the meaning of the sentence.

6. Ⓒ Choice Ⓒ best expresses the idea without changing the intent of the sentence as Ⓔ does. The original and choices Ⓑ and Ⓓ are awkward.

7. Ⓓ *Irregardless* is nonstandard usage. Apart from this error, the original underlined portion is correct and clear. To make sense, choice Ⓒ would require the preposition *of.* Choice Ⓔ contains an agreement error.

8. ⓒ *Fewer readers* is more economical than choice Ⓐ. *Less* in choice Ⓑ is incorrect when the noun (*readers*) can be numbered (for example: fewer gallons, less gasoline; fewer dollars, less money). Since the pronoun refers to the book, not to the author, *it,* not *he,* is correct. Choice Ⓔ incorrectly uses the plural *attract—Gulliver's Travels* is the name of a book and is singular.

9. Ⓔ *Caused* is better than the wordy and pretentious phrase *was causative of* in choices Ⓐ, ⓒ, and Ⓓ. Choice Ⓑ omits two adjectives and unnecessarily changes the tense in *causes.*

AVERAGE

10. Ⓔ Both *commission* and *report* are singular, so the singular pronoun *its* and the singular verb *addresses* must be used. The agreement is correct in choice Ⓓ, but *with that area in mind* is needlessly wordy.

11. ⓒ Along with having inconsistent verb tense and wordiness problems, the original sentence illustrates a long dangling modifier. The underlined portion seems to modify *the university's school of oceanography* and thereby seems to say that the *school* is enjoying *exploring marine life,* etc. Only ⓒ offers an introductory phrase that is both correct and unambiguous. Ⓑ and Ⓓ, although grammatically correct, significantly change the intended meaning of the original sentence.

12. Ⓔ This is the most direct, clear, and economical choice that retains the essential meaning of the original underlined portion. Compared to choice Ⓔ, both Ⓐ and Ⓑ are wordy. Choice ⓒ is a sentence fragment, and Ⓓ distorts the meaning.

13. Ⓓ The use of *would have* and *could have* as the main verbs here does not clearly indicate that buying property twenty years ago is a much earlier action; the verb *had* makes clear the distinction between distant past and recent past. Choice Ⓓ supplies the appropriate verb and eliminates the unnecessary *by.*

14. Ⓒ The error in the original is a diction error. *Effects* (results) is preferable to *affects*. Choices Ⓓ and Ⓔ are economical but change the meaning of the original significantly.

15. Ⓐ The original underlined portion is the most clear and correct choice, resulting in a balanced sentence, with the structure of the second half (that is, the underlined portion) parallel to the structure of the first half: *the more . . . subject . . . active verb*. Choices Ⓑ, Ⓒ, and Ⓓ omit *the more*. In choice Ⓔ, the verb is passive.

16. Ⓐ The original underlined portion is the best choice. Choice Ⓑ is wordy, Ⓒ introduces an agreement error, Ⓓ introduces a comma error, and Ⓔ, by omitting the *while,* changes the meaning.

17. Ⓒ The best choice here arranges the parts of the sentence in the most direct and clear way by keeping the modifiers as close as possible to the words they modify. In addition, choice Ⓒ replaces *when* with a more appropriate and logical term, *after.*

18. Ⓑ Choice Ⓑ is grammatically correct and economical. In choice Ⓒ, *herd* introduces a meaning not in the original, while choice Ⓔ omits details. Choices Ⓐ and Ⓓ are sentence fragments.

19. Ⓑ Choice Ⓑ is the most economical and clear version of the original. Choices Ⓐ and Ⓒ are wordy, containing the unnecessary phrases *when one* and *if one*. Choices Ⓓ and Ⓔ omit the notion of stressing and so change the meaning.

20. Ⓐ The original underlined portion is the best choice. *Whom* is used correctly, as the object of *suspected*. Each of the other choices omits or changes this correct pronoun unnecessarily or changes the meaning of the original.

21. © The original underlined portion contains a verb tense error. *Extends* Ⓐ and *has lasted* Ⓔ are inconsistent with the past tense established through the rest of the sentence. Choice © supplies the simple past tense, *extended,* that agrees with the other verbs in the sentence. Choices Ⓑ and Ⓓ, while grammatically correct, substitute the vaguer *long* for the phrase *for years.*

22. Ⓐ It is an expanse, empty of gods, not an empty expanse of gods—choices Ⓑ and Ⓓ. Choice Ⓔ is needlessly wordy, and © distorts the meaning.

ABOVE AVERAGE TO DIFFICULT

23. Ⓓ *Majority* is a collective noun, which may take either a singular or plural verb, depending on whether the group as a whole or the individuals are emphasized. But *lose* is a clearer and more economical expression than *become defeated.* Choices Ⓑ, ©, and Ⓔ change the meaning of the sentence.

24. Ⓔ *Focusing across* is idiomatically incorrect and also logically unsound (*focusing on* is better). The only choice that is both idiomatically correct and preserves the meaning of the original is Ⓔ.

25. Ⓓ The verbs are the problem in the original underlined portion. The context supplied by the rest of the sentence suggests that the verbs should be simple past tense, both of them indicating what *was* true *in* the fourteenth century. As it stands, the underlined portion is internally contradictory. It states that Europe *had been* Catholic, implying that the region is no longer Catholic, but also states that Catholic influence *continued.* Choice Ⓓ corrects this grammatical/logical problem while retaining the original intended meaning. Choices Ⓑ and Ⓔ are grammatically correct but omit information contained in the original sentence.

26. Ⓐ Although choice Ⓐ is perhaps not the best choice one can imagine, it is decidedly the best choice of the five offered here. *"Buntline Special"* should be placed as close to *gun* as possible.

In choice Ⓑ, the opening phrase modifies *toy stores,* not *gun,* and the phrase *the 1950s* now modifies the *television series* instead of *sold.* Choice Ⓒ also misplaces the phrase *in the 1950s.* Choices Ⓓ and Ⓔ are sentence fragments.

27. Ⓒ The original version is confusing because the clause *which had become tarnished* is awkwardly separated from *dream* and the prepositional phrase *through hard work* is awkwardly separated from the verb it modifies, *earn.* In choices Ⓑ, Ⓓ, and Ⓔ, the prepositional phrase is misplaced.

28. Ⓔ The underlined portion must name Ahab immediately in order to clarify the comparison between Ahab and Macbeth. It is Ahab, *not* the *harpooner,* choices Ⓐ or Ⓒ and *not* the *prophecies,* choice Ⓑ, who is *much like Macbeth.* Choice Ⓓ has the right structure but has an agreement error in *prophecy* and *their.*

29. Ⓑ The original underlined portion presents an illogical comparison, of *areas* to the topic of the first part of the sentence, *air.* Only choice Ⓑ clarifies the air to air comparison without the inappropriate wordiness of choice Ⓔ.

30. Ⓐ The original underlined portion is the best choice. It maintains parallel structure with *to provide.* Each of the other choices makes unnecessary changes in grammar and syntax that do not improve the original.

31. Ⓓ In the original underlined portion, *those* is incorrect. To express respectively two singular points of view, the noun or pronoun which refers to each must be singular; *those* is, of course, plural. Only choice Ⓓ provides a clearly singular reference, *one,* for each viewpoint.

32. Ⓔ The introductory phrase in the original (preceding the comma) properly modifies warheads. Only choice Ⓔ makes this necessary change while retaining the intended meaning of the original.

33. Ⓓ There are several errors in the original version that must be corrected: the preposition *in* for *from,* the adjective *effective* for *effecting,* and the preposition *among* for *between.*

34. Ⓓ The original underlined sentence as well as choices Ⓑ and Ⓒ are unnecessarily wordy. Choice Ⓓ is an efficient, direct, and clear expression that retains the meaning of the original. Choice Ⓔ leaves out essential information from the original.

35. Ⓑ Though choice Ⓑ requires more words, it is the only version that avoids the ambiguous pronouns—*which* in choices Ⓐ and Ⓒ and *that* in choices Ⓓ and Ⓔ—which seem at first to refer to *rectangle*.

INTRODUCTION TO CRITICAL REASONING

The Critical Reasoning questions are similar to Reading Comprehension questions, but the passages are shorter and the questions are reasoning oriented.

ABILITY TESTED

This section tests your ability to read and understand the logic presented in brief passages or conversations.

BASIC SKILLS NECESSARY

Candidates who read critically and understand simple logic and reasoning do well in this section. The ability to isolate the key issue and to identify irrelevant issues is important.

DIRECTIONS

As you read the brief passage, you must follow the line of reasoning using only commonsense standards of logic. No knowledge of formal logic is required. Then you must choose the best answer, realizing that several choices may be possible, but only one will be best.

ANALYSIS

Rely on common sense. No special expertise is necessary.

Use only what is presented or implied by the passage. Do not make leaps in logic to arrive at an answer choice. Don't read anything into the passage that isn't there.

Choose the *best* answer choice. The test makers strongly imply that there may be more than one good answer.

SUGGESTED APPROACH WITH SAMPLES

Preread the question following the passage.

In most instances, each brief passage will be followed by one question. For these one-question passages, it may be time-effective to read the question before reading the passage. Many GMAT candidates have found that prereading the question eliminates having to read the passage a second time while searching for the answer, thus saving valuable minutes. Knowing what the question is before reading the passage enables you to focus on those elements of the passage essential to the question.

Some candidates report that they can effectively preread a question. If you decide to do so, *do not* preread the answer choices. Since four of the five choices are incorrect, scanning them introduces material eighty percent of which is irrelevant and/or inconsistent and therefore incorrect. Prereading the answer choices is a waste of time and energy. Practice will help you determine when prereading is effective for you.

Try reading the *question* about the following passage first; then read the passage:

1. That seniors in the inner cities have inadequate health care available to them is intolerable. The medical facilities in the urban ghetto rarely contain basic medical supplies, and the technology in these hospitals is reflective of the 1960s, if that. Seniors living in the affluent suburbs, however, have available to them state-of-the-art technology and the latest in medical advances, drugs, and procedures.

Which of the following best expresses the primary point of the passage?

Ⓐ Inner-city and suburban seniors should be cared for in hospitals equidistant from both.

Ⓑ Inner-city seniors should be transported to suburban hospitals.

Ⓒ Doctors should treat inner-city and suburban seniors equally.

Ⓓ Better medical care and facilities should be provided for inner-city seniors.

Ⓔ Inner-city seniors should have the same health care as that available to suburban seniors.

Prereading the question helps you to read the passage with a focus; that is, what is the author's point? The main point will be the overall thrust of the entire passage.

The major issue here is health care, and the author's point is that inner-city seniors should have health care better than that available to them now. The heavily charged word *intolerable* in the first sentence indicates that the author feels strongly that inadequate health care for inner-city seniors is not sufficient. Better care should be provided. Choice Ⓓ is the best answer.

Notice that while a comparison is made to suburban seniors having superior health care, no direct argument is made that inner-city seniors should have the *same* health care as suburban seniors. The superior, *state-of-the-art* quality of suburban health care is presented in order to contrast with that of inner-city health care, and the contrast is used simply for that reason: to show how abysmal inner-city health care is in comparison. But nothing in the passage directly indicates that health care for inner-city seniors should necessarily be equivalent with that provided suburban seniors. Inferring this would be beyond the scope of the passage; choice Ⓔ as the author's primary point is incorrect.

Choices Ⓐ and Ⓑ are incorrect because the issues of hospital relocation and transportation are never raised by the passage. And choice Ⓒ not only raises the problematic issue of "equal" treatment (which, as stated previously, is not directly indicated in the passage) but also alters the focus simply to doctors, which in the context of a passage noting medical facilities, technology, supplies, etc., is far too narrow.

Read and analyze all the choices.

Our analysis of this health care question critically assesses each of the answer choices. As you work the Critical Reasoning questions, you should be assessing *all* the choices, eliminating those that are off-topic, irrelevant, inconsistent, or beyond the scope of the passage and retaining and considering those that you think apply. As mentioned above, several choices frequently will appear to be correct. You are to choose the one that answers the question *best,* the one that is most directly relevant to the passage.

Know the Critical Reasoning question prototypes.

Most of the Critical Reasoning questions fall into a small number of categories, or prototypes. These prototypes will be scrambled throughout the verbal section and delivered in different ways. Knowing and anticipating these prototype questions and what they require in terms of an answer will be of great help, especially when a question appears to be long and confusing. Once you can identify the prototype, you can spend the bulk of your time understanding the passage and the answer choices.

Prototype 1: Main Idea—The test may ask you to identify the main idea of a passage, and it may do this in a number of ways. As you can see in the health care passage, the main idea can be expressed as "the primary point of the passage" or "the author's primary point." Most of the time, the main idea will not be directly stated in the passage; you will have to derive it. Be careful to derive only what is most directly indicated by the passage. A jump of logic will take you beyond the scope of the passage (for example, in the previous passage, jumping from "providing better health care" to "providing health care equal to suburban care") and will be incorrect.

Some other ways (but not all the ways) that the main idea prototype can be asked are

- Which of the following best expresses the point the author is attempting to make?
- The author's argument is best expressed as . . .
- Which of the following statements best expresses the author's central point in the passage above?
- In the passage above, the author argues that . . .

2. Whatever else might be said about American elections, they are quite unlike those in totalitarian countries in that Americans make choices. And one choice they can make in this free country is to stay home.

What is the author's point in the above passage?

Ⓐ Americans who do decide to vote make more choices than those who do not.

Ⓑ American elections embody many negative aspects, most of which are not embodied by elections in totalitarian countries.

Ⓒ Choosing not to vote is the prerogative of a free citizen.

Ⓓ All citizens vote in every election in totalitarian countries.

Ⓔ Most American voters are not well informed enough to vote wisely.

When considering the multiple choices, immediately eliminate those items which are (1) irrelevant to the question and/or the major issue of the passage and (2) not at all addressed by the passage. Consider the passage above. The author's point is necessarily connected with the major issue of the passage—in this case, free choice. The author stresses the free choice *not to vote,* by way of making the point. You may eliminate all choices which do not address the free choice not to vote: Ⓐ is irrelevant because it addresses the number of choices rather than the freedom of choice; Ⓑ raises issues scarcely addressed in the passage—that is, the negative aspects of elections. Ⓓ doesn't address the issue of choosing not to vote; though it notes that all citizens in totalitarian countries must vote, it neglects the main point—that Americans don't have to; Ⓔ is irrelevant to the issue of free choice, stressing instead voter information. The best choice is Ⓒ, which addresses the major issue, free choice, and also the author's specific point, the free choice not to vote.

Prototype 2: Inference—The dictionary defines an inference as the act or process of deriving logical conclusions from a line of reasoning. For example, you can infer from the statement "only a minority of children under the age of six have visited a dentist" that a "majority of children under the age of six have not visited a dentist." This type of Critical Reasoning question asks you to determine an inference or implication in a passage.

The distinction between the meanings of "infer" and "imply" is not very important in this section (although it may be in the Sentence Correction section). In actuality, they differ in meaning in the same way as "push" and "pull." A statement implies ("pushes out to you"); you infer ("pull from"). This grammatical distinction is not the operant element in this section; rather, you should be aware that "infers" or "implies" simply means the next logical step in an argument.

Other ways this prototype may be expressed are

- Which of the following can be inferred from the passage?
- The author of the passage implies that . . .
- Which of the following inferences can be most reliably drawn from the passage?
- What can be validly inferred from the facts and premises expressed in the passage?

3. We doubt that the latest government report will scare Americans away from ham, bacon, sausages, hot dogs, bologna, and salami or that it will empty out the bars or cause a run on natural food supplies. If a diet were to be mandated from Washington, Americans probably would order the exact *opposite* course. Therefore, the diet that does make sense is to eat a balanced and varied diet composed of foods from *all* food groups and containing a reasonable caloric intake.

Which of the following is (are) specifically implied by the passage?

   I. Vitamins are necessary to combat disease.
  II. A recent report warned of the risks of meat and alcoholic beverages.
 III. Unorthodox suggestions for a more nutritional diet were recently made by the government.

   Ⓐ I only
   Ⓑ II only
   Ⓒ III only
   Ⓓ I and II only
   Ⓔ II and III only

Since the author doubts that Americans will stop eating meats or visiting bars, one must conclude that the author is referring to the latest government report warning of the risks of meat and alcoholic beverages, statement II. Statement I concerning vitamins may be true but is not specifically implied other than in a very general sense (nutrition). Statement III is not true: there is nothing to suggest that the government report made *unorthodox* suggestions. The correct answer is Ⓑ.

Prototype 3: Assumption—An assumption is an *unstated* notion on which a statement rests. For example, "I don't like people who continually interrupt me; therefore, you may conclude that I don't like Jack." For this argument to be logically valid, it must be assumed that Jack continually interrupts the author. In this type of question, you are asked to determine what assumption lies behind the author's argument.

Other ways this prototype may be expressed are

- Which of the following underlies the passage above?
- The author assumes that . . .
- The argument above logically depends on which of the following assumptions?
- What is the presupposition of the passage above?
- Necessary to the reasoning above is the assumption that . . .

4. In his first message to Congress, Harry Truman said, "The responsibility of the United States is to serve and not dominate the world."

   Which of the following is one basic assumption underlying Truman's statement?

   Ⓐ The United States is capable of dominating the world.
   Ⓑ The United States chooses to serve rather than dominate the world.
   Ⓒ World domination is a virtue.
   Ⓓ One must be decisive when facing a legislative body for the first time.
   Ⓔ The United States, preceding Truman's administration, had been irresponsible.

Truman's statement is not warranted unless one assumes the U.S. capability to dominate the world Ⓐ; that assumed capability makes the choice between serving and dominating possible and is thus a basic assumption.

Prototype 4: Support/Weaken—This question type asks for the answer choice that would support or weaken the passage. For example, the passage may state

> Research comparing children of cigarette-smoking parents in Virginia with children of nonsmoking parents in West Virginia found that children of smoking parents in Virginia have lower test scores than do children of nonsmokers in West Virginia. Therefore, secondhand cigarette smoke is a cause of the lower test scores.

> Which of the following, if true, would weaken the conclusion above?

A correct answer would be "Children in Virginia have lower test scores than children in West Virginia, regardless of whether their parents smoke or not." Notice that if children in Virginia have lower test scores than children in West Virginia, regardless of whether their parents smoke or not, then the cigarette-smoking parents cannot logically be claimed to be a cause of the lower test scores. This choice would weaken the conclusion. However, the question could have been

> Which of the following, if true, would strengthen the logic of the argument?

A correct answer would be "A recent study indicates that, in general, children in any particular state tend to have similar test scores to children in any other state." Notice that this choice would strengthen the logic of the passage. If children in general have similar test scores state to state, then a subpopulation of children from smoking parents having lower test scores than a subpopulation of children from nonsmoking parents strengthens the conclusion that the smoking parents may have been the cause of the difference in scores.

Sometimes the question asks for what would be "relevant" to the reasoning. The choice that would either strengthen or weaken the logic would be the relevant choice.

Notice that this question type may contain the words *if true*. That means accept all of the choices as being true: do not challenge their reasonableness or the possibility of their occurring. Rather, accept all the choices as being true and from there decide which would strengthen or weaken the argument, whatever the question requires.

Other ways this question type may be expressed are

- Which of the following, if true, would support the argument?
- Which of the following, if true, would undermine the conclusion?
- Which of the following, if true, would challenge the logic of the reasoning of the passage?
- Which of the following would confirm the author's conclusion?

5. Experience shows that for every burglar shot by a homeowner there are many more fatal accidents involving small children, family slayings that could have been avoided but for the handy presence of a gun, and thefts of handguns by the criminals they are intended to protect against.

   Which of the following facts, if true, would most seriously weaken the above contention?

   A Criminals tend to sell the handguns they steal during the commission of a burglary.
   B Burglars are also capable of causing fatal accidents.
   C Every burglar shot by a homeowner is stopped from committing scores of further burglaries and injuring scores of other citizens.
   D The number of burglars shot by homeowners is larger than the number of burglars shot by renters.
   E Not all fatal accidents involve guns.

Choice C most directly addresses the argument of the passage. The passage argues that for every burglar shot, there are scores of slayings of the innocent; C argues that for every burglar shot, there are scores of prevented burglaries.

Prototype 5: Conclusion—This prototype question asks for the conclusion that has not yet been stated in the passage. For example,

6. The county legislature has finally, after ten years of legal challenges, passed an antipollution ordinance. From a reading of the language, the legislation promises to be one of the most effective bills in the history of the state.

   Which of the following can be deduced from the passage?

   Ⓐ The pollution problem will be eliminated in the county.
   Ⓑ The pollution problem will be reduced in the county.
   Ⓒ Pollution is not now a problem in the county.
   Ⓓ Pollution will be reduced in the state.
   Ⓔ To reduce pollution, the legislation must now be enforced.

When you are selecting a conclusion for a passage, do not merely choose what may be possible. Usually several of the choices are possible. You are to select the one choice that may necessarily be concluded. So, in the above example, notice that while Ⓐ and Ⓑ are possible, they don't necessarily have to occur; the ordinance, after all, may not be effective despite its tough language. Choices Ⓒ and Ⓓ are even more remote. But of the five choices, Ⓔ is the safest conclusion that can be drawn. When seeking a conclusion, choose the "safest" of the five choices.

Other ways this question type may be presented are

- If the above passage is true, then which of the following must necessarily be true?
- Which of the following is the best deduction based on the passage above?
- If the passage above is true, which of the following must logically follow?
- From the passage above, which of the following can reasonably be deduced?
- Based on the passage above, the author would conclude . . .

7. In the 1940s, the introduction of the 33 rpm long-playing vinyl record completely changed the way we listen to music. The breakable and three-minute 78 rpm record soon disappeared from the marketplace. In our day, the compact disk, superior in quality and convenience, has replaced the vinyl long-playing record and will . . .

Ⓐ increase the size of the record-buying public.
Ⓑ increase the profits of the record industry.
Ⓒ drive the 78 rpm record from the second-hand market.
Ⓓ make the manufacture of phonographs that play 33 rpm records unnecessary.
Ⓔ encourage the growth of computer-generated music.

The passage compares the obsolescence of the 78 rpm record when the 33 rpm was introduced with the present-day situation in which the compact disk replaces the 33 rpm. The passage offers no information on the potential sales of the new disks and tells us nothing of their effect on 78 rpm records or their relation to computer-generated music. If 33 rpm records have become obsolete, it follows that manufacturers will not make the machines to play them Ⓓ.

Prototype 6: Technique—This prototype question asks for the technique of reasoning used in the passage. For example, the passage may use a generalization to prove a specific point, or vice versa. Or it may use an analogy (a comparison) to further an argument. It may present a conclusion without adequately supporting it, or it may contradict its original premise within the passage. As you can see, a line of reasoning may be structured—or may be faulty—in many ways. Be aware that it usually does not matter whether you agree or disagree with the logic presented in the passage because in this case you are not being asked to determine the passage's validity. (That's another question type.) Rather, you need to identify in structural terms how the author has set up the argument.

Ways this prototype may be expressed are

* The author makes her point primarily by . . .
* The author of the passage uses which of the following methods of persuasion?
* In the passage above, the author does which of the following?
* The author is using what line of reasoning to make the point?

8. Tom's writing is always straightforward and honest. After all, whenever he writes a critique, he includes a special note that forewarns us that he will not mince words or make any untruthful statements. Therefore, his prose is direct and always tells the truth.

The statement above uses which of the following to support the argument?

Ⓐ Generalization
Ⓑ Circular reasoning
Ⓒ Specific examples
Ⓓ Deductive reasoning
Ⓔ Formal logic

The statement supports itself by restating its assumption in a slightly different way. This is circular reasoning Ⓑ.

Prototype 7: Error—This prototype asks you to find a logical mistake in the reasoning. As you read the passage, you should look for an inconsistency or flaw in logic. Typically the error will be so striking that, if you are not looking for it, it will cause you to stop in consternation, realizing that the logic of the passage has somehow broken. Prereading the question is effective for this prototype; once you know you're looking for an error, as soon as you reach it, instead of wondering why you're having trouble with the reasoning, you realize you have just discovered the flaw.

Ways that this prototype may be presented are

- The conclusion above is unsound because the author . . .
- Which of the following inconsistencies seriously undermines the author's argument?
- The reasoning in the passage above is flawed because . . .
- Which of the following is an inherent error in logic in the passage above?

9. *Speaker:* One need not look very far to find abundant examples of incivility and brutality in the most genteel corners of American society.

Questioner: Then why don't we step up law enforcement in the slums of our cities?

The question reveals which of the following misunderstandings?

Ⓐ The misunderstanding that incivility and brutality have become more abundant

Ⓑ The misunderstanding that law enforcement is related to the problems of incivility and brutality

Ⓒ The misunderstanding of the speaker's position relative to incivility and brutality

Ⓓ Misunderstanding of the meaning of the word "genteel"

Ⓔ Misunderstanding of the meaning of the words "incivility" and "brutality"

The questioner understands the speaker to be referring to a problem restricted to the slums and so does not understand that *genteel* refers to upper-class situations Ⓓ.

Prototype 8: Parallel—Here you are being asked not to identify how the author structures the line of reasoning or to identify an error in reasoning, but to "parallel" whatever line of reasoning is presented. That is to say, you must select the answer choice that uses either the same method of reasoning or the same type of error as the passage. Here again, whether or not the reasoning is faulty is not the important issue; paralleling the specific reasoning or error in the passage is your concern.

For example,

Since all dogs are animals, and cats are animals, then all cats are dogs.

Which of the following parallels the reasoning in the passage above?

A correct answer would be "All men are human beings, and children are human beings. Therefore all men are children." Notice how this choice is faulty in the same structural way as the original passage.

Other ways this prototype may be expressed are

- Which of the following contains a logical flaw similar to the logical flaw in the passage above?
- The argument above exhibits the same principles of inference as which of the following arguments?
- Which of the following is logically most similar to the argument above?
- Which of the following supports its conclusion in the same way as the passage above?

10. Because cigarette smokers usually have a bad cough and Butch has a bad cough, it follows that Butch is probably a cigarette smoker.

   Which of the following most closely parallels the reasoning used in the argument above?

   Ⓐ Because nonsmokers don't get emphysema and Bud doesn't have emphysema, it follows that Bud is probably not a smoker.
   Ⓑ Because weightlifters usually have large muscles and Bill is a weightlifter, it follows that Bill has large muscles.
   Ⓒ Because diamonds usually have little color and this gem has little color, it follows that this gem is probably a diamond.
   Ⓓ Because people with short hair usually get more haircuts and Al has short hair, it follows that Al recently got a haircut.
   Ⓔ Because coughing spreads germs and Sam is coughing, Sam is spreading germs.

The direct connection between cigarette smoking and coughing made in the passage is not an exclusive connection that would warrant the conclusion that because Butch has a bad cough, he's probably a cigarette smoker. Butch could have a cold. In the same way, just because diamonds have little color, we cannot conclude that a gem with little color probably is a diamond (it could be clear glass). There is a presumption of exclusivity in both instances. Choice Ⓒ is a stronger answer than Ⓐ because the form of the argument is precisely the same in Ⓒ and the original. Also, Ⓐ is an absolute (*don't*), and Ⓒ uses the word *usually* as does the original.

There may be several other Critical Reasoning question types. The inclusion here of only eight does not mean that these are the only question types appearing in the GMAT. However, your understanding and anticipation of these eight should help you more quickly identify what is being asked and therefore allow you to spend the bulk of your time reading and analyzing the passage and the answer choices.

A PATTERNED PLAN OF ATTACK
Critical Reasoning

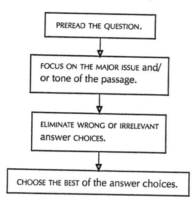

PREREAD THE QUESTION.

↓

FOCUS ON THE MAJOR ISSUE and/or tone of the passage.

↓

ELIMINATE WRONG or IRRELEVANT answer CHOICES.

↓

CHOOSE THE BEST of the answer choices.

PRACTICE CRITICAL REASONING QUESTIONS

EASY TO MODERATE

1. Famous painter James Whistler said, "Industry in art is a necessity—not a virtue—and any evidence of the same, in the production, is a blemish, not a quality."

   Whistler is arguing that

   Ⓐ of necessity, art becomes industrialized
   Ⓑ the qualities of art are its virtues
   Ⓒ blemished paintings are the work of overindustrious artists
   Ⓓ the product reflects the means of production
   Ⓔ the artist must work hard, but the art should look easy

2. Deliberations of our governing bodies are held in public in order to allow public scrutiny of each body's actions and take to task those actions that citizens feel are not, for whatever reason, in their best interests.

   With which of the following statements would the author of the above passage probably agree?

   Ⓐ Deliberations of our governing bodies should be held in public.
   Ⓑ Public scrutiny usually results in the criticism of our governing bodies.
   Ⓒ The best interests of the public usually do not coincide with the motives of our governing bodies.
   Ⓓ No government decisions ought to be kept from the public.
   Ⓔ Citizens in other countries are not cared for by the government.

Questions 3–4

Recent studies indicate that more violent crimes are committed during hot weather than during cold weather. Thus, if we could control the weather, the violent crime rate would drop.

3. The argument above makes which of the following assumptions?

   I. The relationship between weather conditions and crime rate is merely coincidental.
   II. The relationship between weather conditions and crime rate is causal.
   III. The relationship between weather conditions and crime rate is controllable.

   Ⓐ I only
   Ⓑ II only
   Ⓒ I and II only
   Ⓓ II and III only
   Ⓔ I, II, and III

4. The argument would be strengthened if it pointed out that

   Ⓐ the annual crime statistics for New York are higher than those for Los Angeles
   Ⓑ in laboratory tests, increased heat alone accounted for increased aggressive behavior between members of the test group
   Ⓒ poor socioeconomic conditions, more uncomfortable in hot weather than in cold, are the direct causes of increased crime
   Ⓓ weather control will be possible in the near future
   Ⓔ more people leave their doors and windows open during hot weather

5. By appropriating bailout money for the depressed housing industry, Congress is opening the door to a flood of special relief
   programs for other recession-affected businesses.

   The author's attitude toward Congress's action is probably

   Ⓐ neutral
   Ⓑ disapproving
   Ⓒ confused
   Ⓓ supportive
   Ⓔ irate

6. The value of a close examination of the circumstances of an aircraft accident lies not only in fixing blame but in learning les-
   sons.

   The above statement fits most logically into which of the following types of passages?

   Ⓐ A survey of the "scapegoat phenomenon" in modern society
   Ⓑ An argument in favor of including specific details in any
      academic essay
   Ⓒ An argument against the usefulness of the National Trans-
      portation Safety Board
   Ⓓ A brief history of aeronautics
   Ⓔ A description of the causes of a particular aircraft accident

Questions 7–8

The department store owned by my competitor sells green necklaces that glow in the dark. Only those customers of mine wearing
those necklaces must be giving business to the competition.

7. The conclusion could best be strengthened by

   Ⓐ deleting "that glow in the dark"
   Ⓑ changing "sells" to "has sold"
   Ⓒ changing "the competition" to "my competitor."
   Ⓓ inserting "only" as the first word in the first sentence
   Ⓔ changing "wearing" to "owning"

8. The author foolishly assumes that

   Ⓐ the customers might find the necklaces attractive
   Ⓑ customers are not buying other products from the competition
   Ⓒ customers will wear the necklaces in daylight
   Ⓓ a department store should not sell necklaces
   Ⓔ the competition is outselling the author

AVERAGE

9. Without sign ordinances, everyone with the price of a can of spray paint can suddenly decide to publicly create their own personal Picassos, and soon the entire town would start to look like something out of *Alice in Wonderland.* Therefore, we need sign ordinances.

   The author makes which of the following basic assumptions?

   I. Spray paint is used for many signs.
   II. The entire town looking like *Alice in Wonderland* is undesirable.
   III. Sign ordinances are effective.

   Ⓐ I only
   Ⓑ II only
   Ⓒ III only
   Ⓓ I and III only
   Ⓔ I, II, and III

Questions 10–11

In most economies, the government plays a role in the market system. Governments enforce the "rules of the game," impose taxes, and may control prices through price ceilings or price supports. These actions necessarily may create shortages or surpluses. In most developed and interdependent economies, the necessity of the government's playing some role in the economy seldom is disputed.

10. The final sentence in the passage suggests that

  Ⓐ interdependence goes hand in hand with development
  Ⓑ there are underdeveloped countries whose attitude toward government control may be hostile
  Ⓒ disputes over government control usually come from an illiterate populace
  Ⓓ price supports are necessary
  Ⓔ economic success is a sophisticated achievement

11. The author of the passage would probably agree that

  Ⓐ economic surpluses are always good
  Ⓑ market shortages are a necessary evil
  Ⓒ higher prices strengthen the economy
  Ⓓ price ceilings add to the shortages
  Ⓔ surpluses are not usually created intentionally

Questions 12–13

The new vehicle inspection program is needed to protect the quality of the state's air, for us and for our children. Auto exhausts are a leading contributor to coughing, wheezing, choking, and pollution. The state's long-term interests in the health of its citizens and in this area as a place to live, work, and conduct business depend on clean air.

12. Which of the following, if true, would most seriously weaken the argument above?

    Ⓐ Since smog devices were made mandatory automotive equipment by the existing inspection program three years ago, pollution has decreased dramatically and continues to decrease.
    Ⓑ Pollution problems are increasing in other states as well as in this one.
    Ⓒ Sometimes coughing, wheezing, and choking are caused by phenomena other than pollution.
    Ⓓ Vehicle inspectors are not always careful.
    Ⓔ The state should not impose its interests upon the citizenry but should instead allow public health to be regulated by private enterprise.

13. Which of the following is an unstated assumption made by the author?

    Ⓐ Working and conducting business may be different activities.
    Ⓑ The state has been interested in the health of its citizens even before this inspection program was proposed.
    Ⓒ Exhaust emissions contribute to pollution.
    Ⓓ The new inspection program will be effective.
    Ⓔ Our ancestors did not suffer from air pollution.

Questions 14–17

The older we get, the less sleep we should desire. This is because our advanced knowledge and capabilities are most enjoyable when used; therefore, "mindless" sleep becomes a waste of time.

14. Which of the following distinctions is NOT expressed or implied by the author?

   Ⓐ Between sleep and wakefulness
   Ⓑ Between youth and maturity
   Ⓒ Between productivity and waste
   Ⓓ Between a desire and a requirement
   Ⓔ Between more sleep and less sleep

15. The author of this statement assumes that

   Ⓐ less sleep is not desirable
   Ⓑ sleep advances knowledge and capabilities
   Ⓒ mindlessness coincides with wakefulness
   Ⓓ knowledge and capabilities naturally improve with age
   Ⓔ sleep is only for the young

16. This author's statement might be strengthened if he or she pointed out that

   Ⓐ advanced knowledge is often manifested in creative dreams
   Ⓑ the mind is quite active during sleep
   Ⓒ few empirical studies have concluded that sleep is an intellectual stimulant
   Ⓓ advanced capabilities are not necessarily mind-associated
   Ⓔ dreams teach us how to use waking experiences more intelligently

17. The author's statement might be weakened by pointing out that

   Ⓐ eight hours of sleep is a cultural, not a physical, requirement
   Ⓑ the most capable people rarely sleep
   Ⓒ rest is a positive contribution to knowledge and capability
   Ⓓ young children enjoy themselves less than knowledgeable adults
   Ⓔ people rarely waste time during their waking hours

Questions 18–19

It is evident that the methods of science have been highly success-ful. Psychologist B.F. Skinner believes that the methods of science should be applied to the field of human affairs. We are all con-trolled by the world, part of which is constructed by humans. Is this control to occur by accident, by tyrants, or by ourselves? A scientific society should reject accidental manipulation. He asserts that a specific plan is needed to promote fully the development of human beings and society. We cannot make wise decisions if we continue to pretend that we are not controlled.

As Skinner points out, the possibility of behavioral control is offensive to many people. We have traditionally regarded humans as free agents whose behavior occurs by virtue of spontaneous inner changes. We are reluctant to abandon the internal "will," which makes prediction and control of behavior impossible.

18. According to the passage, Skinner would probably agree with each of the following statements EXCEPT:

Ⓒ Rats and pigeons are appropriate animals for behavioristic study.

Ⓓ These behaviors we normally exhibit are not the only ones we are capable of.

Ⓔ The concept of behavioral control has popular appeal.

Ⓕ Inner causes of behavior are more difficult to observe than outer ones.

Ⓖ Positive reinforcement will affect learning in school.

19. The author implies that Skinner feels that the scientific proce-dure he advocates might be effective as

Ⓒ a means of enhancing our future

Ⓓ an explanation of the causes of dictatorships

Ⓔ a means for replacing teachers with computers

Ⓕ a way of identifying characteristics common to rats, pigeons, and humans

Ⓖ a way to understand the human mind

ABOVE AVERAGE TO DIFFICULT

Questions 20–21

Voters on June 8 approved a $495 million bond issue for a state prison construction that is an obvious priority. Now the legislature has voted to put five more general obligation bond issues on the November ballot, adding another $1.5 billion to the state's long-term debt. Those on the November menu include $500 million for building and remodeling public schools, $450 million to extend the veterans home loan program, $200 million to subsidize low-interest mortgages for first-time home buyers, $85 million to acquire land for environmental protection, and $280 million to help counties expand or remodel their jails.

20. Which of the following statements is a point to which the author is most probably leading?

Ⓐ Two of these bond issues are certainly more important than the others.

Ⓑ We must face the obvious conclusion that prison construction is much less important than the improvement of public education and social programs for lawful citizens.

Ⓒ The cost of these bond issues is, on the face of it, negligible.

Ⓓ The voters cannot be expected to help make financial decisions for the state because most voters are suffering from their own severe financial problems.

Ⓔ These five bond proposals are quite enough, and between now and November voters will have to study them carefully to make sure that five are not too many.

21. Which of the following facts would most strongly weaken an argument for approval of the five new bond issues?

Ⓐ Environmental protection is not an overriding concern of the constituency.

Ⓑ The state's long-term debt cannot lawfully exceed $1.5 billion.

Ⓒ Improvements in education, the environment, criminal prosecution, and the real estate market are favored by the voters.

Ⓓ Similar bond proposals in other states have not been successful.

Ⓔ Two bills related to the housing of criminals are quite enough.

22. The state's empty $4 million governor's mansion on the banks of the Capitol River may be sort of a suburban Taj Mahal, as the governor once said. But why shouldn't the state unload it?

Which of the following is one of the author's basic assumptions?

Ⓐ The governor's mansion is out of place in the suburbs.
Ⓑ The reader is aware of the state's intention to "unload" the governor's mansion.
Ⓒ No one has yet lived in the governor's mansion.
Ⓓ The state is trying to sell the governor's mansion.
Ⓔ The governor was correct.

ANSWERS AND EXPLANATIONS FOR THE PRACTICE CRITICAL REASONING QUESTIONS

EASY TO MODERATE

1. Ⓔ Whistler is saying that constant effort (industry) is necessary but that the artwork (production) should not evidence that effort.

2. Ⓐ By describing in very positive terms the effects of public deliberations, the author suggests the opinion that such deliberations *should* be public.

3. Ⓑ The only correct choice is II; it is argued that hot weather *causes* crime. This is not mere coincidence, and the statement does not say that we *can* control the weather.

4. Ⓑ The argument posits an exclusive relationship between hot weather and crime. Ⓐ, Ⓒ, and Ⓔ contradict such an exclusive relationship. Ⓓ is irrelevant to the relationship, but Ⓑ provides evidence supporting and strengthening the heat-crime relationship.

5. Ⓑ By describing the special relief programs as a *flood,* the author gives the programs a negative connotation and suggests disapproval.

6. Ⓔ This choice is related mosst fully to the subject matter of the original statement.

7. Ⓓ Making *only* the first word of the first sentence does not solve all of the logical problems in the passage, but it does strengthen the passage by indicating that customers with green necklaces must have bought them from the competition.

8. Ⓑ The author does not realize that customers not wearing green necklaces may have bought other items from the competition.

AVERAGE

9. Ⓔ All of the statements are assumptions of the author essential to the argument. The author assumes spray paint to be the medium that graffiti painters use and implicitly abhors the possibility of a town looking like *Alice in Wonderland.* In addition, his or her desire for sign ordinances assumes that they work and are effective in deterring spray painting.

10. Ⓑ The last sentence says that it is *developed* or *interdependent* economies that acquiesce to the idea that government must control the economy to some extent. This leaves underdeveloped countries unspoken for and raises the possibility they might *not* acquiesce to government control.

11. Ⓑ The paragraph states that government action *may create shortages* or *surpluses.*

12. Ⓐ The argument for further supervision of vehicle use is most weakened by the statement that present safeguards are already doing the job. Ⓒ and Ⓓ slightly weaken the argument but do not address the overall position of the author.

13. Ⓓ In order to argue for a new inspection program, the author must assume that that particular program, if enacted, will be effective. Ⓒ, the only other choice related to the points of the argument, expresses stated information rather than an unstated assumption.

14. Ⓓ The author does not address the distinction between how much sleep we desire and how much our bodies require. Each of the other distinctions is addressed in the passage.

15. Ⓓ In the passage, becoming older corresponds with <u>advanced knowledge and capabilities</u>. Choices Ⓐ, Ⓑ, and Ⓒ should be eliminated because each is contradicted by the assumptions of the passage (the passage suggests that *more* sleep is undesirable, knowledge and capabilities are connected with *wakefulness,* and mindlessness is connected with *sleep*). Choice Ⓔ is a generalization not at all concerned with amount of sleep and therefore not relevant to the passage.

16. Ⓒ Choices Ⓐ, Ⓑ, and Ⓔ present information that supports the value of sleep, and Ⓓ dissociates advanced capabilities from the mind, thus damaging the author's mind/mindlessness distinction.

17. Ⓒ Only choice Ⓒ asserts the positive value of sleep and thus weakens the author's stance in favor of decreased sleep.

18. Ⓒ In the second paragraph, we read of his recognition that behaviorism is offensive to many people—that it does *not* have popular appeal.

19. Ⓐ The passage discusses the possible application of Skinner's theory to the field of human affairs and in promoting the development of humankind.

ABOVE AVERAGE TO DIFFICULT

20. Ⓔ By listing high costs, the author is probably leading to the conclusion that the state's debt is being strained, a conclusion expressed in Ⓔ. Ⓒ contradicts the author's emphasis on high costs. Ⓐ, Ⓑ, and Ⓓ are neither expressed nor implied by the passage; their choice would rely on extraneous assumptions.

21. Ⓑ This fact indicates that the passage of all the bond measures, which would take the debt over $1.5 billion, is illegal.

22. Ⓑ The author's final question necessarily rests on the assumption that the reader is aware of the state's intention; the author omits information expressing or explaining this intention.

PART III

Full-Length GMAT CAT Practice Test

This section contains a practice simulation GMAT CAT. The practice test is followed by complete answers, explanations, and analysis techniques. The format, levels of difficulty, question structure, and number of questions are similar to those on the actual GMAT CAT. The actual GMAT CAT is copyrighted and may not be duplicated, and these questions are not taken directly from the actual tests.

This simulated GMAT CAT is designed to give you insight into the computer-adaptive test. When taking the simulated test, carefully adhere to the time allotments. Attempt only the questions that you are directed to attempt. Do not skip any questions, and do not go back to any questions. Once you have completed a question, go immediately to the next question. Do not write on the test, except to fill in the oval for an answer. Use scratch paper for any computations.

Remember, on this simulated test, you are directed to specific questions depending on your answer to the previous question. On the actual computer-adaptive GMAT, you will not be directed to questions, but specific questions will appear on the screen. The level of difficulty of these questions will depend on your answers to all previous questions.

Problems in this simulated test have been categorized by approximate levels of difficulty (as were the practice problems earlier in this book). These levels of difficulty are only general approximations based on the levels of GMAT test questions. The actual level of difficulty of a problem is relative to the test taker's background. For example, a certain geometry problem may seem very difficult to most test takers, but if one of your strengths is geometry, the same problem could be very simple for you. Therefore, depending on your strengths and weaknesses, question 5-3 might be easier for you than question 5-2. Use these general level of difficulty categories to assist you in analyzing your strengths and weaknesses.

Note: **On the actual GMAT CAT, the letters Ⓐ, Ⓑ, Ⓒ, Ⓓ, and Ⓔ do NOT appear with the answer choices, and the questions do not have numbers next to them.** To select an answer, you will select the appropriate oval on the computer. Even though the actual test does not label the answer choices with letters or the questions with numbers, letters and numbers are used in this book to assist you in following answers and explanations.

ANALYTICAL WRITING ASSESSMENT

TIME: 60 Minutes
2 Questions

General Directions: In this section, you will have a total time of 60 minutes to plan and write two essays, one for each topic given. The specific time allotted for each essay is 30 minutes.

Analysis of an Issue

TIME: 30 Minutes

Directions: This section will require you to analyze and explain your views on the issue given. Consider many points of view as you develop your own position on the issue. There is no right or wrong answer to the question.

Read the statement and directions carefully. Make any notes or do any prewriting on your scratch paper. Then type your response into the computer.

"Regardless of what business you're in, the better your computer skills, the better your chances of success."

Do you agree with this statement? Using reasons and/or examples from your work experience or from your observations, explain your position.

Analysis of an Argument

TIME: 30 Minutes

<u>Directions</u>: This section will require you to critique the argument given. Questioning underlying assumptions, finding alternative explanations or counterexamples, and delineating evidence to strengthen or weaken an argument are some possible approaches.

Read the argument and directions carefully. Make any notes or do any prewriting on your scratch paper. Then type your response into the computer.

The following advertisement appeared in newspapers throughout New York and New Jersey:

"Try Frostie Lo Calorie Ice Cream to lose weight fast! Seven of ten doctors surveyed recommend Frostie Lo Calorie Ice Cream. You can lose weight and still enjoy your favorite dessert in six delicious lo-calorie flavors."

Write a critique of the argument. You should consider what doubtful assumptions underlie the reasoning, what other explanations might apply and weaken the conclusions, and/or what other evidence would strengthen or weaken the argument. Do NOT write an essay on your views of the issue.

QUANTITATIVE SECTION

TIME: 75 Minutes
   37 Questions

General Directions: Your score on the quantitative section will be based on how well you do on the questions presented and also on the number of questions you answer. You should try to pace yourself so that you have sufficient time to consider every question. If possible, answer all 37 questions in this section. Guess if you need to. Select the best answer choice for each question.

   Note: Because you are checking answers as you go, you should add about 5 to 10 minutes to your testing time.

Directions: Problem Solving

Solve each problem in this section by using the information given and your own mathematical calculations. Then select the correct answer of the five choices given. Use the scratch paper given for any necessary calculations.

   Note: Some problems may be accompanied by figures or diagrams. These figures are drawn as accurately as possible except when it is stated in a specific problem that the figure is not drawn to scale. The figure is meant to provide information useful in solving the problem or problems.

   Unless otherwise stated or indicated, all figures lie in a plane.

   All numbers used are real numbers.

1-3. A sporting goods store sold 64 Frisbees in one week, some for $3 and the rest for $4 each. If receipts from Frisbee sales for the week totaled $204, what is the fewest number of $4 Frisbees that could have been sold?

Ⓐ 24
Ⓑ 12
Ⓒ 8
Ⓓ 4
Ⓔ 2

Answers: 1-3 Ⓑ

If you answered 1-3 **incorrectly, go to 2-2.**
If you answered 1-3 **correctly, go to 2-4.**

2-2. If $\frac{2}{x} = 4$ and if $\frac{2}{y} = 8$, then $x - y =$

Ⓐ $\frac{1}{8}$

Ⓑ $\frac{1}{4}$

Ⓒ $\frac{3}{4}$

Ⓓ 4

Ⓔ 24

2-4. A bus leaves Burbank at 9:00 A.M., traveling east at 50 miles per hour. At 1:00 P.M. a plane leaves Burbank traveling east at 300 miles per hour. At what time will the plane overtake the bus?

Ⓐ 12:45 P.M.

Ⓑ 1:10 P.M.

Ⓒ 1:40 P.M.

Ⓓ 1:48 P.M.

Ⓔ 1:55 P.M.

Answers: 2-2 Ⓑ, 2-4 Ⓓ

If you answered 2-2 **incorrectly**, go to 3-1.
If you answered 2-2 **correctly**, go to 3-3.

If you answered 2-4 **incorrectly**, go to 3-3.
If you answered 2-4 **correctly**, go to 3-5.

3-1. An astronaut weighing 207 pounds on Earth would weigh 182 pounds on Venus. The weight of the astronaut on Venus would be approximately what percent of the astronaut's weight on Earth?

   Ⓐ 50%
   Ⓑ 60%
   Ⓒ 70%
   Ⓓ 80%
   Ⓔ 90%

3-3. If the ratio of the side of cube A to the side of cube B is 2:1, then which of the following is the ratio of the surface areas?

   Ⓐ 1:2
   Ⓑ 2:1
   Ⓒ 3:1
   Ⓓ 4:1
   Ⓔ 8:1

3-5. Three business people wish to invest in a new company. Each person is willing to pay one third of the total investment. After careful calculations, they realize that each of them would pay $7,200 less if they could find two more equal investors. How much is the total investment in the new business?

   Ⓐ $64,000
   Ⓑ $54,000
   Ⓒ $21,000
   Ⓓ $5,400
   Ⓔ $3,600

Answers: 3-1 Ⓔ, 3-3 Ⓓ, 3-5 Ⓑ

If you answered 3-1 **incorrectly, go to 4-1.**
If you answered 3-1 **correctly, go to 4-2.**

If you answered 3-3 **incorrectly, go to 4-2.**
If you answered 3-3 **correctly, go to 4-4.**

If you answered 3-5 **incorrectly, go to 4-4.**
If you answered 3-5 **correctly, go to 4-5.**

4-1. The closest approximation of (69.28 × 0.004)/0.03 is

    Ⓐ   0.092
    Ⓑ   0.92
    Ⓒ   9.2
    Ⓓ   92
    Ⓔ 920

4-2. What is the largest integer if the sum of three consecutive even integers is 318?

    Ⓐ 100
    Ⓑ 104
    Ⓒ 106
    Ⓓ 108
    Ⓔ 111

4-4. A woman invested $1,000, part at 5% and the rest at 6%. Her total investment with interest at the end of the year was $1,053. How much did she invest at 5%?

   (A) $500
   (B) $600
   (C) $700
   (D) $900
   (E) $950

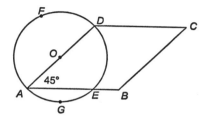

4-5. In the rhombus, $BC = 6$, $AE \cong 4$, and angle $DAE = 45°$. AD is the diameter of the circle. If a man started at C and followed around the outer edge of this figure to D, F, A, G, E, B, and back to C, approximately how far did he travel?

   (A) $14 + \frac{27}{4}\pi$

   (B) $14 + 6\pi$

   (C) $12 + 6\pi$

   (D) $14 + \frac{9}{2}\pi$

   (E) $12 + \frac{9}{2}\pi$

Answers: 4-1 Ⓒ, 4-2 Ⓓ, 4-4 Ⓒ, 4-5 Ⓓ

If you answered 4-1 **incorrectly, go to 5-1.**
If you answered 4-1 **correctly, go to 5-2.**

If you answered 4-2 **incorrectly, go to 5-1.**
If you answered 4-2 **correctly, go to 5-3.**

If you answered 4-4 **incorrectly, go to 5-3.**
If you answered 4-4 **correctly, go to 5-5.**

If you answered 4-5 **incorrectly, go to 5-4.**
If you answered 4-5 **correctly, go to 5-5.**

5-1. Three consecutive traffic signals each show either red or green. How many different arrangements of the three signals are possible? (Note: "Red-red-green" is different from "green-red-red.")

   Ⓐ   10
   Ⓑ   9
   Ⓒ   8
   Ⓓ   7
   Ⓔ   6

5-2. There are 36 students in a certain geometry class. If two thirds of the students are boys and three fourths of the boys are under six feet tall, how many boys in the class are under six feet tall?

   Ⓐ   6
   Ⓑ   12
   Ⓒ   18
   Ⓓ   24
   Ⓔ   27

5-3. How many different three-person committees can be formed from six people?

Ⓐ 2
Ⓑ 18
Ⓒ 20
Ⓓ 36
Ⓔ 108

5-4. A woman has three blouses of different colors, three skirts of different colors, and two different pairs of shoes. She refuses to wear her pink blouse with her green skirt. How many different blouse-skirt-shoe combinations could she wear?

Ⓐ 8
Ⓑ 12
Ⓒ 16
Ⓓ 17
Ⓔ 18

5-5. A drawer contains red socks, black socks, and white socks. What is the least number of socks that must randomly be taken out of the drawer to be sure of having four pairs of socks? (A pair is two socks of the same color.)

Ⓐ 8
Ⓑ 10
Ⓒ 12
Ⓓ 14
Ⓔ 16

Answers: 5-1 ©, 5-2 ©, 5-3 ©, 5-4 ©, 5-5 Ⓑ

If you answered 5-1 **incorrectly, go to 6-1.**
If you answered 5-1 **correctly, go to 6-2.**

If you answered 5-2 **incorrectly, go to 6-1.**
If you answered 5-2 **correctly, go to 6-3.**

If you answered 5-3 **incorrectly, go to 6-2.**
If you answered 5-3 **correctly, go to 6-4.**

If you answered 5-4 **incorrectly, go to 6-3.**
If you answered 5-4 **correctly, go to 6-5.**

If you answered 5-5 **incorrectly, go to 6-4.**
If you answered 5-5 **correctly, go to 6-5.**

<u>Directions</u>: Data Sufficency

Each of the problems below consists of a question and two statements, labeled (1) and (2), in which certain data are given. You must decide whether the data given in the statements are *sufficient* to answer the question. Using the data given in the statements plus your knowledge of mathematics and everyday facts (such as the number of days in July or the meaning of *counterclockwise*), you are to choose oval

Ⓐ if statement (1) ALONE is sufficient, but statement (2) alone is not sufficient to answer the question asked;

Ⓑ if statement (2) ALONE is sufficient, but statement (1) alone is not sufficient to answer the question asked;

Ⓒ if both statements (1) and (2) TOGETHER are sufficient to answer the question asked, but NEITHER statement ALONE is sufficient;

Ⓓ if EACH statement ALONE is sufficient to answer the question asked;

Ⓔ if statements (1) and (2) TOGETHER are NOT sufficient to answer the question asked, and additional data specific to the problem are needed.

6-1. How much precipitation does Springfield need this month to attain its long-term average of 35 inches per year?

   (1) Over the last 11 months, the city has averaged 3 inches of precipitation per month.

   (2) Springfield has accumulated 94.3% of its mean annual precipitation during the last 11 months.

   (A) Statement (1) ALONE is sufficient, but statement (2) alone is not sufficient.

   (B) Statement (2) ALONE is sufficient, but statement (1) alone is not sufficient.

   (C) BOTH statements (1) and (2) TOGETHER are sufficient, but NEITHER statement ALONE is sufficient.

   (D) EACH statement ALONE is sufficient.

   (E) Statements (1) and (2) TOGETHER are NOT sufficient.

6-2. Is a tick longer in duration than a tock?

   (1) There are 48 tocks each day.

   (2) A tick is longer than a minute.

   (A) Statement (1) ALONE is sufficient, but statement (2) alone is not sufficient.

   (B) Statement (2) ALONE is sufficient, but statement (1) alone is not sufficient.

   (C) BOTH statements (1) and (2) TOGETHER are sufficient, but NEITHER statement ALONE is sufficient.

   (D) EACH statement ALONE is sufficient.

   (E) Statements (1) and (2) TOGETHER are NOT sufficient.

6-3. Three spies—Ex, Why, and Zee—together know 19 different secrets. There is no overlap of information. How many secrets does Why know?

(1) Ex knows one more than Why and twice as many as Zee.

(2) Why knows three more secrets than Zee.

Ⓐ Statement (1) ALONE is sufficient, but statement (2) alone is not sufficient.

Ⓑ Statement (2) ALONE is sufficient, but statement (1) alone is not sufficient.

Ⓒ BOTH statements (1) and (2) TOGETHER are sufficient, but NEITHER statement ALONE is sufficient.

Ⓓ EACH statement ALONE is sufficient.

Ⓔ Statements (1) and (2) TOGETHER are NOT sufficient.

6-4. A school play requires 24 actors to be cast among boys, girls, and adults. If no actors may take two roles, how many adult actors are needed?

(1) The ratio of boys needed to girls is 2 to 1.

(2) The ratio of children needed to adults is 3 to 1.

Ⓐ Statement (1) ALONE is sufficient, but statement (2) alone is not sufficient.

Ⓑ Statement (2) ALONE is sufficient, but statement (1) alone is not sufficient.

Ⓒ BOTH statements (1) and (2) TOGETHER are sufficient, but NEITHER statement ALONE is sufficient.

Ⓓ EACH statement ALONE is sufficient.

Ⓔ Statements (1) and (2) TOGETHER are NOT sufficient.

6-5. During 1996, 17,500 patients were admitted to Warehall Hospital, and exactly one sixth of these patients were discharged within one day. Of those patients discharged within one hour, one forth were seen by only one doctor. How many patients during 1996 were seen by only one doctor?

(1) Of the total number of patients admitted to Warehall Hospital in 1996, one ninth were discharged within one hour.

(2) Exactly 11,050 patients were discharged after three days.

Ⓐ Statement (1) ALONE is sufficient, but statement (2) alone is not sufficient.

Ⓑ Statement (2) ALONE is sufficient, but statement (1) alone is not sufficient.

Ⓒ BOTH statements (1) and (2) TOGETHER are sufficient, but NEITHER statement ALONE is sufficient.

Ⓓ EACH statement ALONE is sufficient.

Ⓔ Statements (1) and (2) TOGETHER are NOT sufficient.

Answers: 6-1 Ⓓ, 6-2 Ⓔ, 6-3 Ⓐ, 6-4 Ⓑ, 6-5 Ⓔ

If you answered 6-1 **incorrectly, go to 7-1.**
If you answered 6-1 **correctly, go to 7-2.**

If you answered 6-2 **incorrectly, go to 7-1.**
If you answered 6-2 **correctly, go to 7-3.**

If you answered 6-3 **incorrectly, go to 7-2.**
If you answered 6-3 **correctly, go to 7-4.**

If you answered 6-4 **incorrectly, go to 7-3.**
If you answered 6-4 **correctly, go to 7-5.**

If you answered 6-5 **incorrectly, go to 7-4.**
If you answered 6-5 **correctly, go to 7-5.**

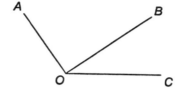

7-1. How many degrees is angle *AOB*?

   (1) Angle $BOC = 35°$.

   (2) $\overline{AO}$ is perpendicular to $\overline{OB}$.

   Ⓐ Statement (1) ALONE is sufficient, but statement (2) alone is not sufficient.

   Ⓑ Statement (2) ALONE is sufficient, but statement (1) alone is not sufficient.

   Ⓒ BOTH statements (1) and (2) TOGETHER are sufficient, but NEITHER statement ALONE is sufficient.

   Ⓓ EACH statement ALONE is sufficient.

   Ⓔ Statements (1) and (2) TOGETHER are NOT sufficient.

7-2. How many degrees is angle *c*?

   (1) *b* is a right angle.

   (2) $a + b = 131°$

   Ⓐ Statement (1) ALONE is sufficient, but statement (2) alone is not sufficient.
   Ⓑ Statement (2) ALONE is sufficient, but statement (1) alone is not sufficient.
   Ⓒ BOTH statements (1) and (2) TOGETHER are sufficient, but NEITHER statement ALONE is sufficient.
   Ⓓ EACH statement ALONE is sufficient.
   Ⓔ Statements (1) and (2) TOGETHER are NOT sufficient.

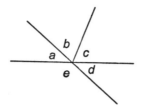

7-3. How many degrees is angle *e*?

   (1) $a + d = 82°$

   (2) $b + d = 111°$

   Ⓐ Statement (1) ALONE is sufficient, but statement (2) alone is not sufficient.

   Ⓑ Statement (2) ALONE is sufficient, but statement (1) alone is not sufficient.

   Ⓒ BOTH statements (1) and (2) TOGETHER are sufficient, but NEITHER statement ALONE is sufficient.

   Ⓓ EACH statement ALONE is sufficient.

   Ⓔ Statements (1) and (2) TOGETHER are NOT sufficient.

7-4. What is the ratio of the area of quadrilateral *BCDE* to the area of triangle *ABE*?

(1) $BC = \frac{1}{2}AC$

(2) Angle *CBE* = 135°.

Ⓐ Statement (1) ALONE is sufficient, but statement (2) alone is not sufficient.

Ⓑ Statement (2) ALONE is sufficient, but statement (1) alone is not sufficient.

Ⓒ BOTH statements (1) and (2) TOGETHER are sufficient, but NEITHER statement ALONE is sufficient.

Ⓓ EACH statement ALONE is sufficient.

Ⓔ Statements (1) and (2) TOGETHER are NOT sufficient.

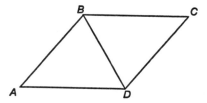

7-5. In rhombus *ABCD,* what is angle *BCD?*

(1) *BC = BD*

(2) Angle *BDA* = 60°.

Ⓐ Statement (1) ALONE is sufficient, but statement (2) alone is not sufficient.

Ⓑ Statement (2) ALONE is sufficient, but statement (1) alone is not sufficient.

Ⓒ BOTH statements (1) and (2) TOGETHER are sufficient, but NEITHER statement ALONE is sufficient.

Ⓓ EACH statement ALONE is sufficient.

Ⓔ Statements (1) and (2) TOGETHER are NOT sufficient.

Answers: 7-1 Ⓑ, 7-2 Ⓑ, 7-3 Ⓐ, 7-4 Ⓐ, 7-5 Ⓓ

If you answered 7-1 **incorrectly, go to 8-1.**
If you answered 7-1 **correctly, go to 8-2.**

If you answered 7-2 **incorrectly, go to 8-1.**
If you answered 7-2 **correctly, go to 8-3.**

If you answered 7-3 **incorrectly, go to 8-2.**
If you answered 7-3 **correctly, go to 8-4.**

If you answered 7-4 **incorrectly, go to 8-3.**
If you answered 7-4 **correctly, go to 8-5.**

If you answered 7-5 **incorrectly, go to 8-4.**
If you answered 7-5 **correctly, go to 8-5.**

8-1. What are the individual prices of three cameras?

(1) The three cameras have an average price of $172.

(2) Two are the same price and sell for $332 together.

Ⓐ Statement (1) ALONE is sufficient, but statement (2) alone is not sufficient.

Ⓑ Statement (2) ALONE is sufficient, but statement (1) alone is not sufficient.

Ⓒ BOTH statements (1) and (2) TOGETHER are sufficient, but NEITHER statement ALONE is sufficient.

Ⓓ EACH statement ALONE is sufficient.

Ⓔ Statements (1) and (2) TOGETHER are NOT sufficient.

8-2. What is the average of ten numbers?

(1) Nine of the numbers sum to 45.

(2) One of the numbers is 15.

Ⓐ Statement (1) ALONE is sufficient, but statement (2) alone is not sufficient.

Ⓑ Statement (2) ALONE is sufficient, but statement (1) alone is not sufficient.

Ⓒ BOTH statements (1) and (2) TOGETHER are sufficient, but NEITHER statement ALONE is sufficient.

Ⓓ EACH statement ALONE is sufficient.

Ⓔ Statements (1) and (2) TOGETHER are NOT sufficient.

8-3. What is the sum of five numbers?

    (1) The average of the numbers is zero.

    (2) Only one of the numbers is positive.

    Ⓐ Statement (1) ALONE is sufficient, but statement (2) alone is not sufficient.

    Ⓑ Statement (2) ALONE is sufficient, but statement (1) alone is not sufficient.

    Ⓒ BOTH statements (1) and (2) TOGETHER are sufficient, but NEITHER statement ALONE is sufficient.

    Ⓓ EACH statement ALONE is sufficient.

    Ⓔ Statements (1) and (2) TOGETHER are NOT sufficient.

8-4. Is the product $xy > 27$?

    (1) $2 < x < 5$

    (2) $6 > y$

    Ⓐ Statement (1) ALONE is sufficient, but statement (2) alone is not sufficient.

    Ⓑ Statement (2) ALONE is sufficient, but statement (1) alone is not sufficient.

    Ⓒ BOTH statements (1) and (2) TOGETHER are sufficient, but NEITHER statement ALONE is sufficient.

    Ⓓ EACH statement ALONE is sufficient.

    Ⓔ Statements (1) and (2) TOGETHER are NOT sufficient.

8-5. Is $x < 2$?

  (1) $x > x^2$

  (2) $\frac{1}{x} > 3$

  Ⓐ Statement (1) ALONE is sufficient, but statement (2) alone is not sufficient.

  Ⓑ Statement (2) ALONE is sufficient, but statement (1) alone is not sufficient.

  Ⓒ BOTH statements (1) and (2) TOGETHER are sufficient, but NEITHER statement ALONE is sufficient.

  Ⓓ EACH statement ALONE is sufficient.

  Ⓔ Statements (1) and (2) TOGETHER are NOT sufficient.

Answers: 8-1 Ⓒ, 8-2 Ⓔ, 8-3 Ⓐ, 8-4 Ⓔ, 8-5 Ⓓ

If you answered 8-1 **incorrectly, go to 9-1.**
If you answered 8-1 **correctly, go to 9-2.**

If you answered 8-2 **incorrectly, go to 9-1.**
If you answered 8-2 **correctly, go to 9-3.**

If you answered 8-3 **incorrectly, go to 9-2.**
If you answered 8-3 **correctly, go to 9-4.**

If you answered 8-4 **incorrectly, go to 9-3.**
If you answered 8-4 **correctly, go to 9-5.**

If you answered 8-5 **incorrectly, go to 9-4.**
If you answered 8-5 **correctly, go to 9-5.**

9-1. What is Toni's typing speed in words per minute?

    (1) She completed a report of 3,150 words in one hour.

    (2) The report had 7 pages, each averaging 450 words.

    Ⓐ Statement (1) ALONE is sufficient, but statement (2) alone is not sufficient.

    Ⓑ Statement (2) ALONE is sufficient, but statement (1) alone is not sufficient.

    Ⓒ BOTH statements (1) and (2) TOGETHER are sufficient, but NEITHER statement ALONE is sufficient.

    Ⓓ EACH statement ALONE is sufficient.

    Ⓔ Statements (1) and (2) TOGETHER are NOT sufficient.

9-2. How long would it take Joan to count the books in a small library?

    (1) She counts twice as fast as Emily.

    (2) Working together, Joan and Emily count the books in 26 hours.

    Ⓐ Statement (1) ALONE is sufficient, but statement (2) alone is not sufficient.

    Ⓑ Statement (2) ALONE is sufficient, but statement (1) alone is not sufficient.

    Ⓒ BOTH statements (1) and (2) TOGETHER are sufficient, but NEITHER statement ALONE is sufficient.

    Ⓓ EACH statement ALONE is sufficient.

    Ⓔ Statements (1) and (2) TOGETHER are NOT sufficient.

9-3. How long would it take Sue to paint the room?

(1) Working with Bob, the project would last 2 hours.

(2) Bob could accomplish the painting alone in $3\frac{1}{4}$ hours.

Ⓐ Statement (1) ALONE is sufficient, but statement (2) alone is not sufficient.

Ⓑ Statement (2) ALONE is sufficient, but statement (1) alone is not sufficient.

Ⓒ BOTH statements (1) and (2) TOGETHER are sufficient, but NEITHER statement ALONE is sufficient.

Ⓓ EACH statement ALONE is sufficient.

Ⓔ Statements (1) and (2) TOGETHER are NOT sufficient.

9-4. Beverage cans are manufactured of steel or aluminum. From the following graphs, what was the approximate percentage change in number of beverage cans manufactured from 1990 to 1995?

Ⓐ Statement (1) ALONE is sufficient, but statement (2) alone is not sufficient.

Ⓑ Statement (2) ALONE is sufficient, but statement (1) alone is not sufficient.

Ⓒ BOTH statements (1) and (2) TOGETHER are sufficient, but NEITHER statement ALONE is sufficient.

Ⓓ EACH statement ALONE is sufficient.

Ⓔ Statements (1) and (2) TOGETHER are NOT sufficient.

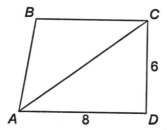

9-5. In the trapezoid *ABCD,* what is the area of triangle *ABC?*

(1) $AC = 10$

(2) $BC = 7$

Ⓐ Statement (1) ALONE is sufficient, but statement (2) alone is not sufficient.

Ⓑ Statement (2) ALONE is sufficient, but statement (1) alone is not sufficient.

Ⓒ BOTH statements (1) and (2) TOGETHER are sufficient, but NEITHER statement ALONE is sufficient.

Ⓓ EACH statement ALONE is sufficient.

Ⓔ Statements (1) and (2) TOGETHER are NOT sufficient.

Answers: 9-1 Ⓐ, 9-2 Ⓒ, 9-3 Ⓒ, 9-4 Ⓒ, 9-5 Ⓒ

If you answered 9-1 **incorrectly, go to 10-1.**
If you answered 9-1 **correctly, go to 10-2.**

If you answered 9-2 **incorrectly, go to 10-1.**
If you answered 9-2 **correctly, go to 10-3.**

If you answered 9-3 **incorrectly, go to 10-2.**
If you answered 9-3 **correctly, go to 10-4.**

If you answered 9-4 **incorrectly, go to 10-3.**
If you answered 9-4 **correctly, go to 10-5.**

If you answered 9-5 **incorrectly, go to 10-4.**
If you answered 9-5 **correctly, go to 10-5.**

10-1. A small college reduced its faculty by approximately 13 percent to 195 professors. What was the original number of faculty members?

 Ⓐ 182
 Ⓑ 208
 Ⓒ 224
 Ⓓ 254
 Ⓔ 302

10-2. If 15 students in a class average 80% on an English exam and 10 students average 90% on the same exam, what is the average in percent for all 25 students?

 Ⓐ 83%

 Ⓑ $83\frac{1}{2}$%

 Ⓒ 84%

 Ⓓ 85%

 Ⓔ $86\frac{2}{3}$%

10-3. The average of 9 numbers is 7 and the average of 7 other numbers is 9. What is the average of all 16 numbers?

Ⓐ 9

Ⓑ 8

Ⓒ $7\frac{7}{8}$

Ⓓ $7\frac{1}{2}$

Ⓔ $7\frac{1}{4}$

10-4. If 20% of a class averages 80% on a test, 50% of the class averages 60% on the test, and the remainder of the class averages 40% on the test, what is the overall class average?

Ⓐ 80%
Ⓑ 74%
Ⓒ 58%
Ⓓ 56%
Ⓔ 50%

10-5. Thirty percent of the women in a college class are science majors, and the non-science majors make up 80% of the class. What percentage of the men are science majors if 40% of the class are men?

Ⓐ 2%
Ⓑ 5%
Ⓒ 28%
Ⓓ 30%
Ⓔ 45%

Answers: 10-1 ©, 10-2 ©, 10-3 ©, 10-4 ©, 10-5 ⑧

If you answered 10-1 **incorrectly, go to 11-1.**
If you answered 10-1 **correctly, go to 11-2.**

If you answered 10-2 **incorrectly, go to 11-1.**
If you answered 10-2 **correctly, go to 11-3.**

If you answered 10-3 **incorrectly, go to 11-2.**
If you answered 10-3 **correctly, go to 11-4.**

If you answered 10-4 **incorrectly, go to 11-3.**
If you answered 10-4 **correctly, go to 11-5.**

If you answered 10-5 **incorrectly, go to 11-4.**
If you answered 10-5 **correctly, go to 11-5.**

11-1. If it takes a machine $\frac{2}{3}$ minute to produce one item, how many items will it produce in 2 hours?

    Ⓐ $\frac{1}{3}$

    Ⓑ $\frac{4}{3}$

    Ⓒ 80

    Ⓓ 120

    Ⓔ 180

11-2. The large square above consists of squares and isosceles right triangles. If the large square has side 4 cm, then the area of the shaded portion in square cm is

    Ⓐ 2
    Ⓑ 4
    Ⓒ 6
    Ⓓ 8
    Ⓔ 12

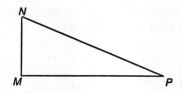

11-3. On △*MNP*, *MN* ⊥ *MP*, *MP* = 24, and *NP* = 26. What is the area of △*MNP* in square units?

Ⓐ 312
Ⓑ 240
Ⓒ 120
Ⓓ   60
Ⓔ   30

11-4. Manny rides a bicycle 6 miles east, 5 miles north, 18 miles west, and 14 miles south, at a rate of 10 miles per hour. If Irv leaves at the same time and from the same place and walks directly to Manny's final destination at a rate of 5 miles per hour, he will arrive

Ⓐ at the same time as Manny
Ⓑ more than one hour before Manny
Ⓒ more than one hour after Manny
Ⓓ less than one hour before Manny
Ⓔ less than one hour after Manny

11-5. In the cube above, *AH* and *BG* are diagonals and the surface area of side *ABFE* is 16. What is the area of rectangle *ABGH*?

(A) $4\sqrt{2}$

(B) $16\sqrt{2}$

(C) $16 + \sqrt{2}$

(D) 16

(E) $15\sqrt{3}$

Answers: 11-1 Ⓔ, 11-2 Ⓓ, 11-3 Ⓒ, 11-4 Ⓑ, 11-5 Ⓑ

If you answered 11-1 **incorrectly, go to 12-1.**
If you answered 11-1 **correctly, go to 12-2.**

If you answered 11-2 **incorrectly, go to 12-1.**
If you answered 11-2 **correctly, go to 12-3.**

If you answered 11-3 **incorrectly, go to 12-2.**
If you answered 11-3 **correctly, go to 12-4.**

If you answered 11-4 **incorrectly, go to 12-3.**
If you answered 11-4 **correctly, go to 12-5.**

If you answered 11-5 **incorrectly, go to 12-4.**
If you answered 11-5 **correctly, go to 12-5.**

12-1. What number times $(\frac{1}{3})^2$ will give the value of 3^3?

   Ⓐ   3
   Ⓑ   9
   Ⓒ   27
   Ⓓ 108
   Ⓔ 243

12-2. If $x = \dfrac{1+y}{y}$, then $y =$

   Ⓐ $\dfrac{1}{x-1}$

   Ⓑ $\dfrac{1}{x+1}$

   Ⓒ $\dfrac{1+x}{x}$

   Ⓓ $\dfrac{1-x}{x}$

   Ⓔ x

12-3. Which of the five choices is equivalent to the expression
$$\frac{x-4}{2x^2-10x+8}?$$

   Ⓐ $\dfrac{1}{2x^2-9x}$

   Ⓑ $\dfrac{1}{2x^2-9x+4}$

   Ⓒ $\dfrac{1}{2x+4}$

   Ⓓ $\dfrac{1}{2x}$

   Ⓔ $\dfrac{1}{2x-2}$

12-4. If $\dfrac{x^2+5x+6}{x^2-4}=\dfrac{3}{2}$, then the value of x is

   Ⓐ -12

   Ⓑ $-2\frac{2}{5}$

   Ⓒ -2

   Ⓓ 2

   Ⓔ 12

12-5. If one root of the equation $x^2 - 5x + m = 0$ is 10, what is the value of $m + 3$?

   Ⓐ 50

   Ⓑ 10

   Ⓒ -5

   Ⓓ -47

   Ⓔ -50

Answers: 12-1 Ⓔ, 12-2 Ⓐ, 12-3 Ⓔ, 12-4 Ⓔ, 12-5 Ⓓ

If you answered 12-1 **incorrectly, go to 13-1.**
If you answered 12-1 **correctly, go to 13-2.**

If you answered 12-2 **incorrectly, go to 13-1.**
If you answered 12-2 **correctly, go to 13-3.**

If you answered 12-3 **incorrectly, go to 13-2.**
If you answered 12-3 **correctly, go to 13-4.**

If you answered 12-4 **incorrectly, go to 13-3.**
If you answered 12-4 **correctly, go to 13-5.**

If you answered 12-5 **incorrectly, go to 13-4.**
If you answered 12-5 **correctly, go to 13-5.**

13-1. The purchase price of an article is $48. In order to include 15% of cost for overhead and to provide $12 of net profit, the markup should be

  Ⓐ 15%
  Ⓑ 25%
  Ⓒ 35%
  Ⓓ 40%
  Ⓔ 45%

13-2. How many 2-inch by 3-inch rectangular tiles are required to tile this shaded region?

  Ⓐ Less than 10
  Ⓑ 10–100
  Ⓒ 101–1,000
  Ⓓ 1,001–1,500
  Ⓔ 1,500+

	60	
70		y
80		x
80		

13-3. The horizontal length of each rectangle is marked within. What is the total horizontal length of $x + y$?

Ⓐ 40
Ⓑ 50
Ⓒ 80
Ⓓ 90
Ⓔ It cannot be determined from the information given.

13-4. If the diameter of circle R is 30% of the diameter of circle S, the area of circle R is what percent of the area of circle S?

Ⓐ 9%
Ⓑ 15%
Ⓒ 30%
Ⓓ 60%
Ⓔ 90%

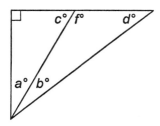

13-5. In the right triangle, $c = 2a$ and $d > 2b$; therefore, which of the following must be true?

Ⓐ $c > b + d$
Ⓑ Angle a is greater than angle b.
Ⓒ Angle a equals angle b.
Ⓓ Angle b is greater than angle a.
Ⓔ Angle d equals twice angle a.

Answers: 13-1 Ⓓ, 13-2 Ⓔ, 13-3 Ⓔ, 13-4 Ⓐ, 13-5 Ⓑ

If you answered 13-1 **incorrectly, go to 14-1.**
If you answered 13-1 **correctly, go to 14-2.**

If you answered 13-2 **incorrectly, go to 14-1.**
If you answered 13-2 **correctly, go to 14-3.**

If you answered 13-3 **incorrectly, go to 14-2.**
If you answered 13-3 **correctly, go to 14-4.**

If you answered 13-4 **incorrectly, go to 14-3.**
If you answered 13-4 **correctly, go to 14-5.**

If you answered 13-5 **incorrectly, go to 14-4.**
If you answered 13-5 **correctly, go to 14-5.**

14-1. How much gross profit did White Store make during its Great Refrigerator Sale?

(1) The store sold 112 refrigerators for $33,060.

(2) The refrigerators cost White an average of $186.

Ⓐ Statement (1) ALONE is sufficient, but statement (2) alone is not sufficient.

Ⓑ Statement (2) ALONE is sufficient, but statement (1) alone is not sufficient.

Ⓒ BOTH statements (1) and (2) TOGETHER are sufficient, but NEITHER statement ALONE is sufficient.

Ⓓ EACH statement ALONE is sufficient.

Ⓔ Statements (1) and (2) TOGETHER are NOT sufficient.

14-2. How much principal and interest are still owed on a home originally sold for $179,000?

(1) The interest rate when the home was purchased was 9%.

(2) The owner has yet to make 84 payments of $1,124 each.

Ⓐ Statement (1) ALONE is sufficient, but statement (2) alone is not sufficient.

Ⓑ Statement (2) ALONE is sufficient, but statement (1) alone is not sufficient.

Ⓒ BOTH statements (1) and (2) TOGETHER are sufficient, but NEITHER statement ALONE is sufficient.

Ⓓ EACH statement ALONE is sufficient.

Ⓔ Statements (1) and (2) TOGETHER are NOT sufficient.

14-3. A savings account earned 1% interest compounded each month, credited on the last day of the month. On December 8 there was $1,115.67 in the account. During which month did the account first exceed $1,100?

(1) $1,000 was deposited on the previous December 31.

(2) There were no deposits or withdrawals this year.

Ⓐ Statement (1) ALONE is sufficient, but statement (2) alone is not sufficient.

Ⓑ Statement (2) ALONE is sufficient, but statement (1) alone is not sufficient.

Ⓒ BOTH statements (1) and (2) TOGETHER are sufficient, but NEITHER statement ALONE is sufficient.

Ⓓ EACH statement ALONE is sufficient.

Ⓔ Statements (1) and (2) TOGETHER are NOT sufficient.

14-4. So far this year, Mr. and Mrs. Dufaa have paid what percent of their annual home expenses?

(1) So far the Dufaas have paid $\frac{1}{2}$ of their annual electricity bill, $\frac{1}{2}$ of their annual gas bill, $\frac{1}{4}$ of their annual water bill, and $\frac{3}{4}$ of their annual trash bill.

(2) The Dufaas' annual home expenses include four items: electricity, gas, water, and trash removal.

Ⓐ Statement (1) ALONE is sufficient, but statement (2) alone is not sufficient.

Ⓑ Statement (2) ALONE is sufficient, but statement (1) alone is not sufficient.

Ⓒ BOTH statements (1) and (2) TOGETHER are sufficient, but NEITHER statement ALONE is sufficient.

Ⓓ EACH statement ALONE is sufficient.

Ⓔ Statements (1) and (2) TOGETHER are NOT sufficient.

14-5. How many people are employed at a certain manufacturing plant with an annual payroll of $2,342,000?

(1) Three-fourths of the employees are clerical, at an average salary of $16,020.

(2) With 8% more employees, the payroll would equal $2,548,000.

(A) Statement (1) ALONE is sufficient, but statement (2) alone is not sufficient.

(B) Statement (2) ALONE is sufficient, but statement (1) alone is not sufficient.

(C) BOTH statements (1) and (2) TOGETHER are sufficient, but NEITHER statement ALONE is sufficient.

(D) EACH statement ALONE is sufficient.

(E) Statements (1) and (2) TOGETHER are NOT sufficient.

Answers: 14-1 Ⓒ, 14-2 Ⓑ, 14-3 Ⓑ, 14-4 Ⓔ, 14-5 Ⓔ

If you answered 14-1 **incorrectly, go to 15-1.**
If you answered 14-1 **correctly, go to 15-2.**

If you answered 14-2 **incorrectly, go to 15-1.**
If you answered 14-2 **correctly, go to 15-3.**

If you answered 14-3 **incorrectly, go to 15-2.**
If you answered 14-3 **correctly, go to 15-4.**

If you answered 14-4 **incorrectly, go to 15-3.**
If you answered 14-4 **correctly, go to 15-5.**

If you answered 14-5 **incorrectly, go to 15-4.**
If you answered 14-5 **correctly, go to 15-5.**

15-1. Is the number *N* an integer?

(1) The factors of *N* are 3, 5, and 7.

(2) *N* cannot be divided evenly by 2.

Ⓐ Statement (1) ALONE is sufficient, but statement (2) alone is not sufficient.

Ⓑ Statement (2) ALONE is sufficient, but statement (1) alone is not sufficient.

Ⓒ BOTH statements (1) and (2) TOGETHER are sufficient, but NEITHER statement ALONE is sufficient.

Ⓓ EACH statement ALONE is sufficient.

Ⓔ Statements (1) and (2) TOGETHER are NOT sufficient.

15-2. Which is greater, *cf* or *fg*?

(1) $c > g$

(2) $f^2 = cg$

Ⓐ Statement (1) ALONE is sufficient, but statement (2) alone is not sufficient.

Ⓑ Statement (2) ALONE is sufficient, but statement (1) alone is not sufficient.

Ⓒ BOTH statements (1) and (2) TOGETHER are sufficient, but NEITHER statement ALONE is sufficient.

Ⓓ EACH statement ALONE is sufficient.

Ⓔ Statements (1) and (2) TOGETHER are NOT sufficient.

15-3. Given that $x = y + z$, where the three values are different positive integers, is x a prime number?

    (1) y and z are odd.

    (2) $z = 3y$

    Ⓐ Statement (1) ALONE is sufficient, but statement (2) alone is not sufficient.

    Ⓑ Statement (2) ALONE is sufficient, but statement (1) alone is not sufficient.

    Ⓒ BOTH statements (1) and (2) TOGETHER are sufficient, but NEITHER statement ALONE is sufficient.

    Ⓓ EACH statement ALONE is sufficient.

    Ⓔ Statements (1) and (2) TOGETHER are NOT sufficient.

15-4. Given $2m^2 + n^2 = 27$, what is the value of m?

    (1) n is positive.

    (2) $m = n$

    Ⓐ Statement (1) ALONE is sufficient, but statement (2) alone is not sufficient.

    Ⓑ Statement (2) ALONE is sufficient, but statement (1) alone is not sufficient.

    Ⓒ BOTH statements (1) and (2) TOGETHER are sufficient, but NEITHER statement ALONE is sufficient.

    Ⓓ EACH statement ALONE is sufficient.

    Ⓔ Statements (1) and (2) TOGETHER are NOT sufficient.

15-5. Given that $m = n + 2$, what is the value of $m^2 - 4m + 4$?

  (1) $n = 20$

  (2) $n^2 = 400$

  Ⓐ Statement (1) ALONE is sufficient, but statement (2) alone is not sufficient.

  Ⓑ Statement (2) ALONE is sufficient, but statement (1) alone is not sufficient.

  Ⓒ BOTH statements (1) and (2) TOGETHER are sufficient, but NEITHER statement ALONE is sufficient.

  Ⓓ EACH statement ALONE is sufficient.

  Ⓔ Statements (1) and (2) TOGETHER are NOT sufficient.

Answers: 15-1 Ⓐ, 15-2 Ⓔ, 15-3 Ⓓ, 15-4 Ⓒ, 15-5 Ⓓ

If you answered 15-1 **incorrectly, go to 16-1.**
If you answered 15-1 **correctly, go to 16-2.**

If you answered 15-2 **incorrectly, go to 16-1.**
If you answered 15-2 **correctly, go to 16-3.**

If you answered 15-3 **incorrectly, go to 16-2.**
If you answered 15-3 **correctly, go to 16-4.**

If you answered 15-4 **incorrectly, go to 16-3.**
If you answered 15-4 **correctly, go to 16-5.**

If you answered 15-5 **incorrectly, go to 16-4.**
If you answered 15-5 **correctly, go to 16-5.**

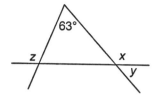

16-1. How many degrees is angle *x*?

(1) $y = 47°$

(2) $z = 110°$

Ⓐ Statement (1) ALONE is sufficient, but statement (2) alone is not sufficient.

Ⓑ Statement (2) ALONE is sufficient, but statement (1) alone is not sufficient.

Ⓒ BOTH statements (1) and (2) TOGETHER are sufficient, but NEITHER statement ALONE is sufficient.

Ⓓ EACH statement ALONE is sufficient.

Ⓔ Statements (1) and (2) TOGETHER are NOT sufficient.

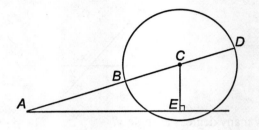

16-2. In the circle with center *C* above, what is the area of right tri-angle *ACE*?

(1) *AE* equals 16 inches.

(2) *BD* equals 12 inches.

Ⓐ Statement (1) ALONE is sufficient, but statement (2) alone is not sufficient.

Ⓑ Statement (2) ALONE is sufficient, but statement (1) alone is not sufficient.

Ⓒ BOTH statements (1) and (2) TOGETHER are sufficient, but NEITHER statement ALONE is sufficient.

Ⓓ EACH statement ALONE is sufficient.

Ⓔ Statements (1) and (2) TOGETHER are NOT sufficient.

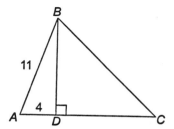

16-3. Given *BD* perpendicular to *AC*, what is the area of triangle *BCD*?

(1) Angle $BAD = 69°$.

(2) $BD = CD$

Ⓐ Statement (1) ALONE is sufficient, but statement (2) alone is not sufficient.

Ⓑ Statement (2) ALONE is sufficient, but statement (1) alone is not sufficient.

Ⓒ BOTH statements (1) and (2) TOGETHER are sufficient, but NEITHER statement ALONE is sufficient.

Ⓓ EACH statement ALONE is sufficient.

Ⓔ Statements (1) and (2) TOGETHER are NOT sufficient.

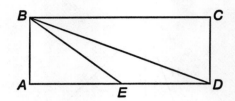

16-4. In the figure above, *ABCD* is a rectangle and *E* is the midpoint of one side. What is the area of triangle *BCD*?

(1) *BE* = 5 inches

(2) *CD* = 3 inches

Ⓐ Statement (1) ALONE is sufficient, but statement (2) alone is not sufficient.

Ⓑ Statement (2) ALONE is sufficient, but statement (1) alone is not sufficient.

Ⓒ BOTH statements (1) and (2) TOGETHER are sufficient, but NEITHER statement ALONE is sufficient.

Ⓓ EACH statement ALONE is sufficient.

Ⓔ Statements (1) and (2) TOGETHER are NOT sufficient.

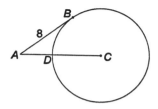

16-5. Given that *AB* is tangent to the circle with center *C*, what is the length of the circle's radius?

(1) $AD = 4$

(2) $AC = 10$

Ⓐ Statement (1) ALONE is sufficient, but statement (2) alone is not sufficient.

Ⓑ Statement (2) ALONE is sufficient, but statement (1) alone is not sufficient.

Ⓒ BOTH statements (1) and (2) TOGETHER are sufficient, but NEITHER statement ALONE is sufficient.

Ⓓ EACH statement ALONE is sufficient.

Ⓔ Statements (1) and (2) TOGETHER are NOT sufficient.

254 GMAT CAT PRACTICE TEST

Answers: 16-1 ⓓ, 16-2 ⓔ, 16-3 ⓑ, 16-4 ⓒ, 16-5 ⓓ

If you answered 16-1 **incorrectly, go to 17-1.**
If you answered 16-1 **correctly, go to 17-2.**

If you answered 16-2 **incorrectly, go to 17-1.**
If you answered 16-2 **correctly, go to 17-3.**

If you answered 16-3 **incorrectly, go to 17-2.**
If you answered 16-3 **correctly, go to 17-4.**

If you answered 16-4 **incorrectly, go to 17-3.**
If you answered 16-4 **correctly, go to 17-5.**

If you answered 16-5 **incorrectly, go to 17-4.**
If you answered 16-5 **correctly, go to 17-5.**

17-1. The first five numbers in a regular sequence are 4, 10, 22, 46, and 94. What is the next number in the sequence?

    Ⓐ 142
    Ⓑ 154
    Ⓒ 176
    Ⓓ 182
    Ⓔ 190

17-2. $2,000 is deposited in a savings account that pays 6% annual interest compounded semiannually. To the nearest dollar, how much is in the account at the end of the year?

    Ⓐ $2,060
    Ⓑ $2,120
    Ⓒ $2,122
    Ⓓ $2,247
    Ⓔ $2,258

17-3. How much tea worth $0.93 per pound must be mixed with tea worth $0.75 per pound to produce 10 pounds worth $0.85 per pound?

Ⓐ $2\frac{2}{9}$

Ⓑ $3\frac{1}{2}$

Ⓒ $4\frac{4}{9}$

Ⓓ $5\frac{5}{9}$

Ⓔ $9\frac{1}{2}$

17-4. In a class of 200 students, 120 study Spanish and 100 study French. If a student must study at least one of these two languages, what percent of the students study French but NOT Spanish?

Ⓐ 80%
Ⓑ 40%
Ⓒ 30%
Ⓓ 20%
Ⓔ 10%

17-5. Which of the following CANNOT be weighed using a balance scale and these unit weights: 1, 4, 7, and 10?

Ⓐ 13
Ⓑ 15
Ⓒ 17
Ⓓ 19
Ⓔ 21

Answers: 17-1 Ⓔ, 17-2 Ⓒ, 17-3 Ⓓ, 17-4 Ⓑ, 17-5 Ⓓ

If you answered 17-1 **incorrectly, go to 18-1.**
If you answered 17-1 **correctly, go to 18-2.**

If you answered 17-2 **incorrectly, go to 18-1.**
If you answered 17-2 **correctly, go to 18-3.**

If you answered 17-3 **incorrectly, go to 18-2.**
If you answered 17-3 **correctly, go to 18-4.**

If you answered 17-4 **incorrectly, go to 18-3.**
If you answered 17-4 **correctly, go to 18-5.**

If you answered 17-5 **incorrectly, go to 18-4.**
If you answered 17-5 **correctly, go to 18-5.**

18-1. A $74.95 lawn chair was sold for $59.95 at a special sale. By approximately what percent was the price decreased?

 Ⓐ 15%
 Ⓑ 20%
 Ⓒ 25%
 Ⓓ 60%
 Ⓔ 80%

18-2. Mr. Smitherly leaves Cedar Rapids at 8 A.M. and drives north on the highway at an average speed of 50 miles per hour. Mr. Dinkle leaves Cedar Rapids at 8:30 A.M. and drives north on the same highway at an average speed of 60 miles per hour. Mr. Dinkle will

 Ⓐ overtake Mr. Smitherly at 9:30 A.M.
 Ⓑ overtake Mr. Smitherly at 10:30 A.M.
 Ⓒ overtake Mr. Smitherly at 11:00 A.M.
 Ⓓ be 30 miles behind at 8:35 A.M.
 Ⓔ never overtake Mr. Smitherly

18-3. On a trip covering 360 miles, a bicyclist travels the first 150 miles at 30 miles per hour and the remainder of the distance at 35 miles per hour. What is the average speed, in miles per hour, for the entire trip?

Ⓐ 28

Ⓑ $32\frac{1}{2}$

Ⓒ $32\frac{8}{11}$

Ⓓ $46\frac{4}{11}$

Ⓔ 65

18-4. A man walks from B to C, a distance of x miles, at 8 miles per hour and returns at 12 miles per hour. What is his average speed?

Ⓐ 10 mph
Ⓑ   9.6 mph
Ⓒ   8.8 mph
Ⓓ   8.4 mph
Ⓔ   4 mph

18-5. The current in a river is 4 mph. A boat can travel 20 mph in still water. How far up the river can the boat travel if the round trip is to take 10 hours?

Ⓐ   69 miles
Ⓑ   88 miles
Ⓒ   96 miles
Ⓓ 100 miles
Ⓔ 112 miles

Answers: 18-1 Ⓑ, 18-2 Ⓒ, 18-3 Ⓒ, 18-4 Ⓑ, 18-5 Ⓒ

If you answered 18-1 **incorrectly, go to 19-1.**
If you answered 18-1 **correctly, go to 19-2.**

If you answered 18-2 **incorrectly, go to 19-1.**
If you answered 18-2 **correctly, go to 19-3.**

If you answered 18-3 **incorrectly, go to 19-2.**
If you answered 18-3 **correctly, go to 19-4.**

If you answered 18-4 **incorrectly, go to 19-3.**
If you answered 18-4 **correctly, go to 19-5.**

If you answered 18-5 **incorrectly, go to 19-4.**
If you answered 18-5 **correctly, go to 19-5.**

19-1. If the radius of a circle is decreased 20%, what happens to the area?

  Ⓐ 10% decrease
  Ⓑ 20% decrease
  Ⓒ 36% decrease
  Ⓓ 40% decrease
  Ⓔ 50% decrease

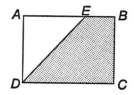

19-2. What is the area of the shaded portion of this rectangle, given that $AD = 6$, $CD = 8$, and $AE = x$?

  Ⓐ $48 - 3x$
  Ⓑ $48 + 3x$
  Ⓒ $3x + 16$
  Ⓓ $24 - 3x$
  Ⓔ $24 + 3x$

19-3. In the figure above, four equal circles are drawn within a square whose perimeter is 32. What is the area of the shaded region?

Ⓐ $32 - 16\pi$
Ⓑ $64 - 16\pi$
Ⓒ $64 - 32\pi$
Ⓓ $32\pi - 32$
Ⓔ $64\pi - 64$

19-4. In the figure above, the centers of four equal circles lie along the diameter of the large circle. If the circumference of the large circle is 64π, what is the area of the shaded region?

Ⓐ 16π
Ⓑ 32π
Ⓒ 64π
Ⓓ 128π
Ⓔ 256π

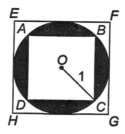

19-5. Square *ABCD* is inscribed in circle *O*, which is inscribed in larger square *EFGH*, as shown in the diagram above. If the radius of circle *O* is 1, then the shaded area is approximately what percent of the area of square *EFGH*?

     Ⓐ   3%
     Ⓑ   4%
     Ⓒ 25%
     Ⓓ 50%
     Ⓔ 75%

Answers: 19-1 ©, 19-2 Ⓐ, 19-3 Ⓑ, 19-4 Ⓔ, 19-5 ©

If you answered 19-1 **incorrectly, go to 20-1.**
If you answered 19-1 **correctly, go to 20-2.**

If you answered 19-2 **incorrectly, go to 20-1.**
If you answered 19-2 **correctly, go to 20-3.**

If you answered 19-3 **incorrectly, go to 20-2.**
If you answered 19-3 **correctly, go to 20-4.**

If you answered 19-4 **incorrectly, go to 20-3.**
If you answered 19-4 **correctly, go to 20-5.**

If you answered 19-5 **incorrectly, go to 20-4.**
If you answered 19-5 **correctly, go to 20-5.**

20-1. $\frac{1}{4}$ of $\frac{3}{5}$ is what percent of $\frac{3}{4}$?

   Ⓐ 15%
   Ⓑ 20%
   © $33\frac{1}{3}$%
   Ⓓ 75%
   Ⓔ 80%

20-2. A sales representative receives a salary of $150 per week and earns a commission of 15% on all sales she makes. How many dollars worth of sales does she need to make in order to bring her total weekly income to $600?

   Ⓐ $3,000
   Ⓑ $3,150
   © $4,000
   Ⓓ $4,150
   Ⓔ $5,000

20-3. A couple who own an appliance store discover that if they advertise a sales discount of 10% on every item in the store, at the end of one month the number of total items sold increases 20%. Their gross income from sales for one month increases by what percent?

Ⓐ   2%
Ⓑ   4%
Ⓒ   5%
Ⓓ   8%
Ⓔ 12%

20-4. A furniture store owner decided to drop the price of her recliners by 20% to spur business. By the end of the week she had sold 50% more recliners. What is the percentage increase of the gross?

Ⓐ 10%
Ⓑ 15%
Ⓒ 20%
Ⓓ 25%
Ⓔ 50%

20-5. The product of x and y is a constant. If the value of x is increased by 50%, by what percentage must the value of y be decreased?

Ⓐ 50%
Ⓑ 40%
Ⓒ $33\frac{1}{3}$%
Ⓓ 25%
Ⓔ $12\frac{1}{2}$%

Answers: 20-1 Ⓑ, 20-2 Ⓐ, 20-3 Ⓓ, 20-4 Ⓒ, 20-5 Ⓒ

If you answered 20-1 **incorrectly**, go to **21-1.**
If you answered 20-1 **correctly**, go to **21-2.**

If you answered 20-2 **incorrectly**, go to **21-1.**
If you answered 20-2 **correctly**, go to **21-3.**

If you answered 20-3 **incorrectly**, go to **21-2.**
If you answered 20-3 **correctly**, go to **21-4.**

If you answered 20-4 **incorrectly**, go to **21-3.**
If you answered 20-4 **correctly**, go to **21-5.**

If you answered 20-5 **incorrectly**, go to **21-4.**
If you answered 20-5 **correctly**, go to **21-5.**

21-1. Assuming that neither m nor n is zero, is the product m^2n positive?

   (1) $m > 0$

   (2) $n > 0$

   Ⓐ Statement (1) ALONE is sufficient, but statement (2) alone is not sufficient.
   Ⓑ Statement (2) ALONE is sufficient, but statement (1) alone is not sufficient.
   Ⓒ BOTH statements (1) and (2) TOGETHER are sufficient, but NEITHER statement ALONE is sufficient.
   Ⓓ EACH statement ALONE is sufficient.
   Ⓔ Statements (1) and (2) TOGETHER are NOT sufficient.

21-2. Is m, which does not equal zero, a positive number?

   (1) $m = m^2$

   (2) $m^2 = m^3$

   Ⓐ Statement (1) ALONE is sufficient, but statement (2) alone is not sufficient.
   Ⓑ Statement (2) ALONE is sufficient, but statement (1) alone is not sufficient.
   Ⓒ BOTH statements (1) and (2) TOGETHER are sufficient, but NEITHER statement ALONE is sufficient.
   Ⓓ EACH statement ALONE is sufficient.
   Ⓔ Statements (1) and (2) TOGETHER are NOT sufficient.

21-3. What is the value of $x + y + z$?

 (1) $y + z = 2x$

 (2) $\dfrac{1}{x} + \dfrac{1}{y} + \dfrac{1}{z} = \dfrac{4}{9}$

 Ⓐ Statement (1) ALONE is sufficient, but statement (2) alone is not sufficient.

 Ⓑ Statement (2) ALONE is sufficient, but statement (1) alone is not sufficient.

 Ⓒ BOTH statements (1) and (2) TOGETHER are sufficient, but NEITHER statement ALONE is sufficient.

 Ⓓ EACH statement ALONE is sufficient.

 Ⓔ Statements (1) and (2) TOGETHER are NOT sufficient.

21-4. If $x < y$, is $(x - y) < yz$?

 (1) $y < 0$

 (2) $z < 0$

 Ⓐ Statement (1) ALONE is sufficient, but statement (2) alone is not sufficient.

 Ⓑ Statement (2) ALONE is sufficient, but statement (1) alone is not sufficient.

 Ⓒ BOTH statements (1) and (2) TOGETHER are sufficient, but NEITHER statement ALONE is sufficient.

 Ⓓ EACH statement ALONE is sufficient.

 Ⓔ Statements (1) and (2) TOGETHER are NOT sufficient.

21-5. Given three different integers, does the exponential quantity $(a - b)^c$ exceed zero?

   (1) $b < a$

   (2) $c = 2a$

   Ⓐ Statement (1) ALONE is sufficient, but statement (2) alone is not sufficient.

   Ⓑ Statement (2) ALONE is sufficient, but statement (1) alone is not sufficient.

   Ⓒ BOTH statements (1) and (2) TOGETHER are sufficient, but NEITHER statement ALONE is sufficient.

   Ⓓ EACH statement ALONE is sufficient.

   Ⓔ Statements (1) and (2) TOGETHER are NOT sufficient.

Answers: 21-1 Ⓑ, 21-2 Ⓓ, 21-3 Ⓔ, 21-4 Ⓒ, 21-5 Ⓓ

If you answered 21-1 **incorrectly, go to 22-1.**
If you answered 21-1 **correctly, go to 22-2.**

If you answered 21-2 **incorrectly, go to 22-1.**
If you answered 21-2 **correctly, go to 22-3.**

If you answered 21-3 **incorrectly, go to 22-2.**
If you answered 21-3 **correctly, go to 22-4.**

If you answered 21-4 **incorrectly, go to 22-3.**
If you answered 21-4 **correctly, go to 22-5.**

If you answered 21-5 **incorrectly, go to 22-4.**
If you answered 21-5 **correctly, go to 22-5.**

22-1. What is the volume of a cylindrical can?

(1) The radius of the can is 3 inches.

(2) The area of the bottom is 9π square inches.

Ⓐ Statement (1) ALONE is sufficient, but statement (2) alone is not sufficient.

Ⓑ Statement (2) ALONE is sufficient, but statement (1) alone is not sufficient.

Ⓒ BOTH statements (1) and (2) TOGETHER are sufficient, but NEITHER statement ALONE is sufficient.

Ⓓ EACH statement ALONE is sufficient.

Ⓔ Statements (1) and (2) TOGETHER are NOT sufficient.

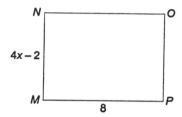

22-2. What is the width *MN* of rectangle *MNOP*?

(1) $OP = x + 4$

(2) The area is 48.

Ⓐ Statement (1) ALONE is sufficient, but statement (2) alone is not sufficient.

Ⓑ Statement (2) ALONE is sufficient, but statement (1) alone is not sufficient.

Ⓒ BOTH statements (1) and (2) TOGETHER are sufficient, but NEITHER statement ALONE is sufficient.

Ⓓ EACH statement ALONE is sufficient.

Ⓔ Statements (1) and (2) TOGETHER are NOT sufficient.

22-3. What is the area of a rectangular field?

(1) The diagonal is twice the width.

(2) The length is 173 feet.

Ⓐ Statement (1) ALONE is sufficient, but statement (2) alone is not sufficient.

Ⓑ Statement (2) ALONE is sufficient, but statement (1) alone is not sufficient.

Ⓒ BOTH statements (1) and (2) TOGETHER are sufficient, but NEITHER statement ALONE is sufficient.

Ⓓ EACH statement ALONE is sufficient.

Ⓔ Statements (1) and (2) TOGETHER are NOT sufficient.

22-4. A farmer wants to fence in a rectangular lot of 3,000 square feet in which to raise pigs. Should the farmer employ configuration X or configuration Y in order to minimize the cost of fencing?

(1) Lot X would be 75 feet long, and lot Y would be 50 feet wide.

(2) Lot X would be $87\frac{1}{2}$ percent longer than wide, and lot Y would be 20 percent longer than wide.

Ⓐ Statement (1) ALONE is sufficient, but statement (2) alone is not sufficient.

Ⓑ Statement (2) ALONE is sufficient, but statement (1) alone is not sufficient.

Ⓒ BOTH statements (1) and (2) TOGETHER are sufficient, but NEITHER statement ALONE is sufficient.

Ⓓ EACH statement ALONE is sufficient.

Ⓔ Statements (1) and (2) TOGETHER are NOT sufficient.

22-5. What is the area of the shaded portion of the half-circle?

   (1) B is the midpoint of $\overset{\frown}{AC}$.

   (2) Angle ABC is a right angle.

   Ⓐ Statement (1) ALONE is sufficient, but statement (2) alone
      is not sufficient.
   Ⓑ Statement (2) ALONE is sufficient, but statement (1) alone
      is not sufficient.
   Ⓒ BOTH statements (1) and (2) TOGETHER are sufficient, but
      NEITHER statement ALONE is sufficient.
   Ⓓ EACH statement ALONE is sufficient.
   Ⓔ Statements (1) and (2) TOGETHER are NOT sufficient.

Answers: 22-1 Ⓔ, 22-2 Ⓓ, 22-3 Ⓒ, 22-4 Ⓓ, 22-5 Ⓐ

If you answered 22-1 incorrectly, go to 23-1.
If you answered 22-1 correctly, go to 23-2.

If you answered 22-2 incorrectly, go to 23-1.
If you answered 22-2 correctly, go to 23-3.

If you answered 22-3 incorrectly, go to 23-2.
If you answered 22-3 correctly, go to 23-4.

If you answered 22-4 incorrectly, go to 23-3.
If you answered 22-4 correctly, go to 23-5.

If you answered 22-5 incorrectly, go to 23-4.
If you answered 22-5 correctly, go to 23-5.

23-1. What is the value of p?

  (1) $2p + 3r = 11$

  (2) $p - r = 5$

  Ⓐ Statement (1) ALONE is sufficient, but statement (2) alone is not sufficient.
  Ⓑ Statement (2) ALONE is sufficient, but statement (1) alone is not sufficient.
  Ⓒ BOTH statements (1) and (2) TOGETHER are sufficient, but NEITHER statement ALONE is sufficient.
  Ⓓ EACH statement ALONE is sufficient.
  Ⓔ Statements (1) and (2) TOGETHER are NOT sufficient.

23-2. What is the value of $\dfrac{14m^4}{s^6}$?

  (1) $m^2 = 3s^3$

  (2) $s^6 = 64$

  Ⓐ Statement (1) ALONE is sufficient, but statement (2) alone is not sufficient.
  Ⓑ Statement (2) ALONE is sufficient, but statement (1) alone is not sufficient.
  Ⓒ BOTH statements (1) and (2) TOGETHER are sufficient, but NEITHER statement ALONE is sufficient.
  Ⓓ EACH statement ALONE is sufficient.
  Ⓔ Statements (1) and (2) TOGETHER are NOT sufficient.

23-3. In the expression $3x - 2y < z$, is y positive?

(1) $x = 3$

(2) $z = 17$

Ⓐ Statement (1) ALONE is sufficient, but statement (2) alone is not sufficient.

Ⓑ Statement (2) ALONE is sufficient, but statement (1) alone is not sufficient.

Ⓒ BOTH statements (1) and (2) TOGETHER are sufficient, but NEITHER statement ALONE is sufficient.

Ⓓ EACH statement ALONE is sufficient.

Ⓔ Statements (1) and (2) TOGETHER are NOT sufficient.

23-4. Is the product cd positive?

(1) $3c = -8d^3$

(2) $d > c + 4$

Ⓐ Statement (1) ALONE is sufficient, but statement (2) alone is not sufficient.

Ⓑ Statement (2) ALONE is sufficient, but statement (1) alone is not sufficient.

Ⓒ BOTH statements (1) and (2) TOGETHER are sufficient, but NEITHER statement ALONE is sufficient.

Ⓓ EACH statement ALONE is sufficient.

Ⓔ Statements (1) and (2) TOGETHER are NOT sufficient.

23-5. What is the value of $x^3 - 2x^2 + 7$?

    (1) $3x^3 - x = 2$

    (2) $x^5 = 1$

    Ⓐ Statement (1) ALONE is sufficient, but statement (2) alone is not sufficient.

    Ⓑ Statement (2) ALONE is sufficient, but statement (1) alone is not sufficient.

    Ⓒ BOTH statements (1) and (2) TOGETHER are sufficient, but NEITHER statement ALONE is sufficient.

    Ⓓ EACH statement ALONE is sufficient.

    Ⓔ Statements (1) and (2) TOGETHER are NOT sufficient.

Answers: 23-1 ©, 23-2 Ⓐ, 23-3 Ⓔ, 23-4 Ⓐ, 23-5 Ⓑ

If you answered 23-1 **incorrectly, go to 24-1.**
If you answered 23-1 **correctly, go to 24-2.**

If you answered 23-2 **incorrectly, go to 24-1.**
If you answered 23-2 **correctly, go to 24-3.**

If you answered 23-3 **incorrectly, go to 24-2.**
If you answered 23-3 **correctly, go to 24-4.**

If you answered 23-4 **incorrectly, go to 24-3.**
If you answered 23-4 **correctly, go to 24-5.**

If you answered 23-5 **incorrectly, go to 24-4.**
If you answered 23-5 **correctly, go to 24-5.**

24-1. In the figure above, $x =$

(A) 15
(B) 25
(C) 35
(D) 45
(E) 55

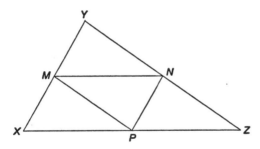

24-2. In $\triangle XYZ$, points M, N, and P are midpoints. If $XY = 10$, $YZ = 15$, and $XZ = 17$, what is the perimeter of $\triangle MNP$?

(A) $10\frac{2}{3}$
(B) 14
(C) 16
(D) 21
(E) 26

24-3. In a circle, a 10-inch chord is drawn at a distance of 12 inches from the center. What is the radius of the circle?

  Ⓐ $2\sqrt{61}$ inches
  Ⓑ 26 inches
  Ⓒ $5\sqrt{3}$ inches
  Ⓓ 13 inches
  Ⓔ $2\sqrt{11}$ inches

24-4. In a triangle, the ratio of two angles is 5:2, and the third angle is equal to the difference between the other two. What is the number of degrees in the smallest angle?

  Ⓐ 18
  Ⓑ $25\frac{2}{7}$
  Ⓒ $25\frac{5}{7}$
  Ⓓ 36
  Ⓔ 54

24-5. If a 32-inch chord is drawn in a circle of radius 20 inches, how far is the chord from the center of the circle?

Ⓐ   4 inches
Ⓑ   6 inches
Ⓒ   8 inches
Ⓓ 10 inches
Ⓔ 12 inches

Answers: 24-1 Ⓑ, 24-2 Ⓓ, 24-3 Ⓓ, 24-4 Ⓓ, 24-5 Ⓔ

If you answered 24-1 **incorrectly, go to 25-1.**
If you answered 24-1 **correctly, go to 25-2.**

If you answered 24-2 **incorrectly, go to 25-1.**
If you answered 24-2 **correctly, go to 25-3.**

If you answered 24-3 **incorrectly, go to 25-2.**
If you answered 24-3 **correctly, go to 25-4.**

If you answered 24-4 **incorrectly, go to 25-3.**
If you answered 24-4 **correctly, go to 25-5.**

If you answered 24-5 **incorrectly, go to 25-4.**
If you answered 24-5 **correctly, go to 25-5.**

25-1. N is a positive integer. When $N + 1$ is divided by 5, the remainder is 4. What is the remainder when N is divided by 5?

Ⓐ 6
Ⓑ 5
Ⓒ 4
Ⓓ 3
Ⓔ 2

25-2. How many two-digit numbers are there whose remainder when divided by 10 is 1, and whose remainder when divided by 6 is 5?

Ⓐ 3
Ⓑ 4
Ⓒ 5
Ⓓ 6
Ⓔ 7

25-3. The denominator of a fraction is 5 greater than the numerator. If the numerator and the denominator are increased by 2, the resulting fraction is equal to $\frac{7}{12}$. What is the value of the original fraction?

Ⓐ $\frac{5}{12}$

Ⓑ $\frac{1}{2}$

Ⓒ $\frac{9}{14}$

Ⓓ $\frac{2}{3}$

Ⓔ $\frac{12}{17}$

25-4. If the numerator of a fraction is tripled, and the denominator of a fraction is doubled, the resulting fraction will reflect an increase of what percent?

Ⓐ $16\frac{1}{6}\%$
Ⓑ 25%
Ⓒ $33\frac{1}{3}\%$
Ⓓ 50%
Ⓔ $66\frac{2}{3}\%$

25-5. If @ is a binary operation defined as the difference between an integer n and the product of n and 5, then what is the largest positive integer n such that the outcome of the binary operation @ of n is less than 10?

Ⓐ 1
Ⓑ 2
Ⓒ 3
Ⓓ 4
Ⓔ 5

Answers: 25-1 ⑩, 25-2 ⒶA, 25-3 ⒷB, 25-4 ⑩, 25-5 ⒷB

If you answered 25-1 **incorrectly, go to 26-1.**
If you answered 25-1 **correctly, go to 26-2.**

If you answered 25-2 **incorrectly, go to 26-1.**
If you answered 25-2 **correctly, go to 26-3.**

If you answered 25-3 **incorrectly, go to 26-2.**
If you answered 25-3 **correctly, go to 26-4.**

If you answered 25-4 **incorrectly, go to 26-3.**
If you answered 25-4 **correctly, go to 26-5.**

If you answered 25-5 **incorrectly, go to 26-4.**
If you answered 25-5 **correctly, go to 26-5.**

26-1. A bookseller sells his books at a 20% markup in price. If he sells a book for $12.00, how much did he pay for it?

Ⓐ $14.40
Ⓑ $14.00
Ⓒ $10.00
Ⓓ $9.60
Ⓔ $5.00

Houses Sold in One Year

Age	Number
1–2	1,200
3–4	1,570
5–6	1,630
7–8	1,440
9–10	1,520

26-2. According to the chart, how many more houses from 5 to 10 years old were sold than those 4 to 8 years old?

Ⓐ 2,455
Ⓑ 1,570
Ⓒ 150
Ⓓ 130
Ⓔ It cannot be determined from the information given.

Products	1986	1988	1990	1992	1994	1996
A	$4.20	$4.60	$5.00	$5.40	$5.80	$6.20
B	$6.30	$6.45	$6.60	$6.75	$6.90	$7.05

26-3. The chart above shows the prices of products A and B from 1986 to 1996. Using the chart, in what year will product A cost 40 cents more than product B?

Ⓐ 2000
Ⓑ 2002
Ⓒ 2003
Ⓓ 2004
Ⓔ 2006

Toys	Cost to Manufacture	Profit per Toy
A	$2.5796	$2.4431
B	$2.5768	$2.4312

26-4. According to the chart above, how many of each toy would have to be manufactured so that the total price of toy A exceeds the total price of toy B by $147.00?

Ⓐ   100
Ⓑ   1,000
Ⓒ   10,000
Ⓓ   100,000
Ⓔ   1,000,000

Station-to-Station and Credit Card	Person-to-Person	Each Additional Minute		
first three minutes	first three minutes	8:00 A.M. to 5:00 P.M. Mon.–Fri.	5:00 P.M. to 11:00 P.M. Mon.–Sat.	11:00 P.M. to 8:00 A.M. Sun.–Fri.
$2.75	$4.35	$0.46	$0.30	$0.19

26-5. Listed above are the rates for operator-assisted telephone calls from San Diego to New York City. On a Friday at 4:17 P.M., Mr. Talbot made a person-to-person phone call from San Diego to New York City. When he received his monthly phone bill, Mr. Talbot noted that this call cost $14.09. To the nearest minute, how long did this call last?

Ⓐ 23
Ⓑ 24
Ⓒ 25
Ⓓ 26
Ⓔ 27

Answers: 26-1 ©, 26-2 ©, 26-3 ©, 26-4 ©, 26-5 ®

If you answered 26-1 **incorrectly, go to 27-1.**
If you answered 26-1 **correctly, go to 27-2.**

If you answered 26-2 **incorrectly, go to 27-1.**
If you answered 26-2 **correctly, go to 27-3.**

If you answered 26-3 **incorrectly, go to 27-2.**
If you answered 26-3 **correctly, go to 27-4.**

If you answered 26-4 **incorrectly, go to 27-3.**
If you answered 26-4 **correctly, go to 27-5.**

If you answered 26-5 **incorrectly, go to 27-4.**
If you answered 26-5 **correctly, go to 27-5.**

27-1. How many rectangular tiles are required for the kitchen floor?

(1) Each tile is 48 square inches.

(2) The kitchen measures 10 feet by 7 feet.

Ⓐ Statement (1) ALONE is sufficient, but statement (2) alone is not sufficient.

Ⓑ Statement (2) ALONE is sufficient, but statement (1) alone is not sufficient.

Ⓒ BOTH statements (1) and (2) TOGETHER are sufficient, but NEITHER statement ALONE is sufficient.

Ⓓ EACH statement ALONE is sufficient.

Ⓔ Statements (1) and (2) TOGETHER are NOT sufficient.

27-2. How much wallpaper is needed to cover the two largest walls of a narrow room that is 9 feet high?

(1) The room is 10 feet wide.

(2) The room is 24 feet long.

Ⓐ Statement (1) ALONE is sufficient, but statement (2) alone is not sufficient.

Ⓑ Statement (2) ALONE is sufficient, but statement (1) alone is not sufficient.

Ⓒ BOTH statements (1) and (2) TOGETHER are sufficient, but NEITHER statement ALONE is sufficient.

Ⓓ EACH statement ALONE is sufficient.

Ⓔ Statements (1) and (2) TOGETHER are NOT sufficient.

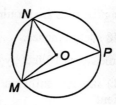

27-3. Within the circle with center O, how many degrees is angle MNO?

(1) Angle $ONP = 31°$.

(2) Angle $NPM = 48°$.

Ⓐ Statement (1) ALONE is sufficient, but statement (2) alone is not sufficient.

Ⓑ Statement (2) ALONE is sufficient, but statement (1) alone is not sufficient.

Ⓒ BOTH statements (1) and (2) TOGETHER are sufficient, but NEITHER statement ALONE is sufficient.

Ⓓ EACH statement ALONE is sufficient.

Ⓔ Statements (1) and (2) TOGETHER are NOT sufficient.

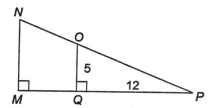

27-4. How long is *MN*?

(1) $ON = 6\frac{1}{2}$

(2) $MQ = 6$

Ⓐ Statement (1) ALONE is sufficient, but statement (2) alone is not sufficient.

Ⓑ Statement (2) ALONE is sufficient, but statement (1) alone is not sufficient.

Ⓒ BOTH statements (1) and (2) TOGETHER are sufficient, but NEITHER statement ALONE is sufficient.

Ⓓ EACH statement ALONE is sufficient.

Ⓔ Statements (1) and (2) TOGETHER are NOT sufficient.

27-5. What is the diameter of the wheel above?

(1) The wheel has rolled 36 feet.

(2) Point *P* has touched the ground 5 times.

Ⓐ Statement (1) ALONE is sufficient, but statement (2) alone is not sufficient.

Ⓑ Statement (2) ALONE is sufficient, but statement (1) alone is not sufficient.

Ⓒ BOTH statements (1) and (2) TOGETHER are sufficient, but NEITHER statement ALONE is sufficient.

Ⓓ EACH statement ALONE is sufficient.

Ⓔ Statements (1) and (2) TOGETHER are NOT sufficient.

Answers: 27-1 Ⓒ, 27-2 Ⓑ, 27-3 Ⓑ, 27-4 Ⓓ, 27-5 Ⓔ

If you answered 27-1 **incorrectly**, go to **28-1.**
If you answered 27-1 **correctly**, go to **28-2.**

If you answered 27-2 **incorrectly**, go to **28-1.**
If you answered 27-2 **correctly**, go to **28-3.**

If you answered 27-3 **incorrectly**, go to **28-2.**
If you answered 27-3 **correctly**, go to **28-4.**

If you answered 27-4 **incorrectly**, go to **28-3.**
If you answered 27-4 **correctly**, go to **28-5.**

If you answered 27-5 **incorrectly**, go to **28-4.**
If you answered 27-5 **correctly**, go to **28-5.**

28-1. A man's suit was discounted to $140. What was its list price?

(1) There would be a $10 fee for alterations.

(2) The sale was at "30% off."

Ⓐ Statement (1) ALONE is sufficient, but statement (2) alone is not sufficient.

Ⓑ Statement (2) ALONE is sufficient, but statement (1) alone is not sufficient.

Ⓒ BOTH statements (1) and (2) TOGETHER are sufficient, but NEITHER statement ALONE is sufficient.

Ⓓ EACH statement ALONE is sufficient.

Ⓔ Statements (1) and (2) TOGETHER are NOT sufficient.

28-2. What is the value of m?

(1) $4m - 5 = 7$

(2) $m^2 + 9 = 6m$

Ⓐ Statement (1) ALONE is sufficient, but statement (2) alone is not sufficient.

Ⓑ Statement (2) ALONE is sufficient, but statement (1) alone is not sufficient.

Ⓒ BOTH statements (1) and (2) TOGETHER are sufficient, but NEITHER statement ALONE is sufficient.

Ⓓ EACH statement ALONE is sufficient.

Ⓔ Statements (1) and (2) TOGETHER are NOT sufficient.

28-3. Does $x = y$?

  (1) $4x - 2y = 80$

  (2) $x = \dfrac{40 + y}{2}$

  Ⓐ Statement (1) ALONE is sufficient, but statement (2) alone is not sufficient.
  Ⓑ Statement (2) ALONE is sufficient, but statement (1) alone is not sufficient.
  Ⓒ BOTH statements (1) and (2) TOGETHER are sufficient, but NEITHER statement ALONE is sufficient.
  Ⓓ EACH statement ALONE is sufficient.
  Ⓔ Statements (1) and (2) TOGETHER are NOT sufficient.

28-4. If a is to b as b is to c, is c positive?

  (1) $c = 2a$

  (2) $b^2 = 32$

  Ⓐ Statement (1) ALONE is sufficient, but statement (2) alone is not sufficient.
  Ⓑ Statement (2) ALONE is sufficient, but statement (1) alone is not sufficient.
  Ⓒ BOTH statements (1) and (2) TOGETHER are sufficient, but NEITHER statement ALONE is sufficient.
  Ⓓ EACH statement ALONE is sufficient.
  Ⓔ Statements (1) and (2) TOGETHER are NOT sufficient.

28-5. The positive integer C is a perfect cube; what is its value?

(1) $30 < C < 100$

(2) C is an even number.

Ⓐ Statement (1) ALONE is sufficient, but statement (2) alone is not sufficient.

Ⓑ Statement (2) ALONE is sufficient, but statement (1) alone is not sufficient.

Ⓒ BOTH statements (1) and (2) TOGETHER are sufficient, but NEITHER statement ALONE is sufficient.

Ⓓ EACH statement ALONE is sufficient.

Ⓔ Statements (1) and (2) TOGETHER are NOT sufficient.

Answers: 28-1 Ⓑ, 28-2 Ⓓ, 28-3 Ⓔ, 28-4 Ⓔ, 28-5 Ⓐ

If you answered 28-1 **incorrectly, go to 29-1.**
If you answered 28-1 **correctly, go to 29-2.**

If you answered 28-2 **incorrectly, go to 29-1.**
If you answered 28-2 **correctly, go to 29-3.**

If you answered 28-3 **incorrectly, go to 29-2.**
If you answered 28-3 **correctly, go to 29-4.**

If you answered 28-4 **incorrectly, go to 29-3.**
If you answered 28-4 **correctly, go to 29-5.**

If you answered 28-5 **incorrectly, go to 29-4.**
If you answered 28-5 **correctly, go to 29-5.**

29-1. What is the volume of a certain box?

    (1) One side of the box has an area of 16 square inches.

    (2) The box is cubical.

    Ⓐ Statement (1) ALONE is sufficient, but statement (2) alone is not sufficient.

    Ⓑ Statement (2) ALONE is sufficient, but statement (1) alone is not sufficient.

    Ⓒ BOTH statements (1) and (2) TOGETHER are sufficient, but NEITHER statement ALONE is sufficient.

    Ⓓ EACH statement ALONE is sufficient.

    Ⓔ Statements (1) and (2) TOGETHER are NOT sufficient.

29-2. Where is the center of a circle on the xy plane?

    (1) The circle passes through both the origin and (0,7).

    (2) The diameter equals 10.

    Ⓐ Statement (1) ALONE is sufficient, but statement (2) alone is not sufficient.

    Ⓑ Statement (2) ALONE is sufficient, but statement (1) alone is not sufficient.

    Ⓒ BOTH statements (1) and (2) TOGETHER are sufficient, but NEITHER statement ALONE is sufficient.

    Ⓓ EACH statement ALONE is sufficient.

    Ⓔ Statements (1) and (2) TOGETHER are NOT sufficient.

29-3. What is the orientation of a line in the *xy* plane?

    (1) The line passes through the point $(5, a)$. .

    (2) $a = -3$

    Ⓐ Statement (1) ALONE is sufficient, but statement (2) alone is not sufficient.

    Ⓑ Statement (2) ALONE is sufficient, but statement (1) alone is not sufficient.

    Ⓒ BOTH statements (1) and (2) TOGETHER are sufficient, but NEITHER statement ALONE is sufficient.

    Ⓓ EACH statement ALONE is sufficient.

    Ⓔ Statements (1) and (2) TOGETHER are NOT sufficient.

29-4. Is the diagonal of square Q a rational number?

    (1) The area equals the side multiplied by itself.

    (2) The side equals $\sqrt{8}$.

    Ⓐ Statement (1) ALONE is sufficient, but statement (2) alone is not sufficient.

    Ⓑ Statement (2) ALONE is sufficient, but statement (1) alone is not sufficient.

    Ⓒ BOTH statements (1) and (2) TOGETHER are sufficient, but NEITHER statement ALONE is sufficient.

    Ⓓ EACH statement ALONE is sufficient.

    Ⓔ Statements (1) and (2) TOGETHER are NOT sufficient.

29-5. The centers of the three circles lie on one line (the circles intersect as shown). What is the area of the shaded part of the figure?

(1) Each of the small circles has a diameter of 5.

(2) The large circle has a radius of 5.

Ⓐ Statement (1) ALONE is sufficient, but statement (2) alone is not sufficient.

Ⓑ Statement (2) ALONE is sufficient, but statement (1) alone is not sufficient.

Ⓒ BOTH statements (1) and (2) TOGETHER are sufficient, but NEITHER statement ALONE is sufficient.

Ⓓ EACH statement ALONE is sufficient.

Ⓔ Statements (1) and (2) TOGETHER are NOT sufficient.

Answers: 29-1 Ⓒ, 29-2 Ⓔ, 29-3 Ⓔ, 29-4 Ⓑ, 29-5 Ⓐ

If you answered 29-1 **incorrectly, go to 30-1.**
If you answered 29-1 **correctly, go to 30-2.**

If you answered 29-2 **incorrectly, go to 30-1.**
If you answered 29-2 **correctly, go to 30-3.**

If you answered 29-3 **incorrectly, go to 30-2.**
If you answered 29-3 **correctly, go to 30-4.**

If you answered 29-4 **incorrectly, go to 30-3.**
If you answered 29-4 **correctly, go to 30-5.**

If you answered 29-5 **incorrectly, go to 30-4.**
If you answered 29-5 **correctly, go to 30-5.**

30-1. $\dfrac{\frac{7}{10}\times 14\times 5\times\frac{1}{28}}{\frac{10}{17}\times\frac{3}{5}\times\frac{1}{6}\times 17}=$

   Ⓐ $\frac{4}{7}$

   Ⓑ 1

   Ⓒ $\frac{7}{4}$

   Ⓓ 2

   Ⓔ $\frac{17}{4}$

30-2. Mary spent $\frac{2}{5}$ of her money on new clothes and then deposited $\frac{1}{2}$ of what remained into her savings account. If she then had $21 left, how much did she have at the start?

   Ⓐ $30
   Ⓑ $35
   Ⓒ $70
   Ⓓ $105
   Ⓔ $210

30-3. Five A's and two B's exactly balance six B's and five C's. One A and four C's exactly balance two A's and four B's. What is the weight of A in terms of C?

Ⓐ $\frac{3}{2}C$

Ⓑ $\frac{6}{5}C$

Ⓒ $\frac{5}{6}C$

Ⓓ $\frac{2}{3}C$

Ⓔ $\frac{1}{2}C$

30-4. Felix earned 30% more per month than Oscar. If Felix's salary is decreased 10% and Oscar's salary is increased 10%, then Felix would be earning what percent more than Oscar?

Ⓐ 10%
Ⓑ 9.09%
Ⓒ 7%
Ⓓ 6.36%
Ⓔ It cannot be determined from the information given.

30-5. In 1995, the Johnsons spent $800 on the family's water bills. Anticipating that water rates would increase in 1996 by 50%, the Johnsons cut back their water usage. By how much must the Johnsons have reduced their 1996 water usage to pay exactly the same amount in 1996 as they paid in 1995?

Ⓐ $33\frac{1}{3}$%
Ⓑ 40%
Ⓒ 50%
Ⓓ $66\frac{2}{3}$%
Ⓔ 100%

Answers: 30-1 Ⓒ, 30-2 Ⓒ, 30-3 Ⓐ, 30-4 Ⓓ, 30-5 Ⓐ

If you answered 30-1 **incorrectly, go to 31-1.**
If you answered 30-1 **correctly, go to 31-2.**

If you answered 30-2 **incorrectly, go to 31-1.**
If you answered 30-2 **correctly, go to 31-3.**

If you answered 30-3 **incorrectly, go to 31-2.**
If you answered 30-3 **correctly, go to 31-4.**

If you answered 30-4 **incorrectly, go to 31-3.**
If you answered 30-4 **correctly, go to 31-5.**

If you answered 30-5 **incorrectly, go to 31-4.**
If you answered 30-5 **correctly, go to 31-5.**

31-1. Given positive integer y, which of the following CANNOT be evenly divisible by y?

  Ⓐ $y + 1$
  Ⓑ $y + 2$
  Ⓒ $2y + 1$
  Ⓓ $y - 1$
  Ⓔ $y + \frac{1}{2}$

31-2. How many positive two-digit numbers, *ab,* are possible such that *ab* is divisible by 8 and the sum of *a* and *b* is divisible by 8?

  Ⓐ 0
  Ⓑ 1
  Ⓒ 2
  Ⓓ 3
  Ⓔ 4

31-3. Given the two equations $3r + s = 17$ and $r + 2s = 9$, by how much does r exceed s?

Ⓐ 3
Ⓑ 4
Ⓒ 5
Ⓓ 6
Ⓔ 7

31-4. $6x - 12 = -6y$

$5y + 5x = 15$

Which of the following is the number of solutions to the system of equations shown above?

Ⓐ More than three
Ⓑ Exactly three
Ⓒ Exactly two
Ⓓ Exactly one
Ⓔ None

31-5. If $x^2 + y^2 = 14$ and $xy = 3$, then $(x - y)^2 =$

Ⓐ 8
Ⓑ 11
Ⓒ 14
Ⓓ 17
Ⓔ 20

Answers: 31-1 Ⓔ, 31-2 Ⓒ, 31-3 Ⓐ, 31-4 Ⓔ, 31-5 Ⓐ

If you answered 31-1 **incorrectly, go to 32-1.**
If you answered 31-1 **correctly, go to 32-2.**

If you answered 31-2 **incorrectly, go to 32-1.**
If you answered 31-2 **correctly, go to 32-3.**

If you answered 31-3 **incorrectly, go to 32-2.**
If you answered 31-3 **correctly, go to 32-4.**

If you answered 31-4 **incorrectly, go to 32-3.**
If you answered 31-4 **correctly, go to 32-5.**

If you answered 31-5 **incorrectly, go to 32-4.**
If you answered 31-5 **correctly, go to 32-5.**

32-1. Simplify: $2 + \dfrac{1}{2 + \frac{1}{2+\frac{1}{2}}}$

Ⓐ $\frac{29}{12}$

Ⓑ $\frac{12}{5}$

Ⓒ $\frac{70}{29}$

Ⓓ $\frac{19}{8}$

Ⓔ $\frac{12}{29}$

32-2. During one season, a tennis team won 21 matches and lost 30% of their matches. What was the number of matches that the team lost?

Ⓐ 70
Ⓑ 30
Ⓒ 9
Ⓓ 7
Ⓔ 5

32-3. Three factories of Conglomerate Corporation are capable of manufacturing hubcaps. Two of the factories can each produce 100,000 hubcaps in 15 days. The third factory can produce hubcaps 30% faster. Approximately how many days would it take to produce a million hubcaps with all three factories working simultaneously?

Ⓐ 38
Ⓑ 42
Ⓒ 46
Ⓓ 50
Ⓔ 54

32-4. Dan can do a job alone in 15 hours. Fred, working alone, can do the same job in just 10 hours. If Dan works alone for 9 hours and then stops, how many hours will it take Fred, working alone, to complete the job?

Ⓐ 4
Ⓑ 5
Ⓒ 6
Ⓓ 12
Ⓔ 12.5

32-5. Machine A can do a certain job in 8 hours. Machine B can do the same job in 10 hours. Machine C can do the same job in 12 hours. All three machines start the job at 9:00 A.M. Machine A breaks down at 11:00 A.M., and the other two machines finish the job. Approximately what time will the job be finished?

Ⓐ Noon
Ⓑ 12:30 P.M.
Ⓒ 1:00 P.M.
Ⓓ 1:30 P.M.
Ⓔ 2:00 P.M.

Answers: 32-1 Ⓐ, 32-2 Ⓒ, 32-3 Ⓒ, 32-4 Ⓐ, 32-5 Ⓒ

If you answered 32-1 **incorrectly, go to 33-1.**
If you answered 32-1 **correctly, go to 33-2.**

If you answered 32-2 **incorrectly, go to 33-1.**
If you answered 32-2 **correctly, go to 33-3.**

If you answered 32-3 **incorrectly, go to 33-2.**
If you answered 32-3 **correctly, go to 33-4.**

If you answered 32-4 **incorrectly, go to 33-3.**
If you answered 32-4 **correctly, go to 33-5.**

If you answered 32-5 **incorrectly, go to 33-4.**
If you answered 32-5 **correctly, go to 33-5.**

33-1. What is the range of a sports car on one tank of gasoline?

(1) The tank holds 50 liters.

(2) It consumes 8 liters of gasoline each 100 kilometers.

Ⓐ Statement (1) ALONE is sufficient, but statement (2) alone is not sufficient.

Ⓑ Statement (2) ALONE is sufficient, but statement (1) alone is not sufficient.

Ⓒ BOTH statements (1) and (2) TOGETHER are sufficient, but NEITHER statement ALONE is sufficient.

Ⓓ EACH statement ALONE is sufficient.

Ⓔ Statements (1) and (2) TOGETHER are NOT sufficient.

33-2. Five persons sat next to each other around a circular table to play cards. Did Grace sit next to Bill?

(1) Dora sat next to Ethyl and Carl.

(2) Grace sat next to Carl.

Ⓐ Statement (1) ALONE is sufficient, but statement (2) alone is not sufficient.

Ⓑ Statement (2) ALONE is sufficient, but statement (1) alone is not sufficient.

Ⓒ BOTH statements (1) and (2) TOGETHER are sufficient, but NEITHER statement ALONE is sufficient.

Ⓓ EACH statement ALONE is sufficient.

Ⓔ Statements (1) and (2) TOGETHER are NOT sufficient.

33-3. An ice-cream stand sells two sizes of cones, Generous and Colossal. How many Colossal cones were sold one day?

(1) The total sales were $209.15.

(2) Generous cones sold for 75 cents, and Colossal cones sold for $1.25.

Ⓐ Statement (1) ALONE is sufficient, but statement (2) alone is not sufficient.

Ⓑ Statement (2) ALONE is sufficient, but statement (1) alone is not sufficient.

Ⓒ BOTH statements (1) and (2) TOGETHER are sufficient, but NEITHER statement ALONE is sufficient.

Ⓓ EACH statement ALONE is sufficient.

Ⓔ Statements (1) and (2) TOGETHER are NOT sufficient.

33-4. If gasoline costs $1.09 per gallon and alcohol costs $1.81, what fraction of each would be used to make Gasohol 99?

(1) The mixture is predominantly gasoline.

(2) A gallon of Gasohol 99 costs $1.22.

Ⓐ Statement (1) ALONE is sufficient, but statement (2) alone is not sufficient.

Ⓑ Statement (2) ALONE is sufficient, but statement (1) alone is not sufficient.

Ⓒ BOTH statements (1) and (2) TOGETHER are sufficient, but NEITHER statement ALONE is sufficient.

Ⓓ EACH statement ALONE is sufficient.

Ⓔ Statements (1) and (2) TOGETHER are NOT sufficient.

33-5. Each of 200 electrical switches controls a separate light bulb. How many of the switches are in the off position?

(1) Forty percent of the bulbs are glowing.

(2) Five percent of the bulbs are burnt out.

Ⓐ Statement (1) ALONE is sufficient, but statement (2) alone is not sufficient.

Ⓑ Statement (2) ALONE is sufficient, but statement (1) alone is not sufficient.

Ⓒ BOTH statements (1) and (2) TOGETHER are sufficient, but NEITHER statement ALONE is sufficient.

Ⓓ EACH statement ALONE is sufficient.

Ⓔ Statements (1) and (2) TOGETHER are NOT sufficient.

Answers: 33-1 Ⓒ, 33-2 Ⓐ, 33-3 Ⓔ, 33-4 Ⓑ, 33-5 Ⓔ

If you answered 33-1 **incorrectly**, go to 34-1.
If you answered 33-1 **correctly**, go to 34-2.

If you answered 33-2 **incorrectly**, go to 34-1.
If you answered 33-2 **correctly**, go to 34-3.

If you answered 33-3 **incorrectly**, go to 34-2.
If you answered 33-3 **correctly**, go to 34-4.

If you answered 33-4 **incorrectly**, go to 34-3.
If you answered 33-4 **correctly**, go to 34-5.

If you answered 33-5 **incorrectly**, go to 34-4.
If you answered 33-5 **correctly**, go to 34-5.

34-1. How many black shoes were sold by Shepard's Shoe Emporium?

   (1) Three-quarters of the shoes sold were brown.

   (2) The Emporium sold 1,284 left shoes.

   Ⓐ Statement (1) ALONE is sufficient, but statement (2) alone is not sufficient.

   Ⓑ Statement (2) ALONE is sufficient, but statement (1) alone is not sufficient.

   Ⓒ BOTH statements (1) and (2) TOGETHER are sufficient, but NEITHER statement ALONE is sufficient.

   Ⓓ EACH statement ALONE is sufficient.

   Ⓔ Statements (1) and (2) TOGETHER are NOT sufficient.

34-2. How much ethylene glycol antifreeze must be mixed with water to fill a car radiator?

   (1) The radiator has a capacity of 3 gallons.

   (2) The solution must be 40% water.

   Ⓐ Statement (1) ALONE is sufficient, but statement (2) alone is not sufficient.

   Ⓑ Statement (2) ALONE is sufficient, but statement (1) alone is not sufficient.

   Ⓒ BOTH statements (1) and (2) TOGETHER are sufficient, but NEITHER statement ALONE is sufficient.

   Ⓓ EACH statement ALONE is sufficient.

   Ⓔ Statements (1) and (2) TOGETHER are NOT sufficient.

34-3. What is Mary's age?

 (1) In two years, Mary will be twice as old as Beth is now.

 (2) Susan's age is the average of Mary's and Beth's ages.

 Ⓐ Statement (1) ALONE is sufficient, but statement (2) alone is not sufficient.

 Ⓑ Statement (2) ALONE is sufficient, but statement (1) alone is not sufficient.

 Ⓒ BOTH statements (1) and (2) TOGETHER are sufficient, but NEITHER statement ALONE is sufficient.

 Ⓓ EACH statement ALONE is sufficient.

 Ⓔ Statements (1) and (2) TOGETHER are NOT sufficient.

34-4. How many years old is Anne?

 (1) Next year, Anne will be half as old as her mother.

 (2) In five years, Anne will be twice as old as a decade ago.

 Ⓐ Statement (1) ALONE is sufficient, but statement (2) alone is not sufficient.

 Ⓑ Statement (2) ALONE is sufficient, but statement (1) alone is not sufficient.

 Ⓒ BOTH statements (1) and (2) TOGETHER are sufficient, but NEITHER statement ALONE is sufficient.

 Ⓓ EACH statement ALONE is sufficient.

 Ⓔ Statements (1) and (2) TOGETHER are NOT sufficient.

34-5. One number is five more than half a second number, which is evenly divisible by a third number. What is the second number?

(1) The first number is one less than the second.

(2) The third number is two less than half the second.

Ⓐ Statement (1) ALONE is sufficient, but statement (2) alone is not sufficient.

Ⓑ Statement (2) ALONE is sufficient, but statement (1) alone is not sufficient.

Ⓒ BOTH statements (1) and (2) TOGETHER are sufficient, but NEITHER statement ALONE is sufficient.

Ⓓ EACH statement ALONE is sufficient.

Ⓔ Statements (1) and (2) TOGETHER are NOT sufficient.

Answers: 34-1 Ⓔ, 34-2 Ⓒ, 34-3 Ⓔ, 34-4 Ⓑ, 34-5 Ⓐ

If you answered 34-1 **incorrectly, go to 35-1.**
If you answered 34-1 **correctly, go to 35-2.**

If you answered 34-2 **incorrectly, go to 35-1.**
If you answered 34-2 **correctly, go to 35-3.**

If you answered 34-3 **incorrectly, go to 35-2.**
If you answered 34-3 **correctly, go to 35-4.**

If you answered 34-4 **incorrectly, go to 35-3.**
If you answered 34-4 **correctly, go to 35-5.**

If you answered 34-5 **incorrectly, go to 35-4.**
If you answered 34-5 **correctly, go to 35-5.**

35-1. If paint costs $3.20 per quart, and a quart covers 20 square feet, how much will it cost to paint the outside of a cube 10 feet on each edge?

   Ⓐ $1.60
   Ⓑ $16.00
   Ⓒ $96.00
   Ⓓ $108.00
   Ⓔ $196.00

35-2. The area of parallelogram *AECD*

   Ⓐ is greater than 24 square units
   Ⓑ is less than 24 square units
   Ⓒ is equal to 24 square units
   Ⓓ is equal to 40 square units
   Ⓔ is equal to 60 square units

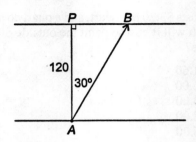

35-3. A boat leaves point A heading directly across the river to point P, 120 yards away. A swift current immediately changes the boat's direction, causing it to land instead at point B. How many yards is point B from the intended destination, P?

Ⓐ 40
Ⓑ 45
Ⓒ 60
Ⓓ 40√3
Ⓔ 60√3

35-4. In the figure above, rectangle ABCD has perimeter 22; the length of DC is 7. What is the area of △DEF?

Ⓐ 12
Ⓑ 8√3
Ⓒ 24
Ⓓ 32
Ⓔ 64

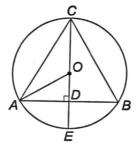

35-5. Equilateral triangle *ABC* is inscribed in a circle with center *O*, as shown. If the radius of the circle is 2, what is the area of triangle *ABC*?

(A) 3
(B) $2\sqrt{3}$
(C) $3\sqrt{2}$
(D) $3\sqrt{3}$
(E) $4\sqrt{2}$

Answers: 35-1 Ⓒ, 35-2 Ⓑ, 35-3 Ⓓ, 35-4 Ⓒ, 35-5 Ⓓ

If you answered 35-1 **incorrectly, go to 36-1.**
If you answered 35-1 **correctly, go to 36-2.**

If you answered 35-2 **incorrectly, go to 36-1.**
If you answered 35-2 **correctly, go to 36-3.**

If you answered 35-3 **incorrectly, go to 36-2.**
If you answered 35-3 **correctly, go to 36-4.**

If you answered 35-4 **incorrectly, go to 36-3.**
If you answered 35-4 **correctly, go to 36-5.**

If you answered 35-5 **incorrectly, go to 36-4.**
If you answered 35-5 **correctly, go to 36-5.**

36-1. Gasoline varies in cost from $0.96 to $1.12 per gallon. If a car's mileage varies from 16 to 24 miles per gallon, what is the difference between the most and least that the gasoline for a 480-mile trip will cost?

   Ⓐ $5.12
   Ⓑ $7.04
   Ⓒ $11.52
   Ⓓ $14.40
   Ⓔ $52.80

36-2. A ferry can transport 78 tons of vehicles. Automobiles range in weight from 1,800 to 3,200 pounds. What is the greatest number of automobiles that can be loaded onto the ferry?

   Ⓐ 23
   Ⓑ 41
   Ⓒ 48
   Ⓓ 62
   Ⓔ 86

36-3. Two quarts containing $\frac{2}{3}$ water and $\frac{1}{3}$ formula are mixed with three quarts containing $\frac{3}{8}$ water and $\frac{5}{8}$ formula. Approximately what percent of the combined five-quart mixture is water?

   Ⓐ 40%
   Ⓑ 45%
   Ⓒ 50%
   Ⓓ 55%
   Ⓔ 60%

36-4. How much water must be added to 10 gallons of 10% brine solution to decrease the concentration to 7%?

   Ⓐ 0–1.5 gal
   Ⓑ 1.5–3 gal
   Ⓒ 3–4.5 gal
   Ⓓ 4.5–6 gal
   Ⓔ 6+ gal

36-5. An incredible punch is composed of buttermilk, orange juice, and brandy. How many pints of orange juice are required to make $7\frac{1}{2}$ gallons of punch containing twice as much buttermilk as orange juice and three times as much orange juice as brandy?

   Ⓐ 16
   Ⓑ 18
   Ⓒ 20
   Ⓓ 22
   Ⓔ 24

Answers: 36-1 Ⓓ, 36-2 Ⓔ, 36-3 Ⓒ, 36-4 Ⓒ, 36-5 Ⓑ

If you answered 36-1 **incorrectly, go to 37-1.**
If you answered 36-1 **correctly, go to 37-2.**

If you answered 36-2 **incorrectly, go to 37-1.**
If you answered 36-2 **correctly, go to 37-3.**

If you answered 36-3 **incorrectly, go to 37-2.**
If you answered 36-3 **correctly, go to 37-4.**

If you answered 36-4 **incorrectly, go to 37-3.**
If you answered 36-4 **correctly, go to 37-5.**

If you answered 36-5 **incorrectly, go to 37-4.**
If you answered 36-5 **correctly, go to 37-5.**

37-1. If $(x + 1)$ times $(2x + 1)$ is an odd integer, then x must be

    Ⓐ an odd integer
    Ⓑ an even integer
    Ⓒ a prime number
    Ⓓ a composite number
    Ⓔ a negative integer

37-2. If x is a positive even number, then each of the following is odd EXCEPT

    Ⓐ $(x + 3)(x + 5)$
    Ⓑ $x^2 + 5$
    Ⓒ $x^2 + 6x + 9$
    Ⓓ $3x^2 + 4$
    Ⓔ $5(x + 3)$

37-3. A corporation triples its annual bonus to 50 of its employees. What percent of the employees' new bonus is the increase?

Ⓐ   50%
Ⓑ $66\frac{2}{3}$%
Ⓒ   100%
Ⓓ   200%
Ⓔ   300%

37-4. To rent an office, each member of a club must pay n dollars. If two more members join the club, the per-member payment would be reduced by two dollars. Which of the following could be the number of members currently in the club?

  I. 16
 II. 17
III. 18

Ⓐ I only
Ⓑ II only
Ⓒ I and III only
Ⓓ II and III only
Ⓔ I, II, and III

37-5. Grace has enough money to buy 45 bricks. If the bricks each cost 10 cents less, Grace could buy 5 more bricks. How much money does Grace have to spend on bricks?

Ⓐ $100
Ⓑ $50
Ⓒ $45
Ⓓ $40
Ⓔ $30

Answers: 37-1 Ⓑ, 37-2 Ⓓ, 37-3 Ⓑ, 37-4 Ⓔ, 37-5 ⒸⒸ

VERBAL SECTION

TIME: *75* Minutes
 41 Questions

General Directions: Your score on the verbal section will be based on how well you do on the questions presented and also on the number of questions you answer. You should try to pace yourself so that you have sufficient time to consider every question. If possible, answer all 41 questions in this section. Guess if you need to. Select the best answer choice for each question.
 Note: Because you are checking answers as you go, you should add about 5 to 10 minutes to your testing time.

Directions: Reading Comprehension

This passage is followed by questions based on its content. After reading the passage, choose the best answer to each question and choose the corresponding oval on the screen. Answer all questions about the passage on the basis of what is *stated* or *implied* in the passage. You may refer back to the passage.

Questions 1–4

Read the passage and answer all four questions that follow.

When the new discipline of social psychology was born at the beginning of this century, its first experiments were essentially adaptations of the suggestion demonstration. The subjects, usually
LINE college students, were asked to give their opinions or preferences
(5) concerning various matters; some time later they were again asked to state their choices, but now they were also informed of the opinions held by authorities or large groups of their peers on the same matters. (Often the alleged consensus was fictitious.) Most of these studies had substantially the same result: confronted with opin-
(10) ions contrary to their own, many subjects apparently shifted their judgments in the direction of the view of the majorities or the experts. Other studies reported that people's evaluations of the merit of a literary passage could be raised or lowered by ascribing the passage to different authors. Apparently the sheer weight of num-

(15)   bers or authority sufficed to change opinions, even when no argu-
       ments for the opinions themselves were provided.

       Now the very ease of success in these experiments arouses sus-
       picion. Did the subjects actually change their opinions, or were
       the experimental victories scored only on paper? On grounds of
(20)   common sense, one must question whether opinions are generally
       as watery as these studies indicate. There is some reason to won-
       der whether it was not the investigators who, in their enthusiasm
       for a theory, were suggestible, and whether the ostensibly gullible
       subjects were not providing answers which they thought good sub-
(25)   jects were expected to give.

       The investigations were guided by the underlying assumptions
       that people submit uncritically and painlessly to external manipu-
       lation by suggestion or prestige, and that any given idea or value
       can be "sold" or "unsold" without reference to its merits. We should
(30)   be skeptical, however, of the supposition that the power of social
       pressure necessarily implies uncritical submission to it; indepen-
       dence and the capacity to rise above group passion are also open to
       human beings. Further, one may question on psychological grounds
       whether it is possible to change a person's judgment of a situation
(35)   or an object without first changing his or her knowledge or as-
       sumptions about it.

1. The first experiments in social psychology appeared to demonstrate all of the following EXCEPT that

   Ⓐ many people will agree with what they believe to be the opin-
       ion held by the majority of their peers
   Ⓑ many people will agree with what they believe to be the opin-
       ion of experts
   Ⓒ many people change their opinions given good arguments
       for doing so
   Ⓓ an individual's evaluation of a literary work can be altered
       by ascribing the work to a different writer
   Ⓔ college students' opinions can be changed

2. The author implies that persons who altered their opinion on a controversial topic have most likely done so because they

    (A) have been influenced by overt social pressures
    (B) have been influenced by covert external manipulation
    (C) have learned more about the topic
    (D) have learned how experts judge the topic
    (E) are incapable of independent thought

3. The main point of the passage is to

    (A) question some assumptions about the influence of social pressures
    (B) show that a judgment of a situation cannot change without a change in the knowledge of the situation
    (C) demonstrate the gullibility of psychological investigators and their subjects
    (D) question the notion that any idea can be "sold" or "unsold"
    (E) support investigations into ideas of propaganda

4. With which of the following ideas would the author be most likely to agree?

    (A) Human beings can be programmed like machines.
    (B) Women are more likely to agree with men than with other women.
    (C) Women are more likely to agree with other women than with men.
    (D) Like women, men are capable of independent thought.
    (E) Like men, women submit uncritically to external manipulation.

Answers: 1 Ⓒ, 2 Ⓒ, 3 Ⓐ, 4 Ⓓ

If you answered **none** of the four reading questions **correctly, go to 5-1.**
If you answered **one** of the four reading questions **correctly, go to 5-2.**
If you answered **two** of the four reading questions **correctly, go to 5-3.**
If you answered **three** of the four reading questions **correctly, go to 5-4.**
If you answered **all four** of the reading questions **correctly, go to 5-5.**

<u>Directions</u>: Sentence Correction

Some part of each sentence is underlined; sometimes the whole sentence is underlined. Five choices for rephrasing the underlined part follow each sentence; the first choice repeats the original, and the other four are different. If the first choice seems better than the alternatives, choose that answer; if not, choose one of the others.

For each sentence, consider the requirements of standard written English. Your choice should be a correct and effective expression, not awkward or ambiguous. Focus on grammar, word choice, sentence construction, and punctuation. If a choice changes the meaning of the original sentence, do not select it.

5-1. As the rising toll of victims at Chernobyl made clear, <u>neither the scientists nor the ecologists knows</u> how to deal with the lethal effects of nuclear power plant accidents.

   Ⓐ neither the scientists nor the ecologists knows
   Ⓑ neither the scientists nor the ecologists know
   Ⓒ neither the scientists or the ecologists know
   Ⓓ neither the scientists together with the ecologists knows
   Ⓔ not the scientists or the ecologists know

5-2. As the shrill, piercing sound of the sirens <u>approached, several of my neighbors' dogs start</u> to howl, waking up every household in the neighborhood.

   Ⓐ approached, several of my neighbors' dogs start
   Ⓑ approached, several of my neighbors' dogs started
   Ⓒ approach, several of my neighbors' dogs starts
   Ⓓ approach, several of my neighbors' dogs start
   Ⓔ approach, several dogs of my neighbor started

5-3. That she neglected the children, that the house remained dirty and cluttered, and poor personal hygiene were reasons for firing the housekeeper.

- Ⓐ That she neglected the children, that the house remained dirty and cluttered, and poor personal hygiene were reasons for firing the housekeeper.
- Ⓑ That she neglected the children, house dirt and clutter, and poor personal hygiene were reasons for firing the housekeeper.
- Ⓒ That she neglected the children, dirty and cluttered house, and not good personal hygiene were reasons for firing the housekeeper.
- Ⓓ Neglect of the children, poor housecleaning, and that she had poor personal hygiene were reasons for firing the housekeeper.
- Ⓔ The housekeeper's neglect of the children, poor housecleaning, and lack of good personal hygiene were reasons for her firing.

5-4. After reconsidering my original judgments, I feel obliged to reread the book I maligned and which initially seemed so inconsequential.

- Ⓐ the book I maligned and which initially seemed so inconsequential
- Ⓑ the book in which I maligned what first seemed so inconsequential
- Ⓒ the maligned book which I initially deemed inconsequential
- Ⓓ the book I malign initially and inconsequentially
- Ⓔ the book I will malign because of its initial inconsequentiality

5-5. After battling hypertension for years, Marvin Murphy was relieved by the results of <u>his doctor's annual physical examination, which</u> indicated his blood pressure was normal.

    Ⓐ his doctor's annual physical examination, which
    Ⓑ his annual physical examination by which it was
    Ⓒ his annual physical examination, which
    Ⓓ an annual physical examination by his doctor, which
    Ⓔ his doctor's annual physical examination that

Answers: 5-1 Ⓑ, 5-2, Ⓑ, 5-3 Ⓔ, 5-4 Ⓐ, 5-5 Ⓓ

If you answered 5-1 **incorrectly, go to 6-1.**
If you answered 5-1 **correctly, go to 6-2.**

If you answered 5-2 **incorrectly, go to 6-1.**
If you answered 5-2 **correctly, go to 6-3.**

If you answered 5-3 **incorrectly, go to 6-2.**
If you answered 5-3 **correctly, go to 6-4.**

If you answered 5-4 **incorrectly, go to 6-3.**
If you answered 5-4 **correctly, go to 6-5.**

If you answered 5-5 **incorrectly, go to 6-4.**
If you answered 5-5 **correctly, go to 6-5.**

6-1. Because they refuse to follow the conventional dress code, neither Barbara nor her friends <u>is invited to pledge the local sorority</u>.

   Ⓐ   is invited to pledge the local sorority
   Ⓑ   are invited to pledge the local sorority
   Ⓒ   is pledging the local sorority
   Ⓓ   are pledging the local sorority
   Ⓔ   will pledge

6-2. <u>The governor understood that if she did not sign the new budget quick, the state</u> might begin the new fiscal year not only with a significant deficit but also with no budgetary guidelines for lessening that deficit.

   Ⓐ   The governor understood that if she did not sign the state budget quick, the state
   Ⓑ   Not signing the new state budget quickly, the governor knew that the state
   Ⓒ   Without a quick signing, the governor new that as far as the budget was concerned, the state
   Ⓓ   The governor understood that if she did not sign the new budget quickly, the state
   Ⓔ   The governor understood that if she did not sign the budget and sign it quickly, that the effects of that action might cause the state to

6-3. If all the local candidates would have participated in the debate, the voters would have a better understanding of the contending points of view.

 Ⓐ If all the local candidates would have participated in the debate
 Ⓑ If all the candidates had engaged in local debate
 Ⓒ If all the local candidates had participated in the debate
 Ⓓ Debating as they should have
 Ⓔ After a debate

6-4. The statement that the consequences of smoking marijuana are no greater than drinking alcohol is an argument often given for legalizing the use of marijuana.

 Ⓐ that the consequences of smoking marijuana are no greater than drinking alcohol
 Ⓑ that the consequences of marijuana are no greater than the consequences of alcohol
 Ⓒ that the consequences of drinking alcohol are as great as the consequences of smoking marijuana
 Ⓓ that the consequences of smoking marijuana are no greater than those of drinking alcohol
 Ⓔ that the consequences of smoking marijuana are as great as drinking alcohol are great

6-5. The vice president of the local bank spoke for a half an hour and told his colleague that he, his colleague, must consider finding a new job, or accept a reduction in salary.

 Ⓐ for a half an hour and told his colleague that he, his colleague, must consider finding a new job
 Ⓑ for a half hour and told his colleague that he must consider to find a new job
 Ⓒ for half an hour and told his colleague that the colleague must get employed by a new bank
 Ⓓ for half an hour telling his colleague that he must find a new job
 Ⓔ for a half hour and told his colleague to consider finding a new job

Answers: 6-1 Ⓑ, 6-2 Ⓓ, 6-3 Ⓒ, 6-4 Ⓓ, 6-5 Ⓔ

If you answered 6-1 **incorrectly, go to 7-1.**
If you answered 6-1 **correctly, go to 7-2.**

If you answered 6-2 **incorrectly, go to 7-1.**
If you answered 6-2 **correctly, go to 7-3.**

If you answered 6-3 **incorrectly, go to 7-2.**
If you answered 6-3 **correctly, go to 7-4.**

If you answered 6-4 **incorrectly, go to 7-3.**
If you answered 6-4 **correctly, go to 7-5.**

If you answered 6-5 **incorrectly, go to 7-4.**
If you answered 6-5 **correctly, go to 7-5.**

7-1. <u>According to legend, while working as an engineer, a train collided with Casey Jones and killed him</u>, but he remains with us as part of a rich American folk history of songs and legends.

    Ⓐ According to legend, while working as an engineer, a train collided with Casey Jones and killed him

    Ⓑ The legendary engineer Casey Jones experienced a collision with another train on the job that killed him

    Ⓒ Engineer Casey Jones was killed when his train collided with another

    Ⓓ Driving the engine, another train killed Casey Jones

    Ⓔ An engineer's work brought Casey Jones to his death when he was hit by a train while working

7-2. Among the members of the legal profession there are <u>many who try to keep their clients out of court</u> and save their clients' money.

    Ⓐ many who try to keep their clients out of court

    Ⓑ ones who try to keep their clients out of court

    Ⓒ they who try to keep their clients out of court

    Ⓓ many of whom try to keep their clients out of court

    Ⓔ a few who try to keep their clients out of court

7-3. Understanding the droning lecturer with comprehension required the intense concentration of the class members present in the lecture hall, all of whom were students.

 Ⓐ Understanding the droning lecturer with comprehension required the intense concentration of the class members present in the lecture hall, all of whom were students.

 Ⓑ Comprehending the droning lecturer with the intense concentration of the class members present.

 Ⓒ To understand the droning lecturer, the students had to concentrate intensely.

 Ⓓ As the lecturer droned on, the students found themselves required to concentrate in order to understand.

 Ⓔ The students listening to the lecturer, who was droning, increased their comprehension by concentrating.

7-4. Clarity and brilliance, in addition to enjoying the beauty: these are the qualities of a beautiful diamond and along with it a beautiful painting.

 Ⓐ Clarity and brilliance, in addition to enjoying the beauty: these are the qualities of a beautiful diamond and along with it a beautiful painting.

 Ⓑ Clarity, brilliance, and beauty: these are the qualities of a beautiful diamond as well as a beautiful painting.

 Ⓒ To be clear, brilliant and beautiful is to be either a beautiful diamond or a beautiful painting.

 Ⓓ Diamonds and paintings give out clarity, brilliance, and beauty.

 Ⓔ Where there are clarity and brilliance and beauty there are the qualities of not only a beautiful diamond but also a beautiful painting.

7-5. With the advent of sound, many stars of silent films found themselves unable to adapt to the "talkies" <u>because their speaking voices were either unattractive or their acting consisted of only exaggerated pantomime.</u>

    (A) because their speaking voices were either unattractive or their acting consisted of only exaggerated pantomime

    (B) because of their voices either being unattractive or their acting being exaggerated pantomime

    (C) with their unattractive voices and exaggerated pantomime

    (D) because of their unattractive voices or exaggerated pantomime that didn't require sound

    (E) because either their voices were unattractive or their acting was only exaggerated pantomime

Answers: 7-1 Ⓒ, 7-2 Ⓐ, 7-3 Ⓒ, 7-4 Ⓑ, 7-5 Ⓔ

If you answered 7-1 **incorrectly**, go to **8-1.**
If you answered 7-1 **correctly**, go to **8-2.**

If you answered 7-2 **incorrectly**, go to **8-1.**
If you answered 7-2 **correctly**, go to **8-3.**

If you answered 7-3 **incorrectly**, go to **8-2.**
If you answered 7-3 **correctly**, go to **8-4.**

If you answered 7-4 **incorrectly**, go to **8-3.**
If you answered 7-4 **correctly**, go to **8-5.**

If you answered 7-5 **incorrectly**, go to **8-4.**
If you answered 7-5 **correctly**, go to **8-5.**

Directions: Critical Reasoning

As you read the brief passage, you must follow the line of reasoning using only commonsense standards of logic. No knowledge of formal logic is required. Then you must choose the best answer, realizing that several choices may be possible, but only one will be best.

8-1. When President Lyndon Johnson signed the Voting Rights Act in 1965, he used fifty pens, handling them out as souvenirs to a joyous gathering in the President's Room of the Capitol, where Abraham Lincoln had signed the Emancipation Proclamation on January 1, 1863. When President Reagan signed an extension of the Voting Rights Act in 1982, he spoke affectionately of "the right to vote," signed with a single pen, and then concluded the four-minute ceremony by rising from his desk, announcing, "It's done."

If the passage above is true, which of the following is most probably true?

Ⓐ The Voting Rights Act did not require an extension.
Ⓑ The Voting Rights Act is not significantly related to the Emancipation Proclamation.
Ⓒ President Reagan saw himself as more like Lincoln than did Johnson.
Ⓓ President Reagan did not regard the extension of the act as an occasion for fanfare.
Ⓔ President Reagan objected strenuously to an extension of the Voting Rights Act.

8-2. Don't spend the night tossing and turning! Take Eezy-Z's for a sound, restful sleep . . . you'll wake up refreshed, energized, with no drugged-up hangover. Remember . . . Eezy-Z's when you need that sleep!

Which of the following is not a claim of Eezy-Z's?

Ⓐ A good night's sleep
Ⓑ Added energy
Ⓒ No aftereffects
Ⓓ Quickly falling asleep
Ⓔ A restful slumber

8-3   Which of the following most logically completes the passage at the blank below?

In a civilized society, members of the community will often defer to others, even against their own better judgment. This situation may occur in public, in gatherings with strangers, or in the household with one's family or friends. It is a sign of a more sophisticated culture that one's immediate interests are thought to be secondary to those of another. On first examination this may seem to be selflessness, but _____.

Ⓐ   actually it is not; it is just ignorance
Ⓑ   rather it may take many names
Ⓒ   actually it is
Ⓓ   to some extent it does serve the ends of the individual concerned
Ⓔ   sometimes it can harbor animosities and hostility

8-4. Which of the following most logically completes the passage at the blank below?

The English language, lacking the rigidity of most European tongues, has been bent and shaped in at least as many ways as there are countries or regions where it is spoken. Though purists often argue that "standard" English is spoken only in certain high-minded enclaves of the American northeast, the fact is that it is the most widely used language in the world and is not likely to yield that distinction for a very long time, if ever. Nevertheless, _____.

Ⓐ   it remains one of the most widely spoken languages throughout the world
Ⓑ   it can be understood in just about very corner of the globe
Ⓒ   even making allowances for regional peculiarities, English as it is spoken has been much abused in recent times
Ⓓ   though we may be proud of these facts, English remains one of the most difficult languages to master
Ⓔ   English, as it is spoken, lacks the rigidity of the classical and more historic European languages

8-5. Of all the petty little pieces of bureaucratic arrogance, it's hard to imagine one smaller than that of the city schools in not admitting a British subject whose father is working—as a legal alien—for a nearby petrochemical company. Someone apparently decided that if the boy had been an illegal alien, a recent U.S. Supreme Court decision in a Texas case would have required the district to admit him, but since he is legal, there is no such requirement. That is nonsense.

Which of the following best expresses the point of the author's argument?

(A) The city schools outside Texas should not base decisions on a precedent set in Texas.

(B) The stability of a parent's job should have no bearing on the educational opportunity offered his or her child.

(C) Bureaucratic arrogance has resulted in unsound legal interpretation.

(D) Legal sense and nonsense are sometimes indistinguishable.

(E) Both legal and illegal aliens should receive equal treatment.

Answers: 8-1 ⓓ, 8-2 ⓓ, 8-3 ⓓ, 8-4 ⓒ, 8-5 ⓒ

Check your answer and continue to the next reading passage.

Questions 9–12

Read the passage and answer all four questions that follow.

In economics, demand implies something slightly different from the common meaning of the term. The layperson uses the term to mean the amount that is demanded of an item. Thus, if the price were to decrease and individuals wanted more of an item, it is commonly said that demand increases. To an economist, demand is a relationship between a series of prices and a series of corresponding quantities that are demanded at these prices. If one reads the previous sentence carefully, it should become apparent that there is a distinction between the quantity demanded and demand. This distinction is often a point of confusion. Demand is a relationship between price and quantities demanded, and therefore suggests the effect of one (e.g., price) on the other (e.g., quantity demanded). Therefore, knowledge of the demand for a product enables one to predict how much more of a good will be purchased if price decreases. But the increase in quantity demanded does not mean demand has increased, since the relationship between price and quantity demanded (i.e., the demand for the product) has not changed. Demand shifts when there is a change in income, expectations, taste, etc., such that a different quantity of the good is demanded at the same price.

In almost all cases, a consumer wants more of an item if the price decreases. This relationship between price and quantity demanded is so strong that it is referred to as the "law of demand." This "law" can be explained by the income and substitution effects. The income effect occurs because price increases reduce the purchasing power of the individual and, thus, the quantity demanded of goods must decrease. The substitution effect reflects the consumer's desire to get the "best buy." Accordingly, if the price of good A increases, the individual will tend to substitute another good and purchase less of good A. The negative correlation between price and quantity demanded is also explained by the law of diminishing marginal utility. According to this law, the additional utility the consumer gains from consuming a good decreases as successively more units of the good are consumed. Because the additional units yield less utility or satisfaction, the consumer is willing to purchase more only if the price of the good decreases.

9. Which of the following is an instance of a shift in demand as it is understood by economists?

   I. A market is selling two pounds of coffee for the price it usually charges for one pound; the *demand* for coffee has increased.
   II. The success of a television program featuring cartoon turtles has increased the *demand* for an oat cereal in turtle shapes.
   III. Because of the rail strike, California lettuce costs more in Chicago, and the *demand* for lettuce has fallen.

   (A) I only
   (B) II only
   (C) III only
   (D) I and III only
   (E) I, II, and III

10. According to the passage, a change in demand, as economists use the term, would occur in which of the following situations?

   (A) The gasoline price increases, resulting in the increased sale of compact cars (whose price remains stable).
   (B) The gasoline price increases, resulting in the increased sale of compact cars (which go on sale in response to increased gas prices).
   (C) The gasoline price decreases on the same day that a new 43-mpg car enters the market.
   (D) A federal order imposes a price ceiling on gasoline.
   (E) A federal order lifts price regulations for gasoline.

11. Assume that firms develop an orange-flavored breakfast drink high in vitamin C that is a good substitute for orange juice but sells for less. Based upon assertions in the passage, which of the following would occur with respect to the demand for orange juice?

Ⓐ Health food stores would resurrect the law of diminishing marginal utility.

Ⓑ Assuming that the price of fresh orange juice remained constant, more orange juice would be consumed.

Ⓒ The law of demand would prevail.

Ⓓ Assuming that the price of fresh orange juice remained constant, the demand would not change.

Ⓔ There is not enough information in the passage to answer this question.

12. The purpose of the passage is to

Ⓐ introduce several important definitions

Ⓑ outline the theory of supply on demand

Ⓒ correct the layperson's economic misapprehensions about prices

Ⓓ introduce a student to a theory of marketing

Ⓔ question a popular misunderstanding of "demand"

Answers: 9 Ⓑ, 10 Ⓐ, 11 Ⓒ, 12 Ⓐ

If you answered **none** of the four reading questions **correctly, go to 13-1.**
If you answered **one** of the four reading questions **correctly, go to 13-2.**
If you answered **two** of the four reading questions **correctly, go to 13-3.**
If you answered **three** of the four reading questions **correctly, go to 13-4.**
If you answered **all four** of the reading questions **correctly, go to 13-5.**

13-1. To the Chair:

At the October 7 meeting it was decided that no two officers would hold positions on the same committee. It has recently come to my attention that both Charles S. Smith and Arnold Krunkle will be serving in some capacity on the Building and Maintenance Committee, and both have been nominated for officer status. As you know, this is in direct disregard for the rules as voted by the membership last October 7. I would hope that sufficient action be taken by the Disciplinary Committee (on which committee both of the above are members) so that this problem will be remedied.

Sincerely, Irving H. Fortnash

Which of the following is the essential flaw that the writer of the letter fails to notice?

Ⓐ Smith and Krunkle are already serving together on the Disciplinary Committee.

Ⓑ The Chairman has no power in the matter.

Ⓒ The membership cannot pass rules limiting members.

Ⓓ Smith and Krunkle are not yet officers.

Ⓔ Building and Maintenance is actually two committees.

13-2. Socrates believed that virtue is the outcome of knowledge and that evil is fundamentally ignorance. This is an early instance of the belief that the intellectual or rational is dominant in man and morally superior.

Socrates' point of view, as described in the passage, implies which of the following conclusions about evil people?

Ⓐ They are ignorant.

Ⓑ They are unable to achieve complete self-knowledge.

Ⓒ They are inherently virtuous but incapable of showing it.

Ⓓ They are often either ignorant or irrational.

Ⓔ They often dominate those who are morally superior.

13-3. To the Chair:

At the October 7 meeting it was decided that no two officers would hold positions on the same committee. It has recently come to my attention that both Charles S. Smith and Arnold Krunkle will be serving in some capacity on the Building and Maintenance Committee, and both have been nominated for officer status. As you know, this is in direct disregard for the rules as voted by the membership last October 7. I would hope that sufficient action be taken by the Disciplinary Committee (on which committee both of the above are members) so that this problem will be remedied.

Sincerely, Irving H. Fortnash

Which of the following most completely and reasonably describes actions that may occur in the near future?

Ⓐ Fortnash resigns his membership.
Ⓑ Either Smith or Krunkle resigns his membership.
Ⓒ Krunkle resigns his committee post on the Building and Maintenance Committee.
Ⓓ Smith resigns his position on the Building and Maintenance Committee.
Ⓔ One of the two (Smith or Krunkle) resigns his position on the Building and Maintenance Committee, and the other resigns his position on the Disciplinary Committee.

13-4. All race-car lovers enjoy classical music.
No backgammon players enjoy classical music.
All those who enjoy classical music also enjoy fine wine.

If each of the above statements is true, which of the following must also be true?

Ⓐ Everyone who plays backgammon enjoys fine wine.
Ⓑ No one who enjoys fine wine plays backgammon.
Ⓒ No backgammon players are race-car lovers.
Ⓓ No backgammon players enjoy fine wine.
Ⓔ No race-car lover enjoys fine wine.

13-5. It has been proven that the "lie detector" can be fooled. If one is truly unaware that one is lying, when in fact one is, then the "lie detector" is worthless.

Without contradicting his or her own statements, the author might present which of the following arguments as a strong point in favor of the lie detector?

(A) The methodology used by investigative critics of the lie detector is itself highly flawed.

(B) Law-enforcement agencies have purchased too many detectors to abandon them now.

(C) Circumstantial evidence might be more useful in a criminal case than is personal testimony.

(D) The very threat of a lie-detector test has led a significant number of criminals to confess.

(E) People are never "truly aware" that they are lying.

Answers: 13-1 Ⓓ, 13-2 Ⓐ, 13-3 Ⓔ, 13-4 Ⓒ, 13-5 Ⓓ

If you answered 13-1 **incorrectly, go to 14-1.**
If you answered 13-1 **correctly, go to 14-2.**

If you answered 13-2 **incorrectly, go to 14-1.**
If you answered 13-2 **correctly, go to 14-3.**

If you answered 13-3 **incorrectly, go to 14-2.**
If you answered 13-3 **correctly, go to 14-4.**

If you answered 13-4 **incorrectly, go to 14-3.**
If you answered 13-4 **correctly, go to 14-5.**

If you answered 13-5 **incorrectly, go to 14-4.**
If you answered 13-5 **correctly, go to 14-5.**

14-1. On a swimming team—
All freestyle swimmers are Olympic winners.
No blue-eyed swimmer is an Olympic winner.
All Olympic winners go on to lucrative professional careers.

If it is determined that all of the above are true, then which of the following must also be true about the swimming team?

Ⓐ All those who go on to professional careers are freestyle swimmers.
Ⓑ Only freestyle swimmers go on to professional careers.
Ⓒ Some blue-eyed swimmers go on to lucrative professional careers.
Ⓓ No blue-eyed swimmer is a freestyle swimmer.
Ⓔ Only blue-eyed swimmers don't go on to lucrative careers.

14-2. A researcher has concluded that women are just as capable as men in math but that their skills are not developed because society expects them to develop other and more diverse abilities.

Which of the following is a basic assumption of the researcher?

Ⓐ Ability in math is more important than ability in more diverse subjects.
Ⓑ Ability in math is less important than ability in more diverse subjects.
Ⓒ Women and men should be equally capable in math.
Ⓓ Women might be more capable than men in math.
Ⓔ Women tend to conform to social expectations.

14-3. The census showed a sharp rise during the last decade in the number of Americans living together as unmarried couples, but a more recent increase in the marriage rate this year, the first of this decade, suggests that matrimony will make a comeback over the next ten years.

Which of the following best refutes the argument above?

Ⓐ One of the causes of more marriages is that people have waited until they were older to marry.

Ⓑ Although information about this year's marriage rate is not complete, most analysts consider it to be reliable.

Ⓒ Many of those marrying this year were couples who had lived together during the previous decade.

Ⓓ The number of Americans living together did not rise at a consistent rate during the previous decade.

Ⓔ The marriage rate increased dramatically ten years ago and fell even more dramatically in following years.

14-4. The census showed a sharp rise during the last decade in the number of Americans living together as unmarried couples, but a more recent increase in the marriage rate this year, the first of this decade, suggests that matrimony will make a comeback over the next ten years.

With which of the following would the author be likely to agree?

Ⓐ Americans should not live together as unmarried couples.

Ⓑ Matrimony is preferable to living together.

Ⓒ Economic circumstances have made matrimony attractive as a way of paying less income tax.

Ⓓ The attitudes of young people now are altogether different from the attitudes of young people during the last ten years.

Ⓔ Prevailing attitudes toward marriage tend to persist for more than one year.

14-5. Money talks as never before in state and local elections, and the main cause is TV advertising. Thirty seconds can go as high as $5000. Political fundraising is one of the few growth industries left in America. The way to stop the waste might be for television to be paid by state and local government, at a standard rate, to provide air time to all candidates to debate the issues. This might be boring at first. But eventually candidates might actually brush up their debating skills and electrify the TV audience with content, not style.

Which of the following presuppositions is (are) necessary to the argument above?

   I. Candidates spend too much money on television advertising.
  II. Television can be used to educate and inform the public.
 III. The freedom of speech doesn't abridge the freedom to spend.

  Ⓐ I only
  Ⓑ II only
  Ⓒ III only
  Ⓓ I and II only
  Ⓔ I, II, and III

Answers: 14-1 ⓓ, 14-2 ⓔ, 14-3 ⓔ, 14-4 ⓔ, 14-5 ⓓ

If you answered 14-1 **incorrectly, go to 15-1.**
If you answered 14-1 **correctly, go to 15-2.**

If you answered 14-2 **incorrectly, go to 15-1.**
If you answered 14-2 **correctly, go to 15-3.**

If you answered 14-3 **incorrectly, go to 15-2.**
If you answered 14-3 **correctly, go to 15-4.**

If you answered 14-4 **incorrectly, go to 15-3.**
If you answered 14-4 **correctly, go to 15-5.**

If you answered 14-5 **incorrectly, go to 15-4.**
If you answered 14-5 **correctly, go to 15-5.**

15-1. The public soon became outraged at <u>the Cabinet member whom betrayed the public trust</u>, and they demanded his ouster by the prime minister.

   Ⓐ the Cabinet member whom betrayed the public trust
   Ⓑ the untrustworthy Cabinet member
   Ⓒ the Cabinet member with whom they betrayed the public trust
   Ⓓ the Cabinet member who, after betraying the public trust
   Ⓔ the Cabinet member who betrayed the public trust

15-2. Arthur was sorry he had agreed to employ his cousin's law firm, because <u>at first meeting with the lawyer, the lawyer seemed indecisive.</u>

   Ⓐ at first meeting with the lawyer, the lawyer seemed indecisive
   Ⓑ at first meeting, the lawyer seemed indecisive
   Ⓒ at first meeting the lawyer seems indecisive
   Ⓓ at first meeting, he seemed an indecisive lawyer
   Ⓔ at first meeting the lawyer, he seems indecisive

15-3. The most recent National Conference of Mathematics Teachers addressed the problem of convincing students who rely on calculators that the ability to calculate mentally or with pencil and paper is important.

Ⓐ The most recent National Conference of Mathematics Teachers addressed the problem of convincing students who

Ⓑ The most recent problem faced by the National Conference of Mathematics Teachers was convincing students who

Ⓒ The most recent National Conference of Mathematics Teachers addressed the problem of convincing students whom

Ⓓ Most recently, the National Conference of Mathematics Teachers addressed the problem of convincing students who

Ⓔ The most recent National Conference of Mathematics Teachers addressed those students who

15-4. No matter what experience you have had with forest fires, if you would have witnessed the fire roaring down through the canyon, you would have been terrified.

Ⓐ if you would have witnessed
Ⓑ if you witnessed
Ⓒ if you could witness
Ⓓ if you had witnessed
Ⓔ when you witnessed

15-5. Recounting a painful childhood experience, the woman remembered that her father was very angry when she failed the fifth grade because she could see him shaking with anger.

   (A) Recounting a painful childhood experience, the woman remembered that her father was very angry when she failed the fifth grade because she could see him shaking with anger.

   (B) Recounting a painful childhood experience, the woman recounted that her father was shaking with anger when she failed the fifth grade.

   (C) Painfully, the woman remembered when she failed the fifth grade and when her father was shaking with anger.

   (D) The failure of the fifth grade and her father's anger were painful for the woman recounting the experience.

   (E) The woman described her father's shaking with anger when he learned that she had failed the fifth grade.

Answers: 15-1 Ⓔ, 15-2 Ⓑ, 15-3 Ⓐ, 15-4 Ⓓ, 15-5 Ⓔ

If you answered 15-1 **incorrectly, go to 16-1.**
If you answered 15-1 **correctly, go to 16-2.**

If you answered 15-2 **incorrectly, go to 16-1.**
If you answered 15-2 **correctly, go to 16-3.**

If you answered 15-3 **incorrectly, go to 16-2.**
If you answered 15-3 **correctly, go to 16-4.**

If you answered 15-4 **incorrectly, go to 16-3.**
If you answered 15-4 **correctly, go to 16-5.**

If you answered 15-5 **incorrectly, go to 16-4.**
If you answered 15-5 **correctly, go to 16-5.**

16-1. Some Detroit car manufacturers promise to give rebates to new customers between June 1 and June 30, <u>granting the returned money during June but not thereafter.</u>

    Ⓐ granting the returned money during June but not thereafter

    Ⓑ during June but not thereafter

    Ⓒ but not thereafter

    Ⓓ no money after that

    Ⓔ denying those who purchase before or after June

16-2. Ella was unable to attend her son's basketball games; because she worked the night shift, <u>arriving at 10 P.M. and leaving at 6 A.M.</u>

    Ⓐ arriving at 10 P.M. and leaving at 6 A.M.

    Ⓑ having arrived at 10 P.M. and leaving at 6 A.M.

    Ⓒ she arrived at 10 P.M. and left at 6 A.M.

    Ⓓ with an arrival at 6 and a departure at 10

    Ⓔ from 10 P.M. to 6 A.M.

16-3. Every year the banker warned his borrowers that <u>planning a career in business is often easier than to pursue it.</u>

   Ⓐ planning a career in business is often easier than to pursue it

   Ⓑ to plan a career in business is often easier than pursuing it

   Ⓒ planning a business career is often easier than pursuing it

   Ⓓ the planning of a business career is often easier than its pursuit

   Ⓔ a business career plan is often easier than a business career

16-4. <u>After having read through the stack of bills laying on my desk,</u> I began wondering whether to file for bankruptcy or to try to consolidate my debts by a new loan.

   Ⓐ After having read through the stack of bills laying on my desk

   Ⓑ Having read through the stack of bills lying on my desk

   Ⓒ Reading through the stack of bills littering my desk

   Ⓓ The stack of bills lying on the desk, after I had read them

   Ⓔ After having read through the stack of bills lying on my desk

16-5. <u>According to statistics, one in every two marriages ends in di-</u><u>vorce, most often involving married couples not wealthy enough</u><u>to "buy" each other's love.</u>

   Ⓐ According to statistics, one in every two marriages ends in divorce, most often involving married couples not wealthy enough to "buy" each other's love.

   Ⓑ Statistically, fifty percent of marriages are divorces, often caused by people not wealthy enough to "buy" each other's love.

   Ⓒ According to statistics, half of all marriages end in divorce, often because the partners are not wealthy enough to "buy" each other's love.

   Ⓓ Statistics tell half of all marriages that they will end in divorce, often because the partners are not wealthy enough to "buy" each other's love.

   Ⓔ Those who cannot "buy" each other's love are destined for divorce in at least half the cases, according to statistics.

358 GMAT CAT PRACTICE TEST

Answers: 16-1 ©, 16-2 ©, 16-3 ©, 16-4 ⑧, 16-5 ©

If you answered 16-1 **incorrectly, go to 17-1.**
If you answered 16-1 **correctly, go to 17-2.**

If you answered 16-2 **incorrectly, go to 17-1.**
If you answered 16-2 **correctly, go to 17-3.**

If you answered 16-3 **incorrectly, go to 17-2.**
If you answered 16-3 **correctly, go to 17-4.**

If you answered 16-4 **incorrectly, go to 17-3.**
If you answered 16-4 **correctly, go to 17-5.**

If you answered 16-5 **incorrectly, go to 17-4.**
If you answered 16-5 **correctly, go to 17-5.**

17-1. Though the receptions at the embassy were usually formal and uneventful, to everyone's surprise a fight broke out when the foreign ambassador <u>took a joke serious and punched the jokester hardly.</u>

  Ⓐ took a joke serious and punched the jokester hardly
  Ⓑ took a joke seriously and hardly punched the jokester
  Ⓒ hardly took a joke and seriously punched the jokester
  Ⓓ took a joke seriously and punched the jokester hard
  Ⓔ gave a hard punch to a serious jokester

17-2. Although there was no contest for senator or governor and voters were expected to be apathetic, the referenda proved so controversial that 90% <u>of those registered showed up at the polls.</u>

  Ⓐ of those registered showed up at the polls
  Ⓑ of the registered showed up at the polls
  Ⓒ of the registered voters showed up at the polls to vote
  Ⓓ were registered to vote
  Ⓔ who were not showed up at the polls

17-3. With pennants waving and the band playing, <u>the huge crowd at the football game cheered the players making the touchdown from the stands</u>.

    Ⓐ the huge crowd at the football game cheered the players making the touchdown from the stands

    Ⓑ the huge crowd from the stands at the football game cheered the players making the touchdown

    Ⓒ making the touchdown, the huge football game crowd cheered the players from the stands

    Ⓓ the huge crowd at the football game cheered from the stands as the players made the touchdown

    Ⓔ cheers arose from the stands as the football game players made the touchdown

17-4. According to the employers, the new union contract forbade <u>working overtime past regular hours, and those who did not comply to this</u> were severely censured.

    Ⓐ working overtime past regular hours, and those who did not comply to this

    Ⓑ working overtime, and those who did so

    Ⓒ working after hours, and those not compliant

    Ⓓ overtime, and those who did not comply with this

    Ⓔ noncompliance with the antiovertime clause

17-5. Because Carla has always been careful to treat all her daycare children affectionately and <u>she likes everyone as much as him</u>, he does not feel special.

    Ⓐ she likes everyone as much as him

    Ⓑ she likes everyone as much as she

    Ⓒ she has a liking for everyone equal to him

    Ⓓ she has a liking for everyone equal to he

    Ⓔ everyone she likes is equal to him

Answers: 17-1 ⓓ, 17-2 ⓐ, 17-3 ⓓ, 17-4 ⓑ, 17-5 ⓐ

Check your answer and continue to the next reading passage.

Questions 18-21

Read the following passage and answer the four questions that follow.

Each method of counting bacteria has advantages and disadvantages; none is 100 percent accurate. Cell counts may be made with a counting chamber, a slide marked with a grid to facilitate count-
LINE ing of cells and to determine the volume of liquid in the area
(5) counted. Counts are made under a microscope and calculations made to determine the number of cells per ml of the original culture. Electronic cell counters can be used to count cells suspended in a liquid medium which passes through a hole small enough to allow the passage of only one bacterial cell at a time. Smear counts
(10) are similar to cell counts: a known volume of culture is spread over a known area (1 cm²) of a slide and then stained. Counts are made from several microscope fields, and calculations are made. In membrane filter counts a known volume of a culture is passed through a filter, which is then examined microscopically for cells.
(15) The advantage of cell counts, smear counts, and membrane filter counts is that they are quickly accomplished with little complicated equipment; however, both living and dead cells are counted.
The serial-dilution method involves the making of a series of dilutions, usually by a factor of 10, into a nutrient medium. The
(20) highest dilution producing growth gives a rough indication of the population of the original culture; for example, if the highest dilution to produce growth is the 1:100 dilution, the original culture had between 100 and 1,000 cells per ml.
Plate counts are made by making serial dilutions (usually in
(25) sterile tap water or an isotonic solution) of the original culture. Samples of known volume of the dilutions are transferred to petri dishes and mixed with nutrient agar. After a suitable incubation period the colonies on the plates with between 30 and 300 colonies are counted. Because each colony is assumed to have arisen
(30) from a single cell, calculations can be made to determine the original population size. Plate counts have the advantage of not including dead cells, and they can be used when the population is so low as to make other methods impractical, but they require more time than direct counts, and they detect only those organisms that can
(35) grow under the conditions of incubation; the development of one colony from more than one cell is also a source of error.

18. The author's purpose in this passage is to

   Ⓐ argue for the development of a fully accurate counting method
   Ⓑ discuss the advantages of several methods of counting cells
   Ⓒ show that new counting methods have surpassed those used in the past
   Ⓓ give instruction in the performance of cell counts
   Ⓔ describe a variety of methods of counting bacteria

19. We can infer that no method of bacteria counting is wholly accurate because

   I. the number of cells is likely to be so large
   II. the cells are microscopic in size
   III. both living and dead cells are counted

   Ⓐ II only
   Ⓑ I and II only
   Ⓒ I and III only
   Ⓓ II and III only
   Ⓔ I, II, and III

20. If we know the total bacteria cell volume in a sample, to determine the bacteria cell count we must also know

    I. the volume of a single cell
    II. the volume of the nutrient culture
    III. the volume of the calibrated centrifuge tube

    Ⓐ I only
    Ⓑ II only
    Ⓒ III only
    Ⓓ I and II only
    Ⓔ II and III only

21. Which of the following best describes the audience to which this passage is probably addressed?

    Ⓐ Advanced students in microbiology
    Ⓑ Casual readers of a scientific magazine
    Ⓒ Elementary school students
    Ⓓ Introductory college biology students
    Ⓔ High school mathematics students

Answers: 18 ⓔ, 19 ⓑ, 20 ⓐ, 21 ⓓ

If you answered **none** of the four reading questions **correctly, go to 22-1.**
If you answered **one** of the four reading questions **correctly, go to 22-2.**
If you answered **two** of the four reading questions **correctly, go to 22-3.**
If you answered **three** of the four reading questions **correctly, go to 22-4.**
If you answered **all four** of the reading questions **correctly, go to 22-5.**

22-1. Most citizens of nineteenth-century London believed that remaining respectable was more important and more difficult than <u>to question</u> the virtues of the age.

Ⓐ to question
Ⓑ questioning
Ⓒ the question of
Ⓓ a question over
Ⓔ all

22-2. Opinions about the ballot issue, of course, <u>varies according with the ethnic and economic status</u> of each voter, and for this reason, the poll of a small sample of voters is of no use.

Ⓐ varies according with the ethnic and economic status
Ⓑ varies according to ethnic and economic status
Ⓒ changes with ethnicity and the economy
Ⓓ vary according to the ethnic and economic status
Ⓔ vary according to ethnic and economical status

22-3. While declaring his support for a nuclear weapons freeze, <u>a small bomb exploded some distance from the Cabinet minister, who was startled but unharmed</u>.

   Ⓐ a small bomb exploded some distance from the Cabinet minister, who was startled but unharmed

   Ⓑ a small bomb startled the Cabinet minister, but did not harm him

   Ⓒ a small bomb startled the Cabinet minister from a distance, but did not harm him

   Ⓓ the Cabinet minister was startled by a bomb that exploded some distance from him, but unharmed

   Ⓔ the Cabinet minister was startled but unharmed by a small bomb that exploded some distance from him

22-4. Having given up hope of influencing the vote, several disgruntled visitors had left the board meeting <u>before it had considered the new municipal tax cut</u>.

   Ⓐ before it had considered the new municipal tax cut

   Ⓑ before it considered the new municipal tax cut

   Ⓒ before the members considered the new municipal tax cut

   Ⓓ with the consideration of the new municipal tax cut yet to come

   Ⓔ previous to the new municipal tax cut

22-5. <u>Not gaining sufficient legislative approval, thousands of women vowed to keep the Equal Rights Amendment alive by continuing their protests.</u>

   Ⓐ Not gaining sufficient legislative approval, thousands of women vowed to keep the Equal Rights Amendment alive by continuing their protests.

   Ⓑ Not gaining sufficient legislative approval, the Equal Rights Amendment had thousands of women vowing to keep it alive with their protests.

   Ⓒ Thousands of women vowed to keep the Equal Rights Amendment alive in spite of failure to gain legislative approval.

   Ⓓ After the Equal Rights Amendment did not gain sufficient legislative approval, thousands of women vowed to keep it alive by continuing their protests.

   Ⓔ Not gaining sufficient legislative approval, protests continued by women who vowed to keep the Equal Rights Amendment alive.

Answers: 22-1 Ⓑ, 22-2 Ⓓ, 22-3 Ⓔ, 22-4 Ⓒ, 22-5 Ⓓ

If you answered 22-1 **incorrectly, go to 23-1.**
If you answered 22-1 **correctly, go to 23-2.**

If you answered 22-2 **incorrectly, go to 23-1.**
If you answered 22-2 **correctly, go to 23-3.**

If you answered 22-3 **incorrectly, go to 23-2.**
If you answered 22-3 **correctly, go to 23-4.**

If you answered 22-4 **incorrectly, go to 23-3.**
If you answered 22-4 **correctly, go to 23-5.**

If you answered 22-5 **incorrectly, go to 23-4.**
If you answered 22-5 **correctly, go to 23-5.**

23-1. Revisionist historians <u>have argued that the entry of the United States into</u> World War II was favored by the Chief Executive and his closest advisors.

    Ⓐ have argued that the entry of the United States into

    Ⓑ arguing about the United States entry into

    Ⓒ entering an argument about the United States and

    Ⓓ had been having an argument that the entry of the United States into

    Ⓔ claim that the entry of the United States into

23-2. Gerrymandering <u>is when a voting area is unfairly divided</u> so that one political party gains advantage, and historically both the Democrats and Republicans have used the gerrymander.

    Ⓐ is when a voting area is unfairly divided

    Ⓑ divides a voting area unfairly

    Ⓒ makes fair voting unfair

    Ⓓ occurs when a voting area is unfairly divided

    Ⓔ is when a voting area is divided unfairly

23-3. None of the applicants could file all of the forms in time because the job application did not state <u>to whom to be sent the
personal references.</u>

    Ⓐ to whom to be sent the personal references
    Ⓑ to who the personal references should be sent
    Ⓒ to whom to send the personal references
    Ⓓ to whom the personal references will be sent
    Ⓔ to whom to send the personal references to

23-4. Though the chief appeal of their program is their disagreement,
<u>movie critics Gene Siskel and Roger Ebert often praise distin-
guished performances even when they are new to the screen.</u>

    Ⓐ movie critics Gene Siskel and Roger Ebert often praise
distinguished performances even when they are new to the
screen
    Ⓑ movie critics Gene Siskel and Roger Ebert, praising dis-
tinguished performances that are new to the screen
    Ⓒ even distinguished performances that are new to the screen
are praised by movie critics Gene Siskel and Roger Ebert
    Ⓓ movie critics Gene Siskel and Roger Ebert often praise
distinguished performances, even those by actors new to
the screen
    Ⓔ with distinguished performances in mind, movie critics
Gene Siskel and Roger Ebert often praise even new screen
actors

23-5. In *Charlotte's Web,* Wilbur is awarded a blue ribbon not because <u>his appearance is superior to the other pigs but also with
reference to the belief that he possesses</u> some sort of "supernatural" power.

Ⓐ his appearance is superior to the other pigs but also with
reference to the belief that he possesses

Ⓑ he looked better than the other pigs but because he was
thought to possess

Ⓒ of his superior appearance but as far as the belief that he
possessed

Ⓓ he looks better than that of the other pigs but because of a
belief in supernatural power

Ⓔ he looks better than the other pigs but because he is thought
to possess

Answers: 23-1 Ⓐ, 23-2 Ⓑ, 23-3 Ⓒ, 23-4 Ⓓ, 23-5 Ⓔ

If you answered 23-1 **incorrectly, go to 24-1.**
If you answered 23-1 **correctly, go to 24-2.**

If you answered 23-2 **incorrectly, go to 24-1.**
If you answered 23-2 **correctly, go to 24-3.**

If you answered 23-3 **incorrectly, go to 24-2.**
If you answered 23-3 **correctly, go to 24-4.**

If you answered 23-4 **incorrectly, go to 24-3.**
If you answered 23-4 **correctly, go to 24-5.**

If you answered 23-5 **incorrectly, go to 24-4.**
If you answered 23-5 **correctly, go to 24-5.**

24-1. <u>After having finished the marathon</u>, both the winner and the losers felt proud of their having completed the course of more than twenty-six miles.

Ⓐ After having finished the marathon
Ⓑ Having finished the marathon
Ⓒ Having been finished after the marathon
Ⓓ Finishing the marathon
Ⓔ The marathon finished

24-2. If a police officer were to mistake the citizen's friendly intentions, <u>and supposes her to be dangerous</u>, he might draw his revolver or call for backup assistance.

Ⓐ and supposes her to be dangerous
Ⓑ and supposed her to be dangerous
Ⓒ and supposes danger from her
Ⓓ and suspect her to be dangerous
Ⓔ and suspected her to be dangerous

24-3. Frank Buck, "the great white hunter," was always portrayed on film as <u>fearless and having great skill in hunting dangerous animals</u>, such as lions, leopards, and Cape buffalo.

Ⓐ fearless and having great skill in hunting dangerous animals

Ⓑ fearless and very skillful in hunting dangerous animals

Ⓒ having no fear and having great skill in hunting dangerous animals

Ⓓ fearless and with skill in hunting dangerous animals

Ⓔ hunting dangerous animals without fear and with skill

24-4. Unaffected by both rising inflation and high interest rates <u>were that type of enterprising American able to create a product</u> adaptable to shifting public tastes.

Ⓐ were that type of enterprising American able to create a product

Ⓑ was that type of enterprising American able to create a products

Ⓒ were the productions of American enterprise

Ⓓ were enterprising Americans who were able to create products

Ⓔ enterprising Americans creating products

24-5. <u>Success in school, according to many of the more cynical critics of public education, is like playing marbles:</u> distinguished achievement depends not upon talent but upon luck.

Ⓐ Success in school, according to many of the more cynical critics of public education, is like playing marbles:

Ⓑ Criticizing success in public education cynically, many compare successful schooling to a successful marble game:

Ⓒ School is a game of marbles, according to many of the more cynical critics of public education

Ⓓ The more cynical critics of public education say that success in school is like playing marbles:

Ⓔ Many of the more cynical critics of public education say that succeeding in school is like playing marbles:

Answers: 24-1 Ⓑ, 24-2 Ⓓ, 24-3 Ⓑ, 24-4 Ⓓ, 24-5 Ⓔ

If you answered 24-1 **incorrectly**, go to 25-1.
If you answered 24-1 **correctly**, go to 25-2.

If you answered 24-2 **incorrectly**, go to 25-1.
If you answered 24-2 **correctly**, go to 25-3.

If you answered 24-3 **incorrectly**, go to 25-2.
If you answered 24-3 **correctly**, go to 25-4.

If you answered 24-4 **incorrectly**, go to 25-3.
If you answered 24-4 **correctly**, go to 25-5.

If you answered 24-5 **incorrectly**, go to 25-4.
If you answered 24-5 **correctly**, go to 25-5.

25-1. The term "articulation disorder" refers to the difficulty an individual has when he uses the speech sounds of the language spoken around him. No communication dysfunction is more familiar to the speech pathologist than the problem of misarticulation. Articulation disorders represent over two thirds of the speech clinician's caseload; a rather sizable percentage when one considers that voice, rhythm, and language disorders also fall under this professional's review.

The passage implies that one of the factors contributing to the importance of articulation disorders is

Ⓐ the speech clinician's practice of treating nonserious disorders
Ⓑ the lack of organic causes of such disorders
Ⓒ the tendency of many children to "outgrow" the disorder
Ⓓ the high incidence of such disorders
Ⓔ the stress placed on such disorders by hospital administrators

25-2. "The sum of behavior is to retain a man's dignity without intruding upon the liberty of others," stated Sir Francis Bacon. If this is the case, then not intruding upon another's liberty is impossible.

The conclusion strongly implied by the author's arguments is that

Ⓐ retaining one's dignity is impossible without intruding upon another's liberty
Ⓑ retaining dignity never involves robbing others of liberty
Ⓒ dignity and liberty are mutually exclusive
Ⓓ there is always the possibility of a "dignified intrusion"
Ⓔ B. F. Skinner's *Beyond Freedom and Dignity* takes its cue from Bacon

GMAT CAT PRACTICE TEST

25-3. The fish *Alpha splendes* usually lives in a lake where there are dissolved alkalies. Lake Huron contains the dissolved alkalies soda and potash. There are no *Alpha splendes* in Lake Huron.

Which of the following could logically complete an argument with the premises given above?

I. Therefore, *Alpha splendes* needs alkalies other than soda and potash.
II. Therefore, there may not be sufficient dissolved alkalies in the lake.
III. Therefore, there will be no *Alpha splendes* living in this lake.

Ⓐ I only
Ⓑ II only
Ⓒ III only
Ⓓ I and II only
Ⓔ II and III only

25-4. "The sum of behavior is to retain a man's dignity without intruding upon the liberty of others," stated Sir Francis Bacon. If this is the case, then not intruding upon another's liberty is impossible.

The author's argument would be weakened if it were pointed out that

I. Bacon's argument has been misinterpreted out of context
II. neither liberty nor dignity can be discussed in absolute terms
III. retaining dignity always involves a reduction of liberty

Ⓐ I only
Ⓑ III only
Ⓒ I and II only
Ⓓ II and III only
Ⓔ I, II, and III

25-5. The dance tonight is a ball, and my child's toy is a ball. Therefore, in addition to the fact that they are called by the same name, there is a way in which the dance and my child's toy are like each other.

Which of the following statements would explain why the conclusion of the argument does not follow from the premises?

    I. The dance tonight may not be a ball.
  II. Something which is neither a dance nor a toy may be a ball.
 III. The dance tonight and my child's toy are not each a ball in the same sense of the word.
 IV. A ball cannot be anything except a dance or a toy.

  Ⓐ II only
  Ⓑ III only
  Ⓒ I and II only
  Ⓓ II and IV only
  Ⓔ I, II, and IV only

Answers: 25-1 ⓓ, 25-2 ⓐ, 25-3 ⓑ, 25-4 ⓒ, 25-5 ⓑ

If you answered 25-1 **incorrectly, go to 26-1.**
If you answered 25-1 **correctly, go to 26-2.**

If you answered 25-2 **incorrectly, go to 26-1.**
If you answered 25-2 **correctly, go to 26-3.**

If you answered 25-3 **incorrectly, go to 26-2.**
If you answered 25-3 **correctly, go to 26-4.**

If you answered 25-4 **incorrectly, go to 26-3.**
If you answered 25-4 **correctly, go to 26-5.**

If you answered 25-5 **incorrectly, go to 26-4.**
If you answered 25-5 **correctly, go to 26-5.**

26-1. Flamo Lighters when you need them! Always reliable, always dependable. In all weather, with ten-year guarantee. Don't get caught without a light—keep a Flamo in your pocket wherever you go!

All of the following are claims made or implied by Flamo Lighters EXCEPT

Ⓐ convenience
Ⓑ dependability
Ⓒ longevity
Ⓓ winter-proof
Ⓔ all-purpose

26-2. In parts of the world where the life spans are short, forty may be regarded as an advanced age. People who live longer are believed to possess special powers. These elders are sometimes treated with a deference based on fear rather than love.

The final statement in the passage is based on which of the following assumptions?

Ⓐ Deference is normally accorded based on love.
Ⓑ Few elders are treated with deference.
Ⓒ People who live shorter lives have no special powers.
Ⓓ People with special powers are not loved.
Ⓔ A deference based on fear is stronger than one based on love.

26-3. All acts have consequences. Given this fact, we may wish to play it safe by never doing anything.

The speaker implies that

(A) we may prefer to live safely
(B) all acts have consequences
(C) consequentiality is not safe
(D) doing nothing has lesser consequences
(E) not doing anything is not an act

26-4. All acts have consequences. Given this fact, we may wish to play it safe by never doing anything.

What conclusion about consequences must we accept if we accept the speaker's statement?

(A) Consequences are significant only for active people.
(B) All consequences are dangerous.
(C) There are some acts that do not produce consequences.
(D) Consequences have moral force.
(E) Inaction has moral force.

26-5. The evolution of the various forms of life from biochemical mass must not be considered a linear progression. Rather, the fossil record suggests an analogy between evolution and a bush whose branches go every which way. Like branches, some evolutionary lines simply end, and others branch again. Many biologists believe the pattern to have been as follows: bacteria emerged first and from them branched viruses, red algae, blue-green algae, and green flagellates. From the latter branched green algae, from which higher plants evolved, and colorless rhizoflagellates, from which diatoms, molds, sponges, and protozoa evolved. From ciliated protozoa (ciliophora) evolved multinucleate (syncytial) flatworms. These branched into five lines, one of which leads to the echinoderms and chordates. The remaining lines lead to most of the other phyla of the animal kingdom.

Which of the following best expresses the analogy between evolution and a bush?

Ⓐ Species is to evolution as bush is to branching.
Ⓑ Species is to branching as bush is to evolution.
Ⓒ Evolution is to species as bush is to branch viruses.
Ⓓ Evolution is to species as bush is to branches.
Ⓔ Evolution is to species as branches is to bush.

Answers: 26-1 Ⓔ, 26-2 Ⓐ, 26-3 Ⓔ, 26-4 Ⓑ, 26-5 Ⓓ

Check your answer and continue to the next reading passage.

Questions 27–30

Read the following passage and answer the four questions that follow.

A growing body of research on sharks and their relatives portrays these creatures as behaving in ways far more sophisticated and complex than was thought possible. Scientists are documenting
LINE elaborate social behaviors among these fish, including never-
(5) before-witnessed mating rituals that seem to be based on electrical signals.

Compared to other fishes, sharks have huge brains. But because sharks are so difficult to study—they are dangerous, far-ranging, and usually inhabit murky waters—scientists only recently have
(10) accumulated enough data to even hint at their behavioral and sensory complexity. In one of the most surprising findings, a researcher discovered a new sense organ, located on top of certain sharks' heads. The organ is a sort of light-gathering "third eye," known in some prehistoric fishes, the lantern fishes, and at least one living
(15) reptile, the tuatara of New Zealand. Its precise function in the six-gilled shark is still uncertain, though sensing light at the deep depths to which they dive is most likely.

Sharks are literally covered in sense organs. Over the last two decades, researchers have found no fewer than four separate sen-
(20) sory systems to detect chemicals in the water. Past researchers have documented that sharks also have good vision and can see in color; they have directional hearing, and although they cannot hear notes much above middle C, they can hear sounds below the threshold of human hearing.

(25) But perhaps the most astounding sense possessed by sharks is their ability to sense electric fields. Elasmobranchs—sharks, skates, and rays—can detect fields so weak they cannot be measured by standard laboratory equipment. All live organisms, immersed in water, have a weak bioelectric field, a current generated between
(30) biological membranes and the surrounding water. Elasmobranch fishes use electroreception to locate prey. Some scientists suspect that sharks, skates, and rays, sensing and interpreting the much larger voltage potentials created by salt-water currents moving

(35) through the earth's magnetic field, use this information to navigate.

(40) Electroreception may also play a key role in the mating system of sharks and the one thousand other fishes in the same taxonomic group. The females use electroreception for some sort of social cues. Receptive females may be advertising their availability by congregating in large, highly visible, unburied piles; but unreceptive females, perhaps already pregnant, may use electroreception to locate other buried females to hide from amorous males in buried aggregation. Field strength intensifies when the fishes open their mouths. Literally, "heavy breathing" could enhance a female's
(45) attraction.

27. The complexity of the shark has been underestimated for which of the following reasons?

    I. Sharks are a very ancient life form.
    II. Sharks are dangerous.
    III. Sharks rarely live in clear waters.

    (A) II only
    (B) I and II only
    (C) I and III only
    (D) II and III only
    (E) I, II, and III

28. It can be inferred from the passage that female sharks hiding in groups from male sharks

    (A) could not be found if they were buried in the sand
    (B) could be discovered by a male shark using his "third eye"
    (C) would emit no bioelectrical signals
    (D) would be easier to detect by electroreception than a female shark hiding alone
    (E) would open their mouths as often as possible

29. According to the passage, sharks may use their electroreceptive ability for all of the following EXCEPT to

Ⓐ locate prey
Ⓑ navigate
Ⓒ gather light
Ⓓ locate other sharks
Ⓔ locate breeding partners

30. Which of the following is most relevant to the research described in the passage?

Ⓐ Certain birds communicate by emitting cries pitched two octaves above middle C.
Ⓑ Certain migrating birds determine their location by detecting variations in the strength of the earth's magnetic field.
Ⓒ Migrating herds of wildebeest can reach their destination in spite of major changes in a landscape from one year to the next.
Ⓓ Some migrating birds and insects appear to arrive at the same place on exactly the same day year after year.
Ⓔ Dogs are capable of hearing sounds at pitches inaudible to human ears.

Answers: 27 Ⓓ, 28 Ⓓ, 29 Ⓒ, 30 Ⓑ

If you answered **none** of the four reading questions **correctly, go to 31-1.**
If you answered **one** of the four reading questions **correctly, go to 31-2.**
If you answered **two** of the four reading questions **correctly, go to 31-3.**
If you answered **three** of the four reading questions **correctly, go to 31-4.**
If you answered **all four** of the reading questions **correctly, go to 31-5.**

31-1. <u>Irregardless of her physical beauty</u>, the judges did not vote for her to represent their state in the Miss America Pageant, but chose the candidate with superior musical abilities.

Ⓐ Irregardless of her physical beauty
Ⓑ In spite of her physical beauty
Ⓒ While her physical beauty was superb
Ⓓ No matter how extraordinary her physical appearance
Ⓔ Regardless how beautiful her physical appearance

31-2. <u>The defendant's refusal to discuss his whereabouts completely convinced the jury of his guilt</u>, even though so many other facts surrounding the crime indicated not only that he was entirely innocent but also that he had been "framed" by members of a local syndicate.

Ⓐ The defendant's refusal to discuss his whereabouts completely convinced the jury of his guilt
Ⓑ Refusing to completely discuss the defendant's whereabouts, the jury was completely convinced of his guilt
Ⓒ The defendant's refusal to complete a discussion of his whereabouts convinced the jury of his guilt
Ⓓ The defendant's refusal to discuss his complete whereabouts convinced the jury that he was guilty
Ⓔ Guilty in the eyes of the jury because his whereabouts had not been completely discussed

31-3. According to a report in the gossip columns, <u>the actor, along with his butler, bodyguard, chauffeur, two maids, and four dogs, are on board</u> the train bound for Cannes.

   Ⓐ the actor, along with his butler, bodyguard, chauffeur, two maids, and four dogs, are on board

   Ⓑ the actor and his butler and also his chauffeur, together with two maids and including four dogs, are on board

   Ⓒ the actor, along with his butler, bodyguard, chauffeur, two maids, and four dogs, is on board

   Ⓓ the actor, along with his butler, bodyguard, chauffeur, two maids, and four dogs, are climbing onto

   Ⓔ the actor's butler, bodyguard, chauffeur, two maids, and four dogs are on board

31-4. Though the Foreign Office claimed the troops were sent to protect innocent civilians, <u>the principle reason for the British invasion was because</u> the sovereignty of British territory had been challenged.

   Ⓐ the principle reason for the British invasion was because

   Ⓑ the principle reason for the British invasion was that

   Ⓒ the principal reason for the British invasion was that

   Ⓓ the British invaded because

   Ⓔ principally, the British staged an invasion because

31-5. Most television is escapist, but <u>reading modern novels continually reminds many people</u> that we live in an age of lost faith and growing anxiety.

   Ⓐ reading modern novels continually reminds many people

   Ⓑ reading modern novels frequently reminds many people

   Ⓒ those who read modern novels continually realize

   Ⓓ those who continually read modern novels realize

   Ⓔ the reading of modern novels is what continually reminds many people

Answers: 31-1 Ⓑ, 31-2 Ⓐ, 31-3 Ⓒ, 31-4 Ⓒ, 31-5 Ⓓ

If you answered 31-1 **incorrectly, go to 32-1.**
If you answered 31-1 **correctly, go to 32-2.**

If you answered 31-2 **incorrectly, go to 32-1.**
If you answered 31-2 **correctly, go to 32-3.**

If you answered 31-3 **incorrectly, go to 32-2.**
If you answered 31-3 **correctly, go to 32-4.**

If you answered 31-4 **incorrectly, go to 32-3.**
If you answered 31-4 **correctly, go to 32-5.**

If you answered 31-5 **incorrectly, go to 32-4.**
If you answered 31-5 **correctly, go to 32-5.**

32-1. <u>Because nuclear weapons had been scorned by so many liberal activists with the power to destroy the world,</u> both of the superpowers began to consider both the limitation and the reduction of their arsenals.

    Ⓐ Because nuclear weapons had been scorned by so many liberal activists with the power to destroy the world

    Ⓑ World-destroying nuclear weapons had been scorned by many liberal activists

    Ⓒ With the power to destroy the world, liberal activists had scorned nuclear weapons

    Ⓓ Because nuclear weapons with the power to destroy the world had been scorned by so many liberal activists

    Ⓔ Liberal activists scorning nuclear weapons

32-2. I'll never forget the tranquil desert resort <u>where having golfed, while I vacationed, in winter, when I was younger.</u>

    Ⓐ where having golfed, while I vacationed, in winter, when I was younger

    Ⓑ where I golfed, while having had vacationed in winter when I was younger

    Ⓒ where I golfed while wintering, when I was younger

    Ⓓ where I having had golf, while I vacationed in winter when I was younger

    Ⓔ where I golfed while I vacationed in winter when I was younger

32-3. Neither the director nor the investors in the second sequel pre-dicts that it will earn less money than the other two films, but they are disturbed by the box-office receipts on its opening weekend.

Ⓐ Neither the director nor the investors in the second sequel predicts

Ⓑ Neither the investors in the second sequel nor its director predicts

Ⓒ The director of the second sequel, along with its investors, predict

Ⓓ Neither the investors nor the directors of the second sequel predicts

Ⓔ About the second sequel, neither the director nor the investors predict

32-4. By composing at the keyboard, the poetry of this century often illustrates a more purposeful alignment of lines and letters made possible by the machine itself.

Ⓐ By composing at the keyboard, the poetry of this century often illustrates a more purposeful alignment of lines and letters made possible by the machine itself.

Ⓑ The poets of this century who compose at the keyboard often take advantage of the machine to arrange lines and letters more purposefully.

Ⓒ The keyboards of the poets of this century align lines and letters more purposefully.

Ⓓ With the keyboard as their means of composition, the poets of this century often align lines and letters more purposefully than the poets before the machine.

Ⓔ With the more purposeful alignment of lines and letters, the poets of this century rely on their machine often.

32-5. <u>I will not object to him joining the fraternity</u> if he is willing to accept its social and academic obligations, to pay his fees on time, and to play on house athletic teams.

    Ⓐ I will not object to him joining the fraternity
    Ⓑ I do not object to his joining the fraternity
    Ⓒ I will make no objection to him joining the fraternity
    Ⓓ I do not object to him joining the fraternity
    Ⓔ I will not object to his joining the fraternity

Answers: 32-1 ⓓ, 32-2 ⓔ, 32-3 ⓑ, 32-4 ⓑ, 32-5 ⓔ

If you answered 32-1 **incorrectly, go to 33-1.**
If you answered 32-1 **correctly, go to 33-2.**

If you answered 32-2 **incorrectly, go to 33-1.**
If you answered 32-2 **correctly, go to 33-3.**

If you answered 32-3 **incorrectly, go to 33-2.**
If you answered 32-3 **correctly, go to 33-4.**

If you answered 32-4 **incorrectly, go to 33-3.**
If you answered 32-4 **correctly, go to 33-5.**

If you answered 32-5 **incorrectly, go to 33-4.**
If you answered 32-5 **correctly, go to 33-5.**

33-1. Beginning this fall, Latino and Asian students will not be allowed to transfer out of bilingual classes (that is, a program in which courses are given in a student's native language) until they pass strict competency tests in math, reading, and writing—as well as spoken English. The board and its supporters say this will protect children from being pushed out of bilingual programs before they are ready. They have hailed this as a victory for bilingual education

The argument above would be most strengthened if the author were to explain

A how efficient the bilingual program is
B how well staffed the bilingual program is
C whether the community supports the bilingual program
D whether any board members do not support the bilingual program
E how the students feel about the bilingual program

33-2. According to a recent study by the National Academy of Public Administration, postal patrons are regularly affronted by out-of-order stamp vending machines, branch post office lobbies locked at night, and thirty-two-cent letters that take as long to get there as eight-cent letters did long ago.

Which of the following transitions probably begins a sentence critical of the argument in the passage?

A However
B In addition
C Despite
D In reality
E Therefore

33-3. Consumers are not so easily manipulated as they are often painted. They may know what they want, and what they want may be greatly different from what other people believe they need.

Which of the following statements, if true, most weakens the above argument?

Ⓐ Most people continue to buy the same brand of a product year after year.

Ⓑ Companies that advertise the most sell the most products.

Ⓒ Store shelves packed with a variety of different brands have the potential to confuse the consumer.

Ⓓ Most consumers know which brand they are going to buy before entering a store.

Ⓔ People who shop with others rarely argue with their companions.

33-4. Voltaire once said, "Common sense is not so common."

Which of the following most nearly parallels Voltaire's statement?

Ⓐ God must have loved the common man; he certainly made enough of them.

Ⓑ The common good is not necessarily best for everyone.

Ⓒ Jumbo shrimp may not actually be very big.

Ⓓ Good people may not necessarily have good sense.

Ⓔ Truth serum cannot contain the truth.

33-5. Beginning this fall, Latino and Asian students will not be allowed to transfer out of bilingual classes (that is, a program in which courses are given in a student's native language) until they pass strict competency tests in math, reading, and writing—as well as spoken English. The board and its supporters say this will protect children from being pushed out of bilingual programs before they are ready. They have hailed this as a victory for bilingual education.

Which of the following, if true, is the strongest criticism of the position of the board?

Ⓐ A foreign student may be quite competent in math without being competent in English.

Ⓑ Some native students already in English-speaking classes are unable to pass the competency tests.

Ⓒ Most foreign students require many months of practice and instruction before mastering English skills.

Ⓓ Many students prefer to transfer out of bilingual classes before they have achieved competency in English.

Ⓔ Holding back students will double the number of students in bilingual classes—twice as many Latino and Asian children isolated from the English-speaking mainstream.

Answers: 33-1 Ⓐ, 33-2 Ⓐ, 33-3 Ⓑ, 33-4 Ⓒ, 33-5 Ⓔ

If you answered 33-1 **incorrectly, go to 34-1.**
If you answered 33-1 **correctly, go to 34-2.**

If you answered 33-2 **incorrectly, go to 34-1.**
If you answered 33-2 **correctly, go to 34-3.**

If you answered 33-3 **incorrectly, go to 34-2.**
If you answered 33-3 **correctly, go to 34-4.**

If you answered 33-4 **incorrectly, go to 34-3.**
If you answered 33-4 **correctly, go to 34-5.**

If you answered 33-5 **incorrectly, go to 34-4.**
If you answered 33-5 **correctly, go to 34-5.**

34-1. *Senator:* Serving a few months as a Capitol page can be an exciting and enriching experience for high school students from around the country.
Student: If the circumstances are right.

The student's response suggests which of the following?

Ⓐ Belligerence
Ⓑ Acquiescence
Ⓒ Skepticism
Ⓓ Disbelief
Ⓔ Ignorance

34-2. *Speaker 1:* The holy passion of friendship is of so sweet and steady and loyal and enduring a nature that it will last through a whole lifetime.
Speaker 2: If not asked to lend money.

The two speakers represent which of the following contrasting attitudes?

Ⓐ Faith and despair
Ⓑ Idealism and cynicism
Ⓒ Idealism and optimism
Ⓓ Socialism and capitalism
Ⓔ Friendship and enmity

34-3. The shortsightedness of our government and our scientists has virtually nullified all of their great discoveries because of their failure to consider the environmental impact. The situation is far from hopeless, but our government agencies must become better watchdogs.

This argument fails to place any blame on

I. consumers who prefer new technology to clean air
II. the ability of government to actually police industry
III. legal loopholes which allow industry abuse of government regulations

Ⓐ I only
Ⓑ II only
Ⓒ III only
Ⓓ I and III only
Ⓔ I, II, and III

34-4. Every speech intended to persuade either argues for a proposition or argues against a proposition. Any speech which argues for a proposition either presents all of the facts or presents a few of the facts, and any speech which argues against a proposition either presents all of the facts or presents a few of the facts. No speech which presents either all of the facts, a few of the facts, or just one fact is uninformative.

If the statements made in the passage above are true, it follows that

Ⓐ every speech presents either all of the facts or a few of the facts
Ⓑ every speech intended to persuade presents many of the facts of the argument
Ⓒ every uninformative speech presents none of the facts
Ⓓ some uninformative speeches present either all of the facts or a few of the facts
Ⓔ some speeches intended to persuade present neither all of the facts nor a few of the facts

34-5. Every speech intended to persuade either argues for a proposition or argues against a proposition. Any speech which argues for a proposition either presents all of the facts or presents a few of the facts, and any speech which argues against a proposition either presents all of the facts or presents a few of the facts. No speech which presents either all of the facts, a few of the facts, or just one fact is uninformative.

Which of the following statements represent a valid conclusion based upon the passage above?

Ⓐ No speech intended to persuade presents some of the facts.
Ⓑ No informative speech both intends to persuade and contains a few of the facts.
Ⓒ No informative speech both argues against a proposition and contains all of the facts.
Ⓓ No informative speech is intended to persuade.
Ⓔ No speech is both intended to persuade and uninformative.

Answers: 34-1 ©, 34-2 ⑧, 34-3 ⑩, 34-4 ©, 34-5 Ⓔ

Check your answer and continue to the next reading passage.

Questions 35–38

Read the following passage and answer the four questions that follow.

Economic growth involves both benefits and costs. The desirability of increasing production has frequently been challenged in recent years, and some have even maintained that economic growth
LINE is merely a quantitative enlargement that has no human meaning
(5) or value. However, economic growth is an increase in the capacity to produce goods and services that people want. Since the product of economic growth can be measured by its value to someone, it is important to ask whose standard of valuation counts.

In the United States, the value of a product is what purchasers
(10) pay for it. This is determined by the purchasers' preferences combined with conditions of supply, which in turn reflect various other factors, such as natural and technological circumstances at any given time and the preferences of those who supply capital and labor. The value by which we measure a product synthesizes all
(15) these factors. Gross National Product (GNP) is the market value of the nation's total output of goods and services.

Gross National Product is not a perfect measure of all the activities involved in economic output. It does not account for deteriorations or improvements in the environment, even when they
(20) are incidental results of the production process. On the other hand, it does not count as "product" many benefits provided as side effects of the economic process; it does not include productive but unpaid work (such as that done by a homemaker); and it does not reckon with such other factors as the burdensomeness of work, the
(25) length of the work week, and so forth.

Nonetheless, the GNP concept makes an important contribution to our understanding of how the economy is working. While it is not a complete measure of economic productivity and even less so of "welfare," the level and rate of increase of the GNP are clearly
(30) and positively associated with what most people throughout the world see as an improvement in the quality of life. In the long run, the same factors result in a growing GNP and in other social benefits: size and competence of population, state of knowledge, amount of capital, and the effectiveness with which these are com-
(35) bined and utilized.

35. The main purpose of the passage is to

   Ⓐ define the limitations of using GNP to measure the nation's well-being
   Ⓑ contrast the American and the European GNPs
   Ⓒ argue for the value of increased economic output
   Ⓓ explain the disadvantages of measuring the quality of life using a scale of material affluence
   Ⓔ define Gross National Product

36. The rhetorical purpose of the third paragraph of the passage (beginning on line 17) is to

   I. anticipate objections to what the GNP fails to take into account
   II. cite examples of "products" the GNP ought to include
   III. develop the definition of paragraph two with specific details

   Ⓐ I only
   Ⓑ II only
   Ⓒ III only
   Ⓓ I and II only
   Ⓔ I, II, and III

37. We can infer from the passage that of the following, the factor that does NOT influence the growth of the GNP is

   Ⓐ the condition of the population
   Ⓑ a dependence on spiritual values
   Ⓒ the capital available in the country
   Ⓓ knowledge related to production of goods and services
   Ⓔ the efficiency of the production process

38. A critic of the limitations of the measurements of the GNP might cite its failure to consider all of the following EXCEPT

   Ⓐ the steady increase in American workers' leisure time
   Ⓑ cooperative baby-sitting projects among parents with young children
   Ⓒ the widespread existence of chemicals in American rivers
   Ⓓ the value of the time a salaried stock broker spends on research
   Ⓔ the valuation of family household management

Answers: 35 Ⓔ, 36 Ⓐ, 37 Ⓑ, 38 Ⓓ

If you answered **none** of the four reading questions **correctly, go to 39-1.**
If you answered **one** of the four reading questions **correctly, go to 39-2.**
If you answered **two** of the four reading questions **correctly, go to 39-3.**
If you answered **three** of the four reading questions **correctly, go to 39-4.**
If you answered **all four** of the reading questions **correctly, go to 39-5.**

39-1. <u>The typical holiday shopper, although seduced by row upon row of novelty gifts, tend to purchase more practical</u> items these days because he or she realizes that frivolous gadgets are often cheaply made.

Ⓐ The typical holiday shopper, although seduced by row upon row of novelty gifts, tend to purchase more practical

Ⓑ As a typical holiday shopper, the tendency to purchase row upon row of novelty gifts is won over by the purchase of more practical

Ⓒ Typically, the holiday shopper who is attracted to novelty gifts tends to remain practical with

Ⓓ The typical holiday shopper, although seduced by row upon row of novelty gifts, tends to purchase more practical

Ⓔ The typical holiday shopper, although seduced by row upon row of novelty gifts, tends to purchase the most practical

39-2. <u>The All-Star Game signals the middle of the baseball season</u> and reminds the losing teams that the time for them to improve their playing is running out.

Ⓐ The All-Star Game signals the middle of the baseball season

Ⓑ With double significance, the All-Star Game occurs midway through

Ⓒ The baseball season is divided in half by the All-Star Game

Ⓓ The baseball All-Star Game signals the middle of the season

Ⓔ With the All-Star Game, half the season is over

39-3. Contrary to the popularly held opinion, painting is a <u>multifaceted, versatile, and a field in which a great deal of artistic diversity is possible.</u>

Ⓐ multifaceted, versatile, and a field in which a great deal of artistic diversity is possible

Ⓑ field in which a lot of multifaceted, versatile artistry is possible

Ⓒ multifaceted field with versatility and diversity also possible

Ⓓ multifaceted, versatile, and artistically diversified field

Ⓔ field of multifaceted versatility and diversified artistry

39-4. <u>On arriving at Dulles International Airport, his friends met him and took him immediately to his speaking engagement</u> in Springfield.

Ⓐ On arriving at Dulles International Airport, his friends met him and took him immediately to his speaking engagement

Ⓑ Arriving at Dulles International Airport, his friends who met him immediately took him to his speaking engagement

Ⓒ When he arrived at Dulles International Airport, his friends met him and took him immediately to his speaking engagement

Ⓓ When he arrived at Dulles International Airport, he was taken immediately to his speaking engagement

Ⓔ After arriving at Dulles International Airport, he was immediately taken to his speaking engagement

39-5. <u>We who graduated from high school in the United States in the early 60's were</u> caught in the middle of the crisis in education created by the Soviet Union's "Sputnik" success.

Ⓐ We who graduated from high school in the United States in the early 60's were

Ⓑ We, who graduated from high school in the United States in the early 60's, were

Ⓒ We who then graduated high school in the United States in the early 60's were

Ⓓ Those of us who then graduated from high school in the United States in the early 60's were

Ⓔ We high school graduates who were in the United States in the early 60's were

Answers: 39-1 ⓓ, 39-2 ⓐ, 39-3 ⓓ, 39-4 ⓒ, 39-5 ⓐ

If you answered 39-1 **incorrectly, go to 40-1.**
If you answered 39-1 **correctly, go to 40-2.**

If you answered 39-2 **incorrectly, go to 40-1.**
If you answered 39-2 **correctly, go to 40-3.**

If you answered 39-3 **incorrectly, go to 40-2.**
If you answered 39-3 **correctly, go to 40-4.**

If you answered 39-4 **incorrectly, go to 40-3.**
If you answered 39-4 **correctly, go to 40-5.**

If you answered 39-5 **incorrectly, go to 40-4.**
If you answered 39-5 **correctly, go to 40-5.**

40-1. By leaving camp an hour before sunrise, the tourists in the Land Rover were able to catch sight of a lion and his mate <u>laying low in the tall jungle grass</u> waiting for the opportunity to capture an unwary antelope.

Ⓐ laying low in the tall jungle grass
Ⓑ the tall jungle grass concealing their low-lying bodies,
Ⓒ that laid low in the tall jungle grass
Ⓓ lying low in the tall jungle grass
Ⓔ was laying in the tall jungle grass

40-2. When the Republican Party was the minority party, <u>its ability to win a presidential election was determined by the number of Democratic and independent voters it attracts.</u>

Ⓐ its ability to win a presidential election was determined by the number of Democratic and independent voters it attracts

Ⓑ its ability to win a presidential election is determined by the number of Democratic and independent voters it attracts

Ⓒ its ability to win a presidential election has been determined by the number of Democratic and independent voters it attracts

Ⓓ the number of Democratic and independent voters it attracts determines its ability to win a presidential election

Ⓔ the number of Democratic and independent voters it attracted determined its ability to win a presidential election

40-3. The boundaries of the Pleasant Valley School District <u>have and will continue to include</u> the small cities of Millerton, Cedarville, Granite, and Homersfield.

    Ⓐ have and will continue to include
    Ⓑ have included and will continue to include
    Ⓒ has included and will continue to include
    Ⓓ has and will continue to include
    Ⓔ include and will include

40-4. One question haunted the swindled, penniless investor: <u>What should his fortune have been if he had not been lured into that last, fateful investment?</u>

    Ⓐ What should his fortune have been if he had not been lured into that last, fateful investment
    Ⓑ What will his fortune have been if he were not lured into that last, fateful investment
    Ⓒ What would his fortune have been if he had not been lured into that last, fateful investment
    Ⓓ What could his fortune have been had not he been lured into that last, fateful investment
    Ⓔ What would his fortune be if he had only resisted the lure of that last fateful investment

40-5. The desert <u>canyon, which in spring had appeared lush with scrub oak and blooming cacti, but grew</u> brown and sere as the hot August winds continued.

Ⓐ canyon, which in spring had appeared lush with scrub oak and blooming cacti, but grew

Ⓑ canyon had appeared lush with scrub oak and blooming cacti and grew

Ⓒ canyon which in spring had appeared lush with scrub oak and blooming cacti grows

Ⓓ canyon in the spring appeared lush with scrub oak and blooming cacti, but has grown

Ⓔ canyon, which in spring had appeared lush with scrub oak and blooming cacti, grew

Answers: 40-1 ⓓ, 40-2 ⓔ, 40-3 ⓑ, 40-4 ⓒ, 40-5 ⓔ

If you answered 40-1 **incorrectly, go to 41-1.**
If you answered 40-1 **correctly, go to 41-2.**

If you answered 40-2 **incorrectly, go to 41-1.**
If you answered 40-2 **correctly, go to 41-3.**

If you answered 40-3 **incorrectly, go to 41-2.**
If you answered 40-3 **correctly, go to 41-4.**

If you answered 40-4 **incorrectly, go to 41-3.**
If you answered 40-4 **correctly, go to 41-5.**

If you answered 40-5 **incorrectly, go to 41-4.**
If you answered 40-5 **correctly, go to 41-5.**

41-1. Which of the following most logically completes this passage?

Several of the survivors discussed their dilemma. They could remain on the island and attempt to survive as best they knew how. Or they could attempt to escape, using the resources available to them. None of the group wished to venture away from their uncertain sanctuary, but all of them knew that help would be a long time coming. Their discussions were thus _____.

Ⓐ futile, arbitrary, and capricious
Ⓑ limited by their imagination and resolve
Ⓒ dampened by a sense of impending doom
Ⓓ possible, but by no means successful
Ⓔ courageous and honorable

41-2. Aristotle said that art represents "general truths" about human nature. Our city councilman is arguing in favor of the artistry—a giant mural in front of a Jeep dealership, portraying a variety of four-wheel-drive vehicles. He cites Aristotle's conception of art as his support.

The passage above raises which of the following questions?

Ⓐ Can a city councilman understand Aristotle?
Ⓑ Which general truths about human nature does a four-wheel-drive mural NOT represent?
Ⓒ Could Aristotle have predicted a modern society filled with sophisticated machines?
Ⓓ To what extent are four-wheel-drive vehicles representative of a general advance in modern technology?
Ⓔ What "general truth" about human nature does a mural of four-wheel-drive vehicles represent?

41-3. Unfortunately, only 11 percent of the driving public uses regular seat belts. Automatic restraints are the answer, and the quicker they are required, the sooner highways deaths will be reduced.

The author's conclusion is based upon which of the following assumptions?

Ⓐ Only 11 percent of the driving public cares about passengers' lives.

Ⓑ The use of restraints reduces highway deaths.

Ⓒ Regular seat belts are inadequate safety devices.

Ⓓ It is unfortunate that 89 percent of the driving public does not use regular seat belts.

Ⓔ Highway deaths occur often enough so that reducing them is a necessity.

41-4. The $464 million "reserve" in the budget adopted by the legislature in June turns out to have been based mainly on wishful thinking. Because of tax cuts approved by voters on the June ballot, along with the continuing economic slump and other events affecting income and expenses, the actual reserve in prospect may be as low as $7 million.

The author is probably leading to which of the following conclusions?

Ⓐ These facts warrant an investigation into who squandered $457 million.

Ⓑ A reserve in the budget is not so necessary as we might wish it to be.

Ⓒ The legislature would be wise not to add any new spending to the budget adopted in June.

Ⓓ The economic slump will probably not last much longer, but while it does the legislature must adjust the budget accordingly.

Ⓔ Legislative budgets are typically careless and unheeding of variable factors which may affect their accuracy.

41-5. According to a recent study by the National Academy of Public Administration, postal patrons are regularly affronted by out-of-order stamp vending machines, branch post office lobbies locked at night, and thirty-two-cent letters that take as long to get there as eight-cent letters did long ago.

Which of the following, if true, would weaken the implication of one of the writer's observations?

Ⓐ Most out-of-order vending machines are located in run-down neighborhoods.

Ⓑ Late-night vandalism has plagued post offices nationwide.

Ⓒ Although postage rates have risen, the cost of first class mail is still cheaper in the U.S. than anywhere else.

Ⓓ As a public corporation, the Postal Service has increased its capital assets by $3 billion.

Ⓔ When stamps cost eight cents, most letters reached their destination within twenty-four hours.

Answers: 41-1 Ⓒ, 41-2 Ⓔ, 41-3 Ⓑ, 41-4 Ⓒ, 41-5 Ⓔ

CHARTING AND ANALYZING YOUR TEST RESULTS

The first step in analyzing your results is to chart your answers. Use the charts on the following pages to do so and to spot your strengths and weaknesses. Complete the process of evaluating your essays and analyzing problems in each area for the practice test. Reexamine your results for trends in types of errors (repeated errors) or poor results in specific subject areas. **This reexamination and analysis is of tremendous importance in helping you maximize your score.** Be sure also to carefully read the answers and explanations that follow these charts.

ANALYTICAL WRITING ASSESSMENT

Analyze your responses using the following charts. Then estimate your score (see the explanation of characteristics of responses at each score level on pages 24-28).

ANALYSIS OF AN ISSUE

Questions	Completely	Partially	No
1. Does the response focus on the assigned topic and cover all of the tasks?			
2. Does the response show an understanding of the complexity of the issue?			
3. Does the response show cogent reasoning and logical position development?			
4. Are there sufficient relevant persuasive supporting details?			
5. Is the response well organized?			
6. Does the response show a command of standard written English?			

ANALYSIS OF AN ARGUMENT

Questions	Completely	Partially	No
1. Does the response focus on the assigned topic and cover all of the tasks?			
2. Does the response carefully analyze the important weaknesses of the argument?			
3. Does the response show cogent reasoning and logical development?			
4. Are there sufficient relevant supporting details of the critique?			
5. Is the response well organized?			
6. Does the response show a command of standard written English?			

Score	Level
6	excellent
5	good
4	competent
3	limited
2	weak
1	poor

QUANTITATIVE SECTION

On the chart that follows, draw a small square around the problems you answered correctly and a small circle around the ones you missed. As you follow the path of your problems, be sure to mark the right/ wrong box to the left of each question. (You may wish to use a highlighter to graphically follow your path.)

Right	Wrong						Problem Type
		18-1 A	18-2 AL	18-3 AL	18-4 AL	18-5 AL	PS
		19-1 G	19-2 G	19-3 G	19-4 G	19-5 G	PS
		20-1 A	20-2 AL	20-3 AL	20-4 AL	20-5 AL	PS
		21-1 AL	21-2 AL	21-3 AL	21-4 AL	21-5 AL	DS
		22-1 G	22-2 G	22-3 G	22-4 G	22-5 G	DS
		23-1 AL	23-2 AL	23-3 AL	23-4 AL	23-5 AL	DS
		24-1 G	24-2 G	24-3 G	24-4 G	24-5 G	PS
		25-1 AL	25-2 A	25-3 AL	25-4 AL	25-5 AL	PS
		26-1 AL	26-2 A	26-3 A	26-4 A	26-5 A	PS
		27-1 G	27-2 G	27-3 G	27-4 G	27-5 G	DS
		28-1 AL	28-2 AL	28-3 AL	28-4 AL	28-5 AL	DS
		29-1 G	29-2 G	29-3 G	29-4 G	29-5 G	DS
		30-1 A	30-2 AL	30-3 AL	30-4 AL	30-5 AL	PS
		31-1 AL	31-2 AL	31-3 AL	31-4 AL	31-5 AL	PS
		32-1 A	32-2 AL	32-3 AL	32-4 AL	32-5 AL	PS
		33-1 A	33-2 A	33-3 AL	33-4 AL	33-5 AL	DS
		34-1 A	34-2 A	34-3 AL	34-4 AL	34-5 AL	DS
		35-1 G	35-2 G	35-3 G	35-4 G	35-5 G	PS
		36-1 A	36-2 A	36-3 A	36-4 AL	36-5 AL	PS
		37-1 AL	37-2 AL	37-3 A	37-4 AL	37-5 AL	PS
		AL	AL	A	AL	AL	

Now that you have completed charting your path, you can tally your responses and review and analyze the results with the following charts.

Average Level Correct

Although the GMAT CAT uses very precise measures to calculate your score, the following calculations will give you a very general approximation of the average level you got right. It is important that you try to finish all 37 questions, and the following score chart assumes that you have done so.

	Number Correct	×	Level of Difficulty
Level 1	_____	×	1 = _____
Level 2	_____	×	2 = _____
Level 3	_____	×	3 = _____
Level 4	_____	×	4 = _____
Level 5	_____	×	5 = _____
		Total =	_____ ÷ 37 = _____

(Average Level)

Type of Problem Missed

Identifying the type of problem you most often miss will help you use your study time efficiently.

	Problem Solving		Data Sufficiency	
	Right	Wrong	Right	Wrong
Arithmetic				
Algebra				
Geometry				
Totals				

VERBAL SECTION

On the chart that follows, draw a small square around the questions you answered correctly and a small circle around the ones you missed. As you follow the path of your questions, be sure to mark the right/wrong box to the left of each question. (You may wish to use a highlighter to graphically follow your path.)

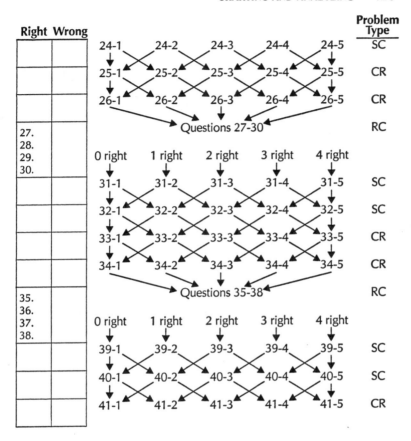

Right	Wrong		Problem Type

Now that you have completed charting your path, you can tally your responses and review and analyze the results with the following charts.

Average Level Correct

Although the GMAT CAT uses very precise measures to calculate your score, the following calculations will give you a very general approximation of the average level you got right.
Note: Count all Reading Comprehension questions as level 3 questions.

It is important that you try to finish all 41 questions, and the following score chart assumes that you have done so.

	Number Correct	×	Level of Difficulty	
Level 1	_____	×	1 = _____	
Level 2	_____	×	2 = _____	
Level 3	_____	×	3 = _____	
Level 4	_____	×	4 = _____	
Level 5	_____	×	5 = _____	
		Total	= _____	÷ 41 = _____
				(Average Level)

Type of Question Missed

Identifying the type of question you most often miss will help you use your study time efficiently.

	Possible	Right	Wrong
RC	20		
SC	13		
CR	8		
Totals	41		

WHERE TO GO FROM HERE

Now that you have completed the chart and analyzed your results, you should return to the simulated computer-adaptive test and work all of the problems in an organized manner. First work all of the problems at the 1 level, that is 4-1, 5-1, 6-1, 7-1, etc. Review the answer to each problem after you work it. Having attempted and reviewed the simpler problems, next work and review all of the level 2 problems, that is 4-2, 5-2, 6-2, 7-2, etc.

Continue this process until you have worked all of the problems available on this simulated exam. Starting with the easier problems will help you build a basis for your review. Following this process will help you prepare to attack the more difficult problems.

QUANTITATIVE SECTION

1-3. Ⓑ Let x be the number of $4 Frisbees. Then $64 - x$ is the number of $3 Frisbees. This gives the equation $3(64 - x) + 4(x) = 204$. Solving gives

$$192 - 3x + 4x = 204$$
$$192 + x = 204$$
$$x = 12$$

Therefore, the fewest number of $4 Frisbees is 12. Note that you could also work from the answers by substituting in each possibility.

2-2. Ⓑ Solving the first equation for x,

$$\frac{2}{x} = 4$$
$$2 = 4x$$
$$\frac{2}{4} = x$$

Therefore, $\frac{1}{2} = x$

Now solving the second equation for y

$$\frac{2}{y} = 8$$
$$2 = 8y$$
$$\frac{2}{8} = y$$

Therefore, $\frac{1}{4} = y$

Substituting these values for $x - y$ gives,

$$\frac{1}{2} - \frac{1}{4} = \frac{2}{4} - \frac{1}{4} = \frac{1}{4}$$

Therefore, $x - y = \frac{1}{4}$, and the correct answer is Ⓑ.

2-4. Ⓓ Set up the equation as follows:

Let t be the length of time it will take the plane to overtake the bus; then $t + 4$ is the time that the bus has traveled before the plane starts. The distance that the bus has traveled by 1 P.M. is $50(t + 4)$, since distance equals rate times time ($d = rt$). The distance the plane will travel is $300t$. Now setting these two equal to each other (they will have to travel the same distance for one to overtake the other) gives $50(t + 4) = 300t$. Solve the equation as follows:

$$50(t + 4) = 300t$$
$$50t + 200 = 300t$$
$$200 = 250t$$

Therefore, $\frac{4}{5} = t$

$\frac{4}{5}$ of an hour ($\frac{4}{5} \times 60$) is 48 minutes. Therefore, it will take 48 minutes for the plane to overtake the bus, and since the plane is starting at 1 P.M., it will overtake the bus at 1:48 P.M.

3-1. Ⓔ Since this is an approximation, round off

$$\frac{\text{Venus weight of } 182}{\text{Earth weight of } 207} \text{ to } \frac{180}{200}, \text{ which is } 90\%$$

3-3. Ⓓ If cube A has side 2, then the surface area is 24 square units, since the area of one face is 2×2, or 4, and there are 6 equal faces to a cube. If cube B has side 1, then the surface area is 6 square units, since the area of one face is 1×1, or 1, and there are 6 faces. Therefore, the ratio could be 24:6, or 4:1.

3-5. Ⓑ If each could save \$7,200, then all three could save \$21,600. Let x stand for the amount each of the five business people invests. Then the difference between the five and three investments would be

$$5x - 3x = 21,600$$
$$2x = 21,600$$
$$x = 10,800$$

Therefore, each of the five invests \$10,800, and the total investment is $5 \times 10,800$, or \$54,000.

Note that answers Ⓒ, Ⓓ, and Ⓔ are not reasonable. Another method uses one of the original investor's savings and works from the equation $(\frac{1}{3}x) - (\frac{1}{5}x) = 7,200$.

4-1. Ⓒ This problem is most easily completed by rearranging and approximating as follows:

$$\frac{69.28 \times 0.004}{0.03} \cong 69 \times \frac{0.004}{0.03} \cong 69 \times 0.1 = 6.9$$

which is the only reasonably close answer to 9.2.

4-2. Ⓓ This problem is most easily answered by dividing 318 by 3 to get 106, which must be the middle number; therefore, the largest is 108. You could also use the equation

$$\begin{array}{ccc} \text{smallest} & \text{middle} & \text{largest} \\ (2x) & + (2x+2) + (2x+4) = 318 \end{array}$$

and work from there.

4-4. Ⓒ Let x be the amount invested at 5%. Then $1,000 - x$ is the amount invested at 6%. This gives the equation $5(x) + 6(1,000 - x) = 5,300$. Solving gives

$$5x + 6,000 - 6x = 5,300$$
$$6,000 - x = 5,300$$
$$-x = -700$$
$$x = 700$$

Therefore, $700 was invested at 5%.

Note that answers Ⓐ, Ⓓ, and Ⓔ are not reasonable.

4-5. Ⓓ Since $ABCD$ is a rhombus, all sides are equal; therefore, $BC = CD = 6$, and $BC + CD = 12$. $AB = 6$, minus $AE \cong 4$ leaves $6 - 4 \cong 2$, which is the approximate length of BE. Adding $12 + 2 = 14$ gives the distance around the rhombus that will be traveled. Now using the formula for circumference of a circle $= 2\pi r$ or πd leaves 6π as the circumference of the complete circle. Because the inscribed angle is 45°, arc DE is 90° (inscribed angle is half of the arc it intercepts). This 90° will not be traveled as it is in the interior of the figure; therefore, only 270° of the 360° in the complete circle will be traveled, or $\frac{3}{4}$ of the circle. $\frac{3}{4} \times 6\pi = 9\pi/2$. This added to the original 14 gives answer Ⓓ $14 + (9\pi/2)$, or $14 + \frac{9}{2}\pi$.

5-1. Ⓒ There are 8 different arrangements, as follows:

red-red-red	green-green-green
red-green-green	green-red-green
green-green-red	green-red-red
red-green-red	red-red-green

5-2. Ⓒ Since two thirds of the students are boys, we have $\frac{2}{3}(36) = 24$ boys in the class.

Out of the 24 boys in the class, three fourths of them are under six feet tall or $\frac{3}{4}(24) = 18$ boys under six feet tall.

5-3. Ⓒ The following are the possible combinations: 123, 124, 125, 126, 134, 135, 136, 145, 146, 156, 234, 235, 236, 245, 246, 256, 345, 346, 356, 456. Thus there are 20 combinations. Using the formula,

$$\binom{6}{3} = \frac{6!}{3!(3!)} = \frac{6 \times 5 \times 4 \times 3 \times 2 \times 1}{3 \times 2 \times 1 \times 3 \times 2 \times 1} = 20$$

The formula is $\binom{n}{r} = \dfrac{n!}{r!(n-r)!}$

5-4. Ⓒ The maximum number of combinations is $3 \times 3 \times 2 = 18$. However, because the woman won't wear her pink blouse and green skirt with either of the two pairs of shoes, two of the combinations are excluded. She could wear $18 - 2 = 16$ different combinations.

5-5. Ⓑ If only nine are picked out, it is possible to get three of each color. Thus the tenth is necessary to be sure of four pairs.

6-1. Ⓓ Either statement allows us to calculate the required precipitation, P.

$$(1) \ P = 35 - 33$$
$$(2) \ P = 35(1 - 0.943)$$

6-2. Ⓔ The first statement implies that a tock equals 30 minutes, but the duration of a tick is indefinite.

6-3. Ⓐ The first statement translates to $Y = X - 1$ and $Z = \frac{1}{2}X$. Given that $X + Y + Z = 19$, substitution yields $X + X - 1 + \frac{1}{2}X = 19$, so $X = 8$. From (1), $Y = 7$ and $Z = 4$.

6-4. Ⓑ From statement (2), let x equal the number of adults and $3x$ equal the number of children.

$$3x + x = 24$$
$$4x = 24$$
$$x = 6 = \text{ number of adults needed}$$

Statement (1) gives a ratio between boys and girls, but no exact numbers can be determined, so the number of adults cannot be determined.

6-5. Ⓔ We have no information concerning the number of patients who stayed more than one hour and were seen by only one doctor.

7-1. Ⓑ Since $\overline{AO}$ is perpendicular to $\overline{OB}$, AOB is a right angle.

7-2. Ⓑ Since the three angles sum to a straight angle, $c = 180° - 131° = 49°$.

7-3. Ⓐ Because vertical angles are equal, $a = d$. From statement (1) we can find that angle $a = 41°$. In the figure, angles a and e are supplementary, so angle $e = 180 - 41 = 139°$.

7-4. Ⓐ Area $BCDE$ equals triangle ACD minus triangle ABE. From the sketch it is clear that the two triangles are similar, as their respective sides are parallel. From (1) we see that the base and height of ABE are half those of ACD; therefore, the area of ABE is one-quarter that of ACD. Consequently, the area $BCDE$ is three times the area of ABE.

7-5. Ⓓ The definition of a rhombus stipulates the equality of its four sides. The first statement reveals that the two triangles are equilateral, so all the angles must be 60°. From the second statement, $CBD = 60°$ (by alternate interior angles); triangle BCD is isosceles with $BC = CD$ (from the definition of a rhombus), so angle $BDC = CBD = 60°$; subtracting those angles from 180° leaves 60° for angle BCD.

8-1.   Ⓒ Statement (1) implies that the three cameras sell for a total price of 3 × $172 = $516. Statement (2) implies that two of the cameras each sell for $\frac{1}{2}$($332) = $166. The third camera must sell for $516 − $332 = $184.

8-2.   Ⓔ To calculate the average, we require the sum of the ten numbers. Statement (1) offers the sum of nine. We do not know whether the number cited in (2) is one of those nine.

8-3.   Ⓐ Because the average is the sum divided by 5, the sum must be the average times 5. Therefore, the sum is zero.

8-4.   Ⓔ From (1), $x < 5$, and from (2), $y < 6$, so $xy < 30$. Therefore, the product may or may not exceed 27.

8-5.   Ⓓ The first statement implies that x is a positive number but less than 1. The second statement yields $x < \frac{1}{3}$. Either statement answers the question that, yes, x is less than 2.

9-1.   Ⓐ From (1), Toni types 3,150/60 = $52\frac{1}{2}$ words per minute.

9-2.   Ⓒ The problem may be solved using both statements. Emily and Joan's joint rate of counting is 1/26 of the books per hour. If y is Emily's rate, then Joan's rate is $2y$, twice as fast. The individual rates sum to the joint rate:

$$2y + y = \frac{1}{26}$$
$$y = \frac{1}{78} \quad \text{Emily's rate}$$
$$2y = \frac{1}{39} \quad \text{Joan's rate}$$

Because rates are the reciprocals of the times, *and conversely*, it would take Joan 39 hours (the reciprocal of her rate) to tally the books alone.

9-3. © Remember that rate = 1/time, so Sue's rate = 1/s, where s is the time for her to paint the room. Since

$$\text{Sue's rate} + \text{Bob's rate} = \text{joint rate}$$
$$1/s + 1/3\tfrac{1}{4} = 1/2$$

which can be solved for $s = 5.2$ hours.

9-4. © To solve the problem, it is necessary to know the *total* number of beverage cans manufactured in both 1990 and 1995. Graph (1) has the data for aluminum cans, and graph (2) has the data for steel cans. The data from the two graphs must be added together.

9-5. © In the trapezoid, $\overline{BC}$ is evidently parallel to $\overline{AD}$. The first statement reveals that triangle ACD is a 6-8-10 right triangle, with angle $ADC = 90°$. Because $\overline{BC}$ is parallel to $\overline{AD}$, angle BCD must also equal 90°. Consider triangle ABC with base $\overline{BC}$. The altitude to vertex A equals $\overline{CD}$, because $\overline{CD}$ is perpendicular to $\overline{BC}$. Then the area = $\tfrac{1}{2}bh = \tfrac{1}{2}(\overline{BC})(\overline{CD}) = \tfrac{1}{2} \times 7 \times 6 = 21$.

10-1. © Since the reduction was approximately 13 percent, the 195 professors are 87 percent of the original number.

$$195 = 0.87n$$
$$n = \tfrac{195}{0.87} \cong 224$$

10-2. © In this type of problem (weighted average) you must multiply the number of students times their respective scores and divide this total by the number of students as follows:

$$15 \times 80\% = 1{,}200$$
$$\underline{10} \times 90\% = \underline{\ 900}$$
$$25 \qquad\quad 2{,}100$$

Now divide 25 into 2,100. This gives an average of 84%; therefore, the correct answer is ©.

10-3. Ⓒ If the average of 9 numbers is 7, then the sum of these numbers must be 9 × 7, or 63.

If the average of 7 numbers is 9, then the sum of these numbers must be 7 × 9, or 63.

The sum of all 16 numbers must be 63 + 63, or 126.

Therefore, the average of all 16 numbers must be

$$126 \div 16 = \tfrac{126}{16} = 7\tfrac{14}{16} = 7\tfrac{7}{8}$$

Notice that answers Ⓐ and Ⓔ are not reasonable.

10-4. Ⓒ We look at total percentage points.

$$(20)(80) + (50)(60) + (30)(40) = 5{,}800 = 58\%$$

Notice that answers Ⓐ and Ⓑ are not reasonable.

10-5. Ⓑ Begin by using an arbitrary number, say 100, for the total number of students in the class. Therefore, there are 40 men and 60 women. Of the 60 women, 30%, or 18, are science majors. Since non-science majors make up 80% of the class, then there are 80 non-science majors and 20 science majors. We already know that 18 science majors are women, so the remaining 2 science majors must be men. Among the 40 men, there are 2 science majors, so 5% of the men are science majors.

11-1. Ⓔ First change 2 hours into 120 minutes.

(Always get a common unit of measurement.)

Then dividing 120 by $\tfrac{2}{3}$ gives

$$\overset{60}{\cancel{120}} \times \frac{3}{\underset{1}{\cancel{2}}} = 180$$

The correct answer is Ⓔ, 180 items. Notice that choices Ⓐ and Ⓑ are not reasonable.

11-2. ⓓ Since the large square has side 4 cm, then its area must be 16. By careful grouping of areas, you will see that there are four unshaded smaller squares and four shaded smaller squares (match the shaded parts to four squares). Therefore one half of the area is shaded, or 8 sq cm.

11-3. ⓒ The area of $\triangle MNP = \frac{1}{2}bh = \frac{1}{2}(MP)(MN)$.

Since $\triangle MNP$ is a right triangle, the Pythagorean theorem says

$$c^2 = a^2 + b^2$$
$$(NP)^2 = (MP)^2 + (MN)^2$$
$$26^2 = 24^2 + (MN)^2$$
$$676 = 576 + (MN)^2$$
$$(MN)^2 = 100$$
$$MN = \sqrt{100} = 10$$

So the area of
$$MNP = \frac{1}{2}(MN)(MP)$$
$$= \frac{1}{2}(10)(24)$$
$$= 120$$

11-4. ⓑ The following diagram shows Manny's bicycling path and Irv's walking path.

Manny traveled 43 miles at 10 miles per hour, so it took him 4.3 hours. The distance Irv travels is calculated by subtracting travel in opposite directions and using the Pythagorean theorem. 6 east and 18 west leaves 12 west, while 5 north and 14 south leaves 9 south. The right triangle has legs of 9 and 12. Therefore, the hypotenuse must be 15 (3:4:5 ratio), or using the theorem,

$$a^2 + b^2 = c^2$$
$$9^2 + 12^2 = c^2$$
$$81 + 144 = c^2$$
$$225 = c^2$$
$$15 = c$$

Irv must travel 15 miles at 5 miles per hour, or 3 hours. Since they both start at the same time, Irv arrives over one hour earlier than Manny.

11-5. Ⓑ Since the surface area of side *ABFE* is 16, then each side is 4. Now use the Pythagorean theorem to find the length of the diagonal that is also the length of the rectangle.

$$4^2 + 4^2 = AH^2$$
$$16 + 16 = AH^2$$
$$32 = AH^2$$
$$\sqrt{32} = AH$$

Simplifying

$$\sqrt{32} = \sqrt{16+2} = \sqrt{16} \times \sqrt{2} = 4\sqrt{2}$$

Now multiplying length times width gives

$$4 \times 4\sqrt{2} = 16\sqrt{2}$$

Notice that you might recognize the ratio of a 45°:45°:90° triangle as 1:1:$\sqrt{2}$ and find the diagonal quickly using 4:4:$4\sqrt{2}$.

12-1. Ⓔ First simplify 3^3, which is $3 \times 3 \times 3 = 27$. Then simplify $(\frac{1}{3})^2$, which is $\frac{1}{3} \times \frac{1}{3} = \frac{1}{9}$. Now divide 27 by $\frac{1}{9}$, which is the same as $27 \times \frac{9}{1} = 243$.

12-2. Ⓐ We solve for y as follows:

$$x = \frac{1+y}{y}$$
$$xy = 1 + y$$
$$xy - y = 1$$
$$y(x-1) = 1$$
$$y = \frac{1}{x-1}$$

12-3. Ⓔ Since the five choices all have a numerator of 1, the denominator of the correct choice times $(x-4)$ will equal $(2x^2 - 10x + 8)$. That denominator may be found by dividing polynomials:

$$
\begin{array}{r}
2x - 2 \quad\quad \leftarrow \textit{denominator of answer} \\
x-4 \overline{\smash{)}2x^2 - 10x + 8} \\
\underline{2x^2 - 8x} \quad\quad\;\; \\
-2x + 8 \\
\underline{-2x + 8}
\end{array}
$$

12-4. Ⓔ Factoring both numerator and denominator of the left side gives

$$\frac{\overset{1}{\cancel{(x+2)}}(x+3)}{\underset{1}{\cancel{(x+2)}}(x-2)} = \frac{3}{2}$$

Thus

$$\frac{x+3}{x-2} = \frac{3}{2}$$

Cross multiplying gives

$$2(x+3) = 3(x-2)$$
$$2x+6 = 3x-6$$
$$6 = x-6$$
$$12 = x$$

12-5. ⓓ If one root of the equation is 10, then the factored form of $x^2 - 5x + m = 0$ is $(x-10)(x + ?) = 0$. Since the middle term of the quadratic is $-5x$, then ? must be 5. So the factored version is $(x - 10)(x + 5)$. To check this, multiply the means and extremes together and add them

$$+5x$$
$$\overbrace{-10x}$$
$$(x-10)(x+5)$$

Therefore, m would have the value of -10×5, or -50. But the problem asks for $m + 3$, which is $50 + 3$, or 47.

13-1. ⓓ The net profit is 25%, since $12 is 25% of $48. Now add in 15% for overhead and you have 25% + 15% = 40%.

13-2. ⓔ First find the area of the shaded region. The difference of the outer rectangle ($6 \times 12 = 72$) and the inner rectangle ($2 \times 3 = 6$) is 66 square feet. Since it takes 24 2-inch by 3-inch tiles to cover one square foot, the correct answer is $24 \times 66 = 1,584$.

13-3. ⓔ The horizontal length of x cannot be determined because there is no indication of the overlapping length of the rectangle to the left of x. If x cannot be determined, then $x + y$ cannot be determined.

13-4. Ⓐ Ratio of diameters = ratio of radii.

$$\frac{d_1}{d_2} = \frac{r_1}{r_2} = \frac{30}{100} = \frac{3}{10}$$

Ratio of area = (ratio of radii)².

$$\frac{A_1}{A_2} = \left(\frac{r_1}{r_2}\right)^2$$

$$\frac{A_1}{A_2} = \frac{9}{100}$$

So the area of circle R, is 9/100, or 9%, of the area of circle S.

13-5. Ⓑ In the right triangle, if $c = 2a$, then angle $a = 30°$ and $c = 60°$. Since angle f is supplementary to angle c, angle f must be 120°. If angle f is 120°, then there are 60° left to be divided between angles d and b (remember, there are 180° in a triangle). Since $d > 2b$, then b must be less than 30°; therefore, the correct answer is Ⓑ—angle a (30°) is greater than angle b (less than 30°).

Notice the way you should have marked the diagram to assist you.

14-1. Ⓒ From the second statement, the refrigerators cost 112 × $186 = $20,832. Subtraction from the sale revenue in (1) leaves a gross profit of $12,228.

14-2. Ⓑ Statement (2) is sufficient. Since 84 payments of $1,124 each are still to be paid, simply multiply 84 times 1,124 to find the principal and interest still owed.

14-3. Ⓑ The month is uniquely determined only if there were no deposits or withdrawals from the account. Otherwise, any month is possible. With the restriction, the account exceeded $1,100 first on October 31, when the interest credited brought the account up to $1,104.62.

14-4. Ⓔ No exact dollar amounts are given for the individual bills. Had the Dufaas paid $\frac{1}{2}$ of each of the bills, 50% would be the answer, but since they paid different fractional amounts of some of the bills, with each bill potentially a different dollar amount, the percent paid of the total amount can differ, depending upon the relative amounts of the different bills. (For example, if the Dufaas' annual trash bill was significantly larger than the other bills, the total percent paid on all the bills would be closer to 75% than 25%.)

14-5. Ⓔ The information is insufficient to determine the number of workers at the plant. Statement (1) is inadequate without the average salary of the remaining workers. Statement (2) is inadequate because the extra employees may not earn the same average salary as the original employees.

15-1. Ⓐ The product of the factors is 105. N must be an integer that is an odd multiple of 105. The very mention of factors in (1) implies that N is an integer.

15-2. Ⓔ From (2), the product cg is positive; therefore, c and g have the same sign: f could be either positive or negative. Assume all three numbers are positive, and from (1) $cf > cg$. However, if we assume c and g are positive but f is negative, then from (1) $cf < cg$. The contradiction makes the problem indeterminate.

15-3. Ⓓ No, x is not prime. From the first statement we know that x is even, or divisible by 2. From the second statement we deduce that $x = y + 3y = 4y$, so 4 is a factor of x.

15-4. Ⓒ From the second statement, $3m^2 = 27$, $m^2 = 9$, and $m = \pm 3$. But from both statements, since n is positive, so must be m.

15-5. Ⓓ Substituting $n = 20$ into the equation $m = n + 2$, it is found that $m = 22$. That value can be substituted into the quadratic expression:

$$m^2 - 4m + 4 = (22)^2 - 4(22) + 4 = 400$$

Statement (2) gives two values for m (+22, −18), each of which when substituted into the expression $m^2 - 4m + 4$ yields 400, so either statement (1) or (2) alone is sufficient.

16-1. Ⓓ From the first statement, $x = y = 47°$, for vertical angles are equal. From the second statement, the interior angle adjacent to z is 70°, because that angle and z sum to a straight angle. Since the interior angles of a triangle add to 180°, you can write the equation $x + 63° + 70° = 180°$, permitting the determination of x.

16-2. Ⓔ The area of the right triangle equals half the product of the two legs, AE and CE. The length of AE is given (1). But point E is not on the circle, so CE is less than $\frac{1}{2}(BD)$, the diameter (2). Lacking the length of CE, one cannot calculate the area.

16-3. Ⓑ From the Pythagorean theorem we know that $AD^2 + BD^2 = AB^2$, so $BD^2 = 16 + 121$, and $BD = \sqrt{137}$. The second statement tells us that the base and height of the triangle are equal, so $A = \frac{1}{2}bh = \frac{1}{2}\sqrt{137} \times \sqrt{137} = \frac{137}{2}$.

16-4. Ⓒ In the rectangle, $BA = CD = 3$ inches. So two sides of right triangle BAE are known, and the length of side AE can be found with the Pythagorean theorem to be 4 inches. As point E is the midpoint of AD, the length of the rectangle is twice AE, or 8 inches. The area of the right triangle BCD is half the product of the sides adjacent to the right angle:

$$A = \tfrac{1}{2}bh = \tfrac{1}{2}(8)(3) = 12 \text{ in}^2$$

16-5. Ⓓ The radius BC must be perpendicular to the tangent AB, so ABC is a right triangle. The second statement implies it is a 6-8-10 right triangle, so the radius is 6. We can solve from the first statement with the Pythagorean theorem:

$$(AC)^2 = (AB)^2 + (BC)^2$$
$$(4+r)^2 = 8^2 + r^2$$
$$16 + 8r + r^2 = 64 + r^2$$
$$r = \tfrac{48}{8} = 6$$

17-1. Ⓔ The given sequence more than doubles at each step, so it is fundamentally a geometric (multiplicative) sequence rather than an arithmetic (additive) sequence. Each term is two more than double the preceding term. The next number in the sequence would be $2 + 2(94) = 190$.

17-2. Ⓒ A 6% annual interest rate, compounded semiannually (every half year) is the same as a 3% semiannual interest rate. At the end of first half of year: Interest on $2,000 at 3% =$2,000 × 0.03 = $60. New balance at end of first half year = $2,000 + $60 = $2,060. At the end of first full year: Interest on $2,060 at 3% = $2,060 × 0.03 = $61.80 $\cong$ $62. New balance at end of first full year = $2,060 + $62 = $2,122.

17-3. ⓓ The only reasonable answer is $5\frac{5}{9}$, since 85¢ per pound is slightly closer to 93¢ per pound than 75¢ per pound. Then slightly more than half of the 10 pounds must be 93¢ per pound.

Algebraically, let x stand for the pounds of 93¢ tea. Then $10 - x$ is the 75¢ tea. This leads to the equation

$$0.93x + 0.75(10 - x) = 0.85(10)$$

Solving gives

$$93x + 750 - 75x = 850$$
$$18x = 100$$
$$x = \frac{100}{18}$$

Therefore, $\qquad\qquad x = 5\frac{5}{9}$

17-4. ⓑ Since 100 plus 120 is 220, there must be 20 students who study both languages. Thus, of the 100 who study French, 80 do not study Spanish. 80 is 40% of the total of 200.

17-5. ⓓ Only the 19 cannot be weighed. To get 13, place 10 and 4 on one side and 1 on the other. To get the 15, place the 10, 4, and 1 on one side. To get the 17, place the 10 and 7 on one side. To get the 21, place the 10, 7, and 4 on one side.

18-1. ⓑ Percent change is found by using the formula

$$\text{percent decrease or increase} = \frac{\text{change}}{\text{starting point}}$$

The change was $75 - 60 = 15$. (Notice that rounding off is possible.) The starting point was 75. Thus, $\frac{15}{75} = \frac{1}{5} = 20\%$.

18-2. ⓒ Let x be the length of time Mr. Dinkle travels. Then $x + \frac{1}{2}$ is the time Mr. Smitherly travels. This gives the equation $50(x + \frac{1}{2}) = 60x$, to see when they will meet. Solving gives

$$50x + 25 = 60x$$
$$25 = 10x$$
$$2.5 = x$$

Therefore, it will take Mr. Dinkle $2\frac{1}{2}$ hours to overtake Mr. Smitherly. Since Mr. Dinkle starts at 8:30 A.M., he will overtake Mr. Smitherly at 11:00 A.M.

Note that answers Ⓐ, Ⓓ, and Ⓔ are not reasonable.

18-3. Ⓒ Average speed is total distance/total time. The total distance is 360 miles. Time for the first 150 miles is 150/30 = 5 hours. The time for the remaining 210 miles is 210/35 = 6 hours. Thus the average speed is 360/(5 +6) = 360/11 = $32\frac{8}{11}$ mph.

18-4. Ⓑ Average speed is total distance/total time. The total distance is $2x$. Time going is $x/8$. Time coming back is $x/12$. Thus the average speed is

$$\frac{2x}{x/8 + x/12} = \frac{2x}{3x/24 + 2x/24}$$

$$= \frac{2x}{5x/24} = \frac{2x}{1} \cdot \frac{24}{5x} = \frac{48}{5} = 9.6$$

Notice that answers Ⓒ, Ⓓ, and Ⓔ are not reasonable.

18-5. Ⓒ We can set up the following chart

	D	=	R	×	T
Up	D		16		$\frac{D}{16}$
Down	D		24		$\frac{D}{24}$

Since the time is 10 hours for the whole trip,

$\frac{D}{16} + \frac{D}{24} = 10$ Multiply by 48, $3D + 2D = 480$

$$5D = 480$$
$$D = 96$$

19-1. Ⓒ If the radius of a circle is 1, and it is reduced by 20%, it becomes 0.8. Since the area formula squares the radius, the original factor remains 1, but the new factor becomes 0.64, which is a 36% decrease.

19-2. Ⓐ The shaded area is the difference between the entire rectangle (with an area of $6 \times 8 = 48$) and the white triangle (with an area of $(6 \times x)/2 = 3x$). Thus, $48 - 3x$.

19-3. Ⓑ Since the perimeter of the square is 32, each side of the square is 8.

Area of square $= 8^2 = 64$

Note that $\quad 4r = 8$ or $r = 2$

Area of 1 circle $= \pi r^2$

$\qquad\qquad\qquad = \pi \times 2^2$

$\qquad\qquad\qquad = 4\pi$

Area of 4 circles $= 4 \times$ (area of 1 circle)

$\qquad\qquad\qquad = 4(4\pi)$

$\qquad\qquad\qquad = 16\pi$

Then shaded area $=$ (area of square) $-$ (area of 4 circles)

$\qquad\qquad\qquad = 64 - 16\pi$

19-4. Ⓔ The circumference of the large circle is 64π.

Since circumference $= 2\pi r$

$\qquad\qquad 64\pi = 2\pi r$

$\qquad\qquad\quad 32 = r$

Radius of large circle $= 32$

Diameter of 2 small circles $= 32$

So diameter of 1 small circle $= 16$

Radius of small circle $= 8$

Area of small circle $= \pi r^2$

$\qquad\qquad\qquad = \pi \times 8^2$

$\qquad\qquad\qquad = 64\pi$

So area of 4 small circles $= 4 \times$ (area of 1 small circle)

$$= 4(64\pi)$$

$$= 256\pi$$

19-5.   Ⓒ The area of any square equals one-half the product of its diagonals. Thus, the area of square $ABCD = \frac{1}{2}(2)(2) = 2$. The area of circle O equals $\pi r^2 \cong 3 \times 1 = 3$. The shaded area = the area of circle O minus the area of square $ABCD$, or $3 - 2 = 1$. Notice that to find the area of square $EFGH$, you may move the radius as follows:

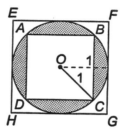

Thus the sides of square $EFGH$ are each 2, so its area is $2 \times 2 = 4$. Therefore, the shaded area is approximately 1 out of 4, or 25% of square $EFGH$. You may also simply eliminate answer choices Ⓐ, Ⓑ, Ⓓ, and Ⓔ by inspection. Every choice except Ⓒ is not reasonable. Be aware that this type of elimination by inspection is possible only if the diagram is drawn close to scale and if the answer choices are far enough apart to allow approximating.

20-1. Ⓑ First note that $\frac{1}{4}$ of $\frac{3}{5}$ = $\frac{3}{20}$. We then have: $\frac{3}{20}$ is what percent of $\frac{3}{4}$?

$$\frac{\text{is number}}{\text{of number}} = \frac{\text{percent}}{100}$$

$$\frac{\frac{3}{20}}{\frac{3}{4}} = \frac{P}{100}$$

Cross multiplying gives

$$\frac{3}{4}P = \frac{3}{\overset{}{\underset{1}{20}}}(\overset{5}{\cancel{100}})$$

$$\frac{3}{4}P = 15$$

$$P = \frac{4}{\overset{}{\underset{1}{\cancel{3}}}}(\overset{5}{\cancel{15}})$$

$$P = 20$$

Thus Ⓑ 20% is the correct answer.

20-2. Ⓐ The desired weekly income is $600. $600 − $150 (weekly salary) = $450 (amount to be made up from commission). Let x = number of dollars in sales for one week. Since the sales representative earns 15% on all sales, this gives the equation

$$0.15x = 450$$
$$x = \frac{450}{0.15}$$
$$x = 3,000$$

Therefore, she must make sales totaling $3,000.

20-3. Ⓓ Begin with an arbitrary number of items sold, say 10, for a gross income of $1,000. By reducing the price 10% to $90, the owners sell 20% more items, or now 12. Now their gross income is 12 × $90 = $1,080. The percent increase is 80/1,000, or 8%.

20-4. Ⓒ The best way to solve this problem is by using simple numbers. If the recliners originally sold at $100 each, then a 20% reduction would leave a price of $80 each. If the owner sold 50% more recliners, it would be the same as $40 more for each original sale. This would be $120, ($80 + $40), which is 20% more than $100 per recliner.

An alternate method would be to let $\frac{3}{2}$ represent a 50% increase. Then $\frac{3}{2}$ times 80% = 120%, which is a 20% increase over the original 100%.

20-5. Ⓒ If x is increased by 50%, we can represent it by $\frac{3}{2}x$. We must multiply this by $\frac{2}{3}y$ in order to keep the product equal to xy. Since $\frac{2}{3}$ is a $\frac{1}{3}$ reduction, answer Ⓒ is the correct response. You could also try using some values for x and y.

21-1. Ⓑ Whether m is positive or negative, m^2 must be positive. So the sign of n determines the sign of the product.

21-2. Ⓓ The sole solution is $m = 1 = 1 \times 1 = 1 \times 1 \times 1$ and so m is positive. Note that $-1 \neq (-1)(-1) \neq (-1)(-1)(-1)$.

21-3. Ⓔ Neither statement permits the calculation of $x + y + z$. Especially, the second statement cannot be inverted to obtain $\frac{9}{4}$, for the summation of fractions requires a common denominator:

$$\frac{yz + xz + xy}{xyz} = \frac{4}{9}$$

21-4. Ⓒ The question can be answered with both pieces of information. With $x < y$ and $y < 0$, then $(x-y)$ is negative. With $y < 0$ and $z < 0$, then the product yz is positive. Given both statements, $(x-y)$ is less than yz.

21-5. Ⓓ If $b < a$, statement (1), then $(a - b) > 0$ and, for any c, $(a-b)^c$ is positive. Incidentally, if $c = 0$, the entire exponential quantity equals 1, by definition. Also, if $c = 2a$, statement (2), then c is an even integer and the entire exponential quantity is positive, even if $(a - b)$ is negative.

22-1. Ⓔ Volume is the product of three dimensions. For the can, volume equals its base area (two dimensional) times its height; but the height is not stated.

22-2. Ⓓ From the first statement, $x + 4 = 4x - 2$, because opposite sides of a rectangle are equal. So $x = 2$ and the width $x + 4 = 6$. Or we can use the area of the second statement, as width = area/length = $\frac{48}{8}$ = 6.

22-3. Ⓒ The first statement implies that the diagonal divides the field into two 30°-60° right triangles, with sides in the ratio $1:2:\sqrt{3}$. Employing that ratio to find the width with a length of 173 feet, the width equals 100 feet. Then the area equals 17,300 square feet.

22-4. Ⓓ This problem may be solved swiftly with knowledge of the principle that for quadrilaterals of equal area, the square has the shortest perimeter. Then the farmer would need less fencing for the stubbier configuration, approaching a square. Statement (2) yields that information immediately. Since the area of 3,000 equals the length times the width, statement (1) implies that lot X would be 75×40 and lot Y would be 60×50. From either statement, lot Y would have the shorter perimeter.

22-5. Ⓐ Angle ABC, inscribed on a diameter, is necessarily 90°, so the second statement adds nothing new. But the first statement implies the triangle has an altitude equal to the circle's radius, 6. So the shaded area equals the area of the semicircle, $(\frac{1}{2} \times \pi \times 6^2)$ minus the area of the triangle $(\frac{1}{2}bh = \frac{1}{2} \times 12 \times 6 = 36)$.

23-1. Ⓒ Since there are two unknowns, we need two equations to solve for p and r. From (2), $p = r + 5$. Substituting that for p in (1) yields $2r + 10 + 3r = 11$, or $r = \frac{1}{5}$. Since $p = r + 5$, $p = \frac{1}{5} + 5 = \frac{26}{5}$.

23-2. Ⓐ From the first statement, $m^2/s^3 = 3$, and squaring each side, $m^4/s^6 = 9$. Substituting into the original expression, $14(m^4/s^6) = 14 \times 9 = 126$.

23-3. Ⓔ Making substitutions from both statements yields the expression $9 - 2y < 17$. To solve for y, we first subtract 9 from both sides and then divide by –2; the latter operation reverses the sense of the inequality. The solution $y > -4$ records that y may be positive, zero, or negative (between 0 and –4).

23-4. Ⓐ From statement (1), $3c$ and $8d^3$ have opposite signs. Hence c and d^3 have opposite signs. With the odd exponent, the sign of d will be the same as d^3. So statement (1) is sufficient to answer the question, even though the answer is "no."

23-5. Ⓑ We cannot solve the first equation by elementary methods. The second equation implies $x = 1$. Hence $x^3 - 2x^2 + 7 = 6$.

24-1. Ⓑ In $\triangle ABD$, the sum of $\angle A$, $\angle B$, and $\angle BDA$ is 180°. If $\angle B = 90°$ and $\angle BDA = 50°$, then $\angle A = 40°$. Since $\angle A = x° + 15°$, we have

$$40° = x° + 15°$$
$$25° = x°$$

Therefore, $\qquad x = 25$

24-2. ⃝ Perimeter of $\triangle MNP = \frac{1}{2}$(perimeter of $\triangle XYZ$)

$$= \frac{1}{2}(XY + YZ + XZ)$$
$$= \frac{1}{2}(10 + 15 + 17)$$
$$= \frac{1}{2}(42)$$

Perimeter of $\triangle MNP = 21$

24-3. ⃝ From the figure and using the Pythagorean theorem, we find the radius is 13 inches.

$$5^2 + 12^2 = r^2$$
$$24 + 144 = r^2$$
$$169 = r^2$$
$$13 = r$$

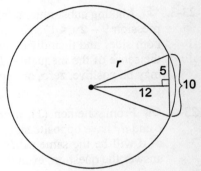

Alternate method: If you recognized the 5-12-13 right triangle, you could quickly find r to be 13.

24-4. ⃝ Let

$$5x = \text{first angle}$$
$$2x = \text{second angle}$$
$$5x - 2x = 3x = \text{third angle}$$

Since the sum of the angles in any triangle is 180°, we have

$$5x + 2x + 3x = 180°$$
$$10x = 180°$$
$$x = 18°$$

Therefore,

$$5x = 90°$$
$$2x = 36°$$
$$3x = 54°$$

The smallest angle has a measure of 36°.

24-5. Ⓔ From the figure, we use the Pythagorean theorem and find the missing side, x, is 12 inches. Thus, Ⓔ is correct.

$$a^2 + b^2 = c^2$$
$$16^2 + x^2 = 20^2$$
$$256 + x^2 = 400$$
$$x^2 = 400 - 256$$
$$x^2 = 144$$
$$x = 12$$

25-1. Ⓓ When $N + 1$ is divided by 5, the remainder is 4. When N (which is one less than $N + 1$) is divided by 5, the remainder should be 3 (which is one less than 4).

25-2. Ⓐ The two-digit numbers whose remainder is 1 when divided by 10 are: 11, 21, 31, 41, 51, 61, 71, 81, and 91. When divided by 6, the remainder is 5 for the numbers 11, 41, and 71. Therefore, 3 numbers satisfy the conditions of the problem.

25-3. Ⓑ Set up the problem as follows

$$\frac{x+(2)}{x+5+(2)} = \frac{7}{12}, \text{ or } \frac{x+2}{x+7} = \frac{7}{12}$$

By observation $x = 5$ since $\dfrac{5+2}{5+7} = \dfrac{7}{12}$

Substituting into the original fraction $\dfrac{x}{x+5}$ gives

$$\frac{5}{5+5} = \frac{5}{10} = \frac{1}{2}$$

A simpler method is

$$\frac{7-2}{12-2} = \frac{5}{10} = \frac{1}{2}$$

25-4. ⓓ Begin by choosing a simple fraction, say 100/100. If the numerator is tripled and the denominator is doubled, the resulting fraction will be 300/200, or $1\frac{1}{2}$. So the new fraction represents a 50% increase over the original fraction.

25-5. ⓑ The @ of 2 = (2)(5) − 2 = 8. So 2 is the largest positive integer n such that @ of n will be less than 10.

26-1. ⓒ If x represents the cost of the book, then we have the following equation:

$$x + 0.20x = \$12.00$$
$$1.2x = \$12.00$$
$$x = \$10.00$$

26-2. ⓔ Since the chart does not distinguish how many houses are 3 years old or 4 years old, the answer cannot be determined.

26-3. ⓔ Simply continue the chart as follows, adding 40¢ for each two years to Product A and 15¢ for each two years to Product B:

Products	1998	2000	2002	2004	2006
A	$6.60	$7.00	$7.40	$7.80	$8.20
B	$7.20	$7.35	$7.50	$7.65	$7.80

It is evident that the correct answer is 2006.

26-4. ⓒ The total price of toy A is $5.0227 [$2.5796 + $2.4431], and the total price of toy B is $5.0080 [$2.5768 + $2.4312]. Toy A exceeds toy B by $0.0147; therefore 10,000 of each must be manufactured to have a $147.00 difference.

26-5. Ⓑ Mr. Talbot's charge for the call $14.09
       Cost of first 3 minutes of a
          person-to-person call   −$4.35
       Cost of additional minutes $9.74

       Cost of additional minutes $9.74
       Cost of each additional minute   ———— ≅ 21 minutes
                                        $0.46

       Total length of call = first 3 minutes + additional minutes
                            = 3 + 21 = 24 minutes

27-1. Ⓒ The number of tiles would equal the area of the kitchen divided by the area of one tile, or $(120 \times 84)/48 = 210$ tiles.

27-2. Ⓑ The amount of wallpaper can be measured in square feet, the area of the two largest walls. Each large wall has an area equal to the length of the room times the height of the room. The total amount of wallpaper required is $2 \times 24 \times 9 = 432$ square feet.

27-3. Ⓑ The central angle MON must be 96°, twice the inscribed angle NPM. Further, the triangle MNO has two radii as sides, so it is isosceles, and angle $OMN = MNO$. Therefore, $2(MNO) + 96° = 180°$, and one may solve for $MNO = 42°$.

27-4. Ⓓ Either statement suffices to determine MN to be $7\frac{1}{2}$. Because of similar triangles, $MN:OQ = MP:QP = NP:OP$. From the Pythagorean theorem, $OP = 13$. By addition, $NP = ON + OP = 6\frac{1}{2} + 13 = 19\frac{1}{2}$; also $MP = 18$. Therefore, $MN:5 = 18:12 = 19\frac{1}{2}:13$ and we can solve for MN.

27-5. Ⓔ Since P is not now touching the ground, all we know is that the wheel has traveled more than 5 circumferences but less than $5\frac{1}{4}$. So, $5\pi d < 36 < 5\frac{1}{4}\pi d$. Therefore, the diameter is uncertain, somewhere in the range 2.18 to 2.29 feet.

28-1. (B) The sale price equaled the list price L minus 30%. So $140 = 0.7L$, and $L = 140/0.7 = \$200$.

28-2. (D) To solve the first expression, we add 5 to both sides and divide by 4. The second expression is solved by collecting terms on the left, $m^2 - 6m + 9 = 0$, and factoring, $(m-3)^2 = 0$. From either expression, $m = 3$.

28-3. (E) No relationship can be determined between x and y, since the two equations are the same. (Multiply the second equation by 4.)

28-4. (E) The first statement reveals only that c and a have the same sign. From the initial proportion and the second statement, $ac = b^2 = 32$, but the sign of c is indeterminate.

28-5. (A) The first five perfect cubes are 1, 8, 27, 64, and 125. Therefore, $C = 64$.

29-1. (C) If the box is cubical, then each side is square. An edge of the box would be the square root of the side, or 4 inches. The volume equals the edge cubed, or 64 cubic inches.

29-2. (E) The first statement lists two points through which the circle passes, but many circles could pass through any two points. Knowing the diameter would still not yield a unique circle.

29-3. (E) Combining both statements, all we know is that the line passes through the point $(5, -3)$, and the orientation is unspecified.

29-4. (B) Necessarily, the diagonal equals the side times $\sqrt{2}$, so from the second statement, $d = \sqrt{8} \times \sqrt{2} = \sqrt{16} = 4$, a rational number.

29-5. Ⓐ The shaded part equals the area of the large circle minus the areas of the two small circles. For any circle, $A = \pi r^2$ and we can ascertain the radii of the circles from statement (1) alone. The small circles are of equal size, with radii of $2\frac{1}{2}$. Because the small circles are equal, their diameter is the radius of the large circle. Shaded area $= 25\pi - 2(25/4)\pi = (25/2)\pi$.

30-1. Ⓒ

$$\dfrac{\dfrac{\cancel{7}^{\,1}}{\cancel{10}_{\,2}} \times \dfrac{14}{1} \times \dfrac{\cancel{5}^{\,1}}{1} \times \dfrac{1}{\cancel{28}_{\,4}}}{\dfrac{\cancel{10}}{\cancel{11}_{\,1}} \times \dfrac{\cancel{3}}{\cancel{5}_{\,1}} \times \dfrac{1}{\cancel{6}_{\,2}} \times \dfrac{\cancel{11}}{1}} = \dfrac{\dfrac{14}{8}}{\dfrac{2}{2}} = \dfrac{\dfrac{7}{4}}{1} = \dfrac{7}{4}$$

30-2. Ⓒ Having spent $\frac{2}{5}$ of her money on clothes, Mary has $\frac{3}{5}$ of her money left. Then $\frac{1}{2}$ of $\frac{3}{5}$, or $\frac{3}{10}$, is placed in her savings account. She has now spent $\frac{2}{5} + \frac{3}{10} = \frac{7}{10}$ of her money. Thus, she has $\frac{3}{10}$ remaining. If m is the money she started with, and she has only $21 left, we have the equation

$$\left(\tfrac{3}{10}\right)m = 21$$
$$m = 21\left(\tfrac{10}{3}\right)$$
$$m = 70$$

30-3. Ⓐ Set up two equations.

$$5A + 2B = 6B + 5C \qquad 1A + 4C = 2A + 4B$$
$$5A = 4B + 5C \qquad\qquad 4C = A + 4B$$
$$4C - A = 4B$$

Substitute $4C - A$ for $4B$ in the other equation.

$$5A = 4C - A + 5C$$
$$6A = 9C$$
$$A = \tfrac{9}{6}C$$
$$= \tfrac{3}{2}C$$

30-4. Ⓓ Since Felix earns 30% more than Oscar, let x = Oscar's salary and $1.3x$ = Felix's salary. If Felix's salary is reduced by 10%, he is now earning $1.3x - 0.13x = 1.17x$. If Oscar's salary is increased 10%, he is now earning $1x + 0.1x = 1.1x$. Felix is now earning $(0.07x/1.1x) = 6.36\%$ more than Oscar.

30-5. Ⓐ Let x equal 1995's amount used; let y equal 1995's rate. Therefore, xy = 1995's water expenditure. For 1996, instead of y, use $1.5y$ for the new rate, and let p equal the new fraction of x (water used) to set up the equation:

$$\text{expenditure in 1995} = \text{expenditure in 1996}$$
$$xy = (px)(1.5y)$$
$$xy = xy(1.5p)$$
$$1 = 1.5p$$
$$1/1.5 = p$$
$$0.66\tfrac{2}{3} = p$$

Since for 1996, the Johnsons must use only $66\tfrac{2}{3}\%$ of 1995's amount, they must reduce their 1995 usage by $33\tfrac{1}{3}\%$.

31-1. Ⓔ If y is a positive integer, y could be 1. Choices Ⓐ, Ⓑ, Ⓒ, and Ⓓ are all evenly divisible by 1. Only choice Ⓔ, $1\tfrac{1}{2}$, is not divisible by 1.

31-2. Ⓒ Two 2-digit numbers, 80 and 88, are each divisible by 8, and the sums of their digits are divisible by 8.

31-3. Ⓐ You must solve the two simultaneous linear equations for both variables.

$$
\begin{array}{ll}
3r + s = 17 & \text{The first equation} \\
\underline{-3r - 6s = -27} & \text{The second equation times } -3 \\
{-5s} = -10 & \text{Adding two equations} \\
s = 2 & \text{Solution for } s
\end{array}
$$

$$3r + 2 = 17 \quad \text{Substituting into the first equation}$$
$$3r = 15$$
$$r = 5 \quad \text{Solution for } r$$

So r exceeds s by 3.

31-4. Ⓔ First rearrange and simplify the first equation as follows:

Add $+12$ and $+6y$ to both sides of the equation $6x - 12 = -6y$ and you get

$$\begin{array}{rl} 6x - 12 & = -6y \\ +12 + 6y & = +6y + 12 \\ \hline 6x \quad + 6y & = \quad 12 \end{array}$$

Now dividing through by 6 leaves $x + y = 2$.

Next, rearrange and simplify the second equation as follows:

$5y + 5x = 15$ is the same as $5x + 5y = 15$. Dividing through by 5 leaves $x + y = 3$.

The equations $x + y = 2$ and $x + y = 3$ have no solutions in common because you can't add the same two numbers and get two different answers.

31-5. Ⓐ Note that $(x - y)^2 = x^2 - 2xy + y^2$
$$= x^2 + y^2 - 2xy$$
$$= 14 - 2(3)$$
$$= 14 - 6$$
$$= 8$$

32-1. Ⓐ Start at the lower right, and add the whole number 2 with the fraction. Change to an improper fraction, invert, and continue.

$$2 + \cfrac{1}{2 + \cfrac{1}{2\frac{1}{2}}}$$

$$2 + \cfrac{1}{2 + \cfrac{1}{\frac{5}{2}}}$$

$$2 + \cfrac{1}{2 + \frac{2}{5}}$$

$$2 + \cfrac{1}{2\frac{2}{5}}$$

$$2 + \cfrac{1}{\frac{12}{5}}$$

$$2 + \frac{5}{12}$$

$$2\frac{5}{12} = \frac{29}{12}$$

32-2. Ⓒ Since 21 is 70% of the total, the total must be 30. Thus the team lost 9 matches.

$$21 = 70\% \text{ of } x$$
$$21 = 0.7x$$
$$\frac{21}{0.7} = x$$
$$30 = x$$
$$30 - 21 = 9$$

Notice that answers Ⓐ and Ⓑ are not reasonable.

32-3. Ⓒ Calculate the rates of production per day. Two of the factories each make $100{,}000/15 \cong 6{,}667$ hubcaps per day. The third plant makes $1.3 \times 6{,}667 \cong 8{,}667$ hubcaps per day. The total production rate is $8{,}667 + 2(6{,}667) = 22{,}001$ hubcaps per day. At that rate it would take 45.5 days to produce a million hubcaps.

32-4. Ⓐ Since it takes Dan 15 hours to complete the job, then in 9 hours he will be able to do only $\frac{9}{15}$, or $\frac{3}{5}$, of the job. This leaves $\frac{2}{5}$ of the job to be finished by Fred. Since Fred takes 10 hours to do the *whole* job by himself, to do only $\frac{2}{5}$ of the job, it would take Fred $\frac{2}{5} \times 10 = 4$ hours.

32-5. Ⓒ Since machine A worked for 2 hours and could do the entire job in 8 hours, machine A must have done $\frac{1}{4}$ of the job. We have the following formula in which the value of x represents the time actually worked.

$$\underset{\underline{\text{A}}}{\frac{2}{8}} + \underset{\underline{\text{B}}}{\frac{x}{10}} + \underset{\underline{\text{C}}}{\frac{x}{12}} = 1$$

$$\frac{x}{10} + \frac{x}{12} = \frac{3}{4}$$

$$6x + 5x = 45$$

$$11x = 45$$

$$x = 4\tfrac{1}{11}$$

9:00 A.M. $+ 4\frac{1}{11}$ hours $\cong$ 1:00 P.M.

33-1. Ⓒ The question asks how far the car can travel, and the answer would be $\frac{50}{8} \times 100 = 625$ kilometers. It is essential to realize that liters measure volume and kilometers measure distance.

33-2. Ⓐ Since Ethyl, Dora, and Carl are consecutive, Grace and Bill must be in the remaining adjacent seats.

33-3. Ⓔ The question is indeterminate because many different combinations of the two cone prices can sum to $209.15. The question could be answered if you also knew *either* the number of Generous cones *or* the number of all cones.

33-4. ⑧ Let g be the fraction of gasoline. Then the fraction of alcohol is $1-g$. So for the mixture, $1.09g + 1.81(1-g) = 1.22$, and we can solve for $g = 0.82$. Gasohol 99 is 82% gasoline and 18% alcohol.

33-5. ⓔ The question cannot be answered, even with both statements, because any burnt-out bulb could have its switch either ON or OFF.

34-1. ⓔ The second statement means that the Emporium sold a total of 2,568 shoes. You cannot assume from the first statement that one-quarter of those shoes were black, because some shoes are neither black nor brown.

34-2. ⓒ The radiator requires 60% antifreeze in its 3 gallons, or 1.8 gallons antifreeze.

34-3. ⓔ The two statements may be translated into the equations

$$(1) \ M + 2 = 2b$$
$$(2) \ S = (M + B)/2$$

As two equations are insufficient to determine three variables, Mary's age is indeterminate.

34-4. ⑧ The first statement translates to the equation $A + 1 = \frac{1}{2}(M + 1)$, which has two unknowns and cannot be solved for A. But the second statement means $A + 5 = 2(A - 10)$, and we can solve for Anne's age, 25 years.

34-5. ⓐ Let's symbolize the first number as f and the second as s. The main clause of the first sentence of the question yields the equation $f = 5 + \frac{1}{2}s$, and statement (1) is the equation $f = s - 1$. Those two linear equations with two unknowns can be solved for both the first number ($f = 11$) and the second number ($s = 12$).

35-1. ⓒ The six faces of the cube each have an area of $10 \times 10 =$ 100 square feet. That is a total of 600 square feet. Since it takes one quart for each 20 square feet, you need 30 quarts. Take 30 $\times$ \$3.20 = \$96.00

35-2. Ⓑ Notice that in triangle *BCE* the angle at *B* equals 94°. Therefore, any perpendicular dropped from *C* to line *AB* must be less than 3 (see diagram below). Since the area of a parallelogram = base $\times$ height, then the area of parallelogram *AECD* = 8 $\times$ (a height less than 3) = an area less than 24.

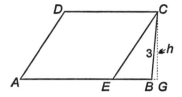

35-3. Ⓓ Points *A, B,* and *P* form a 30°-60°-90° triangle, the sides of which are in a 1-$\sqrt{3}$-2 relationship. A proportion can therefore be established:

$$\frac{120}{\sqrt{3}} = \frac{?}{1}$$

Solving:

$$\frac{120}{\sqrt{3}} = \frac{x}{1}$$

$$x = \frac{120}{\sqrt{3}}$$

$$x = \frac{120}{\sqrt{3}} \cdot \frac{\sqrt{3}}{\sqrt{3}} = \frac{120\sqrt{3}}{3} = 40\sqrt{3}$$

35-4. © Since the perimeter of rectangle $ABCD$ is 22 and $DC = 7$, we have

$$22 = 2(AD) + 2(7)$$
$$22 = 2(AD) + 14$$
$$8 = 2(AD)$$
$$4 = AD$$

Next note that $\triangle ADE$ is a 30°-60°-90° triangle with side ratios $1:\sqrt{3}:2$. Since the side across from 30° is 4, the side across from 60° is $4\sqrt{3}$. Thus $DE = 4\sqrt{3}$. Also note that $\triangle DEF$ is a 45°-45°-90° triangle with side ratios $1:1:\sqrt{2}$. Since $DE = 4\sqrt{3}$, then $EF = 4\sqrt{3}$. Then the area of DEF

$$= \tfrac{1}{2}(EF)(DE)$$
$$= \tfrac{1}{2}\left(4\sqrt{3}\right)\left(4\sqrt{3}\right)$$
$$= \tfrac{1}{2} \times 16 \times 3$$
$$= 24$$

35-5. ⓓ Since arc AC is 120°, then arc AE equals 60°. Therefore, $\angle AOE$ is 60° and $\triangle AOD$ is a 30°-60°-90° triangle and its sides are in the proportion $1\text{-}\sqrt{3}\text{-}2$. Since AO is 2, AD equals $\sqrt{3}$, and OD is 1. So the base of $\triangle ABC$ is $2\sqrt{3}$, and its height is $1 + 2 = 3$. So the area of $ABC = \tfrac{1}{2}bh = \tfrac{1}{2}(2\sqrt{3})(3) = 3\sqrt{3}$.

36-1. ⓓ The most the trip will cost is when gas costs $1.12 and the mileage is 16 mph. Thus $1.12 × (480/16) = $33.60. The least would be $0.96 × (480/24) = $19.20. The difference is $14.40.

36-2. ⓔ The ferry can transport the maximum number of cars when they are all the minimum weight, 1,800 pounds. Each of those cars weighs 1,800/2,000 = 0.9 tons. The number of those automobiles that can be transported by the ferry is its capacity divided by the weight of one car: 78/0.9 = 86.67 automobiles.

36-3. © Looking at the water, we have $\tfrac{2}{3}$ of 2 quarts $= \tfrac{4}{3}$ quarts, and $\tfrac{3}{8}$ of 3 quarts $= \tfrac{9}{8}$ quarts. These add together to give $2\tfrac{11}{24}$, which is very close to 50% of 5 quarts.

36-4. Ⓒ Set up an equation for the amount of salt.

$$10\% \text{ of } 10 \quad \text{plus} \quad 0\% \text{ of } x \quad \text{equals} \quad 7\% \text{ of } (10+x)$$
$$1.0 \quad + \quad 0 \quad = \quad (0.7+0.07x)$$
$$1 = 0.7 + 0.07x$$
$$0.3 = 0.07x$$
$$\frac{0.3}{0.07} = x$$
$$\frac{30}{7} = x$$

Solving for x, we get $4\frac{2}{7}$.

36-5. Ⓑ Since there are 8 pints per gallon, the volume of punch is 60 pints. If we call the amount of orange juice J, then the amount of buttermilk is $2J$ and the amount of brandy is $J/3$. All the ingredients add to 60 pints.

$$J + 2J + \frac{J}{3} = 60$$
$$\frac{3J + 6J + J}{3} = 60$$
$$3J + 6J + J = 180$$
$$10J = 180$$
$$J = 18 \text{ pints of orange juice}$$

37-1. Ⓑ Solve this problem by plugging in simple numbers. Start with 1, an odd integer.

$$(1+1) \text{ times } (2 \cdot 1) + 1 =$$
$$(2) \text{ times } (2+1) =$$
$$2 \quad \times \quad 3 \quad = 6 \text{ Not odd}$$

Now try 2, an even integer.

$$(2+1) \text{ times } (2 \cdot 2) + 1 =$$
$$(3) \text{ times } (4+1) =$$
$$3 \quad \times \quad 5 \quad = 15 \text{ Odd}$$

37-2. Ⓓ Examining each choice,

Ⓐ $(x+3)(x+5)$ Since x is even, both $x+3$ and $x+5$ are odd; then (odd)(odd) = odd.

Ⓑ x^2+5 Since x is even, x^2 is even, and x^2+5 is odd.

Ⓒ x^2+6x+9 Since x is even, x^2 is even and $6x$ is even; then (even) + (even) + (odd) = odd.

Ⓓ $3x^2+4$ Since x is even, $3x^2$ is even; then (even) + (even) = *even*.

Ⓔ $5(x+3)$ Since x is even, $x+3$ is odd; then (odd)(odd) = odd.

37-3. Ⓑ If the annual bonus were normally $100, tripled it would be $300. Therefore, the increase ($200) is $\frac{2}{3}$ of the new bonus ($300). Two thirds is $66\frac{2}{3}\%$.

37-4. Ⓔ Any number of members is possible as long as the number of dollars per member is two more than the number of members.

37-5. Ⓒ Let c = cost of each brick. Let M = total money. Thus $M = 45c$ and $M = 50(c-10)$.

Therefore,
$$45c = 50(c-10)$$
$$45c = 50c - 500$$
$$500 = 5c$$
$$100 = c$$

Thus $M = 4,500$ cents, or $45.00.

VERBAL SECTION

1. Ⓒ The first paragraph supports answers Ⓐ, Ⓑ, Ⓓ, and Ⓔ. One of the points of the experiments described is to show that people will change their opinions *without* being given good reasons to do so.

2. Ⓒ The passage concludes that a change of judgment is likely to be based on a change of knowledge or assumptions about the topic.

3. Ⓐ Though the passage refers to ideas in choices Ⓑ, Ⓒ, and Ⓓ, only Ⓐ is the main point of the *whole* passage.

4. Ⓓ The passage gives us no information on the author's views of men as opposed to women. Answer Ⓓ, referring to both men and women, is clearly implied by the last paragraph.

5-1. Ⓑ Choice Ⓑ correctly supplies the plural *know,* which agrees with *ecologists.* The subject closest to the verb determines the number of the verb in this case. Choice Ⓑ also retains the necessary *neither . . . nor.*

5-2. Ⓑ Choice Ⓑ corrects the verb agreement problem in the original wording. The verbs must both be past tense or both be present tense. No other choice uses proper tense without introducing a subject-verb agreement error.

5-3. Ⓔ Choice Ⓔ best expresses the parallel form called for in this sentence (*neglect, housecleaning, lack*—all nouns). The other choices contain the same "unparallel" structure of the original wording.

5-4. Ⓐ The original is better than any of the alternatives. All other choices are less direct, create ambiguities, or change the meaning of the original.

5-5. Ⓓ Choice Ⓓ clarifies whose physical examination is in question—Marvin's or the doctor's. Choice Ⓒ is straightforward and concise, also leaving no doubt as to whose examination it is; however, the *doctor* is not mentioned, and because one cannot assume that all physical examinations are administered by a doctor, this information must be included.

6-1. Ⓑ Choice Ⓑ contains the correct verb form *are* for the *neither . . . nor* construction. The verb in this case should be plural to match *friends,* which is the closer of the two subjects to the verb. Choice Ⓓ correctly uses *are* but changes the meaning of the original.

6-2. Ⓓ In the original sentence, the adjective *quick* is used incorrectly to modify an *action,* signing. Actions are modified by adverbs—in this case, *quickly.* This is the only necessary change.

6-3. Ⓒ In order to indicate that participation in the debate precedes voter understanding, the verb *had* must replace *would have.* None of the other choices retains the original meaning clearly and fully.

6-4. Ⓓ Choice Ⓓ correctly states the comparison by adding *those.* The alternative wordings do not clearly express the comparison. Choice Ⓑ is wordy and imprecise, and Ⓒ changes the meaning of the original sentence.

6-5. Ⓔ Choice Ⓔ best simplifies the awkward wording of the original sentence. Choices Ⓒ and Ⓓ change the meaning slightly by eliminating the notion of *consider,* and choice Ⓑ is not idiomatic.

7-1. Ⓒ The original is constructed so that *a train* seems to be *working as an engineer.* Also, the phrase *according to legend* repeats information supplied later in the sentence. Choice Ⓒ is both economical and clearly constructed.

7-2. Ⓐ The original wording is the best expression of this idea. Choice Ⓔ changes the meaning slightly. The other choices are either stylistically awkward or ungrammatical.

7-3. Ⓒ The original is extremely wordy, filled with repetitious phrases (for instance, *understanding . . . with comprehension* and *class members . . . were students*). All choices except Ⓒ retain some of the original wordiness or are grammatically unacceptable.

7-4. Ⓑ Two major errors weaken the original. (1) Faulty parallelism—*enjoying the beauty* is not parallel in structure with *clarity* and *brilliance.* (2) Vague wordiness—*and along with it* might suggest that the diamond and the painting are being perceived together, but the more logical meaning is that they are phenomena that are generally similar to one another. Ⓑ is syntactically and logically correct and retains the intended meaning of the original.

7-5. Ⓔ *Either* is misplaced in the original so that it does not refer to *voices* as well as *acting.* Ⓔ corrects this error, eliminates the repetitious term *speaking,* and changes *consisted of* to *was* to produce a more economical, parallel structure.

8-1. Ⓓ Choices Ⓑ and Ⓔ are contradicted by the passage, and the passage does not support the probability of Ⓐ or Ⓒ. Choice Ⓓ is reasonable, plausible, and probable, given the information in the passage.

8-2. Ⓓ The commercial either explicitly states or implies all but Ⓓ. It makes no reference to how long it will take to fall asleep or how quickly the drug works. It does, however, claim to provide a restful, good night's sleep, with added energy and no aftereffects the next morning.

8-3. Ⓓ The passage sets up the thesis that sometimes individuals yield to others' interests. Choices Ⓐ and Ⓔ are unsubstantiated or not mentioned in the passage; Ⓒ does not fit the structure of the sentence; Ⓑ could possibly be the correct answer, but Ⓓ more nearly completes the thought of the passage and is neatly juxtaposed with the first part of the incomplete sentence.

8-4. Ⓒ The transitional word *nevertheless* establishes a juxtaposition of the phrases immediately before and after it. Therefore, Ⓐ and Ⓑ are incorrect. Choice Ⓓ may be a good answer, but Ⓒ is better, as it addresses a concern initially introduced in the paragraph and brings the passage full circle.

8-5. Ⓒ Geographic location and employment status are irrelevant issues, so Ⓐ and Ⓑ should be eliminated. Ⓓ and Ⓔ are too general and vague. Only Ⓒ makes explicit the point of the author's argument, that interpretation of the Texas law is arrogant and unsound.

9. Ⓑ Demand, as economists use the word, requires the relationship between price and the quantity demanded to remain unchanged. In both I and III the price has changed, rising in III and falling in I.

10. Ⓐ Initially, the passage emphasizes a distinction between *demand* and *quantity demanded,* concluding that *demand shifts when there is a change in income, expectations, taste, etc., such that a different quantity of the good is demanded at the same price.* This statement fits Ⓐ precisely. All other choices include or allow for a changing price.

11. Ⓒ This situation establishes a relationship between price and quantity that parallels the paragraph's explanation of the *law of demand.* This section discusses *the consumer's desire to get the "best buy"* and goes on to say that *if the price of good A increases, the individual will tend to substitute another good*

and purchase less of good A. Since the appearance of a lower-priced breakfast drink makes orange juice more "expensive" in relation, the law of demand as so described would prevail.

12. Ⓐ The passage defines a number of important economic terms. Though it does question a popular misunderstanding Ⓔ, it does so only in the first paragraph. The passage does not deal with supply Ⓑ or marketing Ⓓ.

13-1. Ⓓ The letter fails to note that the decision concerns *officers,* and Smith and Krunkle have been merely nominated to be officers and are not yet such. The other choices are either not stated in the letter or are not essential to the argument.

13-2. Ⓐ This question draws from a simple, explicit statement: *Socrates believed . . . that evil is fundamentally ignorance.* Each of the other choices is an unwarranted complication or extension of this statement.

13-3. Ⓔ Answers Ⓑ, Ⓒ, and Ⓓ are only partial descriptions and, although they may be correct, are not as complete a description of possible future action as answer Ⓔ. Nothing in the letter would imply the action stated in Ⓐ.

13-4. Ⓒ All race-car lovers enjoy classical music. Since there are no backgammon players who enjoy classical music, then none of the backgammon players are race-car lovers. Ⓓ is false because the third statement does not necessarily exclude those who don't enjoy classical music from enjoying fine wine.

13-5. Ⓓ Only this choice both represents a *strong* point *and* is not contradictory. Ⓐ, Ⓒ, and Ⓔ contradict the argument, and Ⓑ is not a relatively strong point.

14-1. ⓓ Since no blue-eyed swimmer is an Olympic winner, then no blue-eyed swimmer may be a freestyle swimmer, since *all* freestyle swimmers are Olympic winners. ⓑ and ⓔ are false because they exclude other possibilities that may, in fact, exist.

14-2. ⓔ The researcher concluded that women could be just as capable as men in math but that they develop other abilities because of social pressures. Thus, the researcher assumes that women do conform to social expectations.

14-3. ⓔ Choices ⓐ, ⓒ, and ⓓ are irrelevant to the argument, and ⓑ actually strengthens the argument. ⓔ suggests that the evidence from one year cannot reliably predict a long-term trend.

14-4. ⓔ This is implied in the final sentence. Each of the other choices requires assumptions or beliefs extraneous to the passage.

14-5. ⓓ The argument presupposes both that candidates are spending too much on television advertising (*the waste*) and that television can be used to inform the public (*provide air time to all candidates to debate the issues*). Statement III is irrelevant to the argument.

15-1. ⓔ The correct pronoun in this case is *who,* the subject of *betrayed.*

15-2. ⓑ Choice ⓑ is correct because it is both concise and clear. The other choices are ambiguous or unnecessarily change the past tense of the original to the present tense. Choice ⓓ is a less direct, more wordy way to express what choice ⓑ does more concisely.

15-3. ⓐ The original is more correct, clear, and logical than any of the other choices.

15-4. Ⓓ Choice Ⓓ supplies the correct verb form *had witnessed* called for by the original sentence.

15-5. Ⓔ The original suggests that she failed the fifth grade possibly because of her father's shaking. Ⓑ is clearer in this respect but repetitious with its use of both *recounting* and *recounted*. Choice Ⓔ is the clearest and most economical of the choices. The fact that such an experience would be painful is obvious, and since the experience happened in fifth grade, it is clearly a childhood experience. The sentence is not harmed by the lack of these details.

16-1. Ⓒ *Granting the returned money during June* is repetitious, and of the choices offered, Ⓒ is the clearest and most economical expression.

16-2. Ⓒ With the semicolon, the second part of the original sentence is a fragment; so are choices Ⓑ, Ⓓ, and Ⓔ.

16-3. Ⓒ The original is flawed by faulty parallelism. *Planning* is not parallel to *to pursue* (the former a gerund, the latter an infinitive). Choice Ⓒ corrects this problem; *planning* is parallel to *pursuing.*

16-4. Ⓑ The original contains two errors. *After having read* is redundant (*having read* already contains the *after* meaning), and *laying* (which means *putting*) is incorrect (*lying* is correct).

16-5. Ⓒ The original is not the best choice here because it is not as economical and clear as Ⓒ. Each of the other choices is either too wordy, vague, or illogical.

17-1. Ⓓ Both errors in the original result from a confusion of adjectives and adverbs. *Seriously,* an adverb, correctly modifies the verb *took; hard,* used as an adverb meaning *with strength,* correctly modifies *punched.* Choices Ⓑ, Ⓒ, and Ⓔ significantly change the meaning of the original.

17-2. Ⓐ The original is better than any of the alternatives.

17-3. Ⓓ *From the stands,* in the original, is a misplaced modifier suggesting that the players made the touchdown from the stands, which is impossible. Choice Ⓔ leaves *crowd* out of the sentence (a significant omission), and all other choices except Ⓓ contain misplaced modifiers.

17-4. Ⓑ The original contains two important errors. *Overtime* and *past regular hours* are repetitious, and *comply to this* is both vague and nonidiomatic. Choice Ⓑ corrects both of these weaknesses. Ⓓ is a correct expression but retains the vague pronoun *this,* which possibly refers to either the contract or the overtime.

17-5. Ⓐ The original is correct. The sentence abbreviates "She likes everyone as much as *she likes* him." All other choices are either ungrammatical or change the meaning of the sentence.

18. Ⓔ Though the passage alludes to the advantage of one method, the excerpt as a whole is concerned with describing several methods used to count bacteria.

19. Ⓑ Though some methods count both living and dead cells, one method that is described counts only living cells.

20. Ⓐ If we know the total volume of the bacteria cells and the volume of one cell, we can divide the former by the latter to determine the total number of cells.

21. Ⓓ The passage is too advanced for options Ⓑ or Ⓒ but not so technical as we would expect for advanced students Ⓐ. The subject of the passage is not mathematics Ⓔ.

22-1. Ⓑ *To question* is not parallel with *remaining;* only Ⓑ corrects this problem.

22-2. Ⓓ The original contains two errors. *Varies* does not agree with the plural subject, *opinions,* and *according with* is not idiomatic. Ⓒ is a correct phrase but changes and obscures the meaning of the sentence.

22-3. Ⓔ The introductory phrase is a dangling modifier, corrected by following *freeze* with *the Cabinet minister* to make clear to whom the introductory phrase refers. Choice Ⓓ is not best because *but unharmed* is left in an awkward position.

22-4. Ⓒ The original contains two errors. *It* suggests that the meeting, not the members, does the considering, and *had considered* is a verb tense simultaneous with *had left* and does not indicate that considering the tax cut occurred after the visitors had left. Choice Ⓓ is unnecessarily wordy and leaves unsaid who did the considering.

22-5. Ⓓ The introductory phrase is a dangling modifier, making it seem as if the *women* did not gain legislative approval. Only choice Ⓓ both clarifies the relationship between the Equal Rights Amendment and legislative approval and indicates that the failure of the amendment precedes the protests logically and chronologically.

23-1. Ⓐ The original is better than any of the alternatives.

23-2. Ⓑ *Is when* is not acceptable because *gerrymandering* is not a time; choice Ⓔ repeats this error. Ⓓ is not best because it leaves vague whether gerrymandering is synonymous with unfair division. Ⓒ is very general and vague.

23-3. Ⓒ Choice Ⓒ best corrects the awkward wording in the original sentence. Choice Ⓓ, although grammatically correct, changes the meaning of the original.

23-4. Ⓓ The pronoun *they* is not used clearly in the original; it is illogical to conclude that *they* refers to *distinguished performances* because all performances are *new to the screen.* (Each performance is done only once even though it may be shown many times.) New *performers* (as opposed to veteran actors) may be new to the screen, however, and the use of *actors* in choice Ⓓ provides this clear, logical reference.

23-5. Ⓔ The conventions of standard written English dictate that *but also* be preceded by *not only,* which is not the case in the original here. Additionally, the underlined portion illogically compares *appearance* to *other pigs* and relies on a vague, wordy phrase, *with reference to the belief.* Choice Ⓔ remedies all of these problems by simplifying the structure and clarifying the diction. Ⓑ is not a good choice because it employs the past tense. The original is in present tense, and there is no reason to change it because present tense is appropriate when one discusses "timeless" works of art and literature.

24-1. Ⓑ *Having finished* expresses the past tense by itself, so *after* is repetitious (its meaning is already implied in *having finished*). None of the other choices expresses the past tense both economically and clearly.

24-2. Ⓓ *Supposes* is not the correct verb tense; in order to be parallel with *to mistake,* the verb in the underlined portion must also connect idiomatically with *to. Suspect* is the only possible choice.

24-3. Ⓑ The original is flawed by faulty parallelism. *Fearless* is not parallel to *having great skill.* Choice Ⓑ corrects this problem. *Fearless* is parallel to *skillful.* Ⓒ and Ⓔ are both unnecessarily wordy.

24-4. Ⓓ In the original, the verb *were* does not agree with the subject, *type.* Ⓑ is incorrect because it uses the plural *products* with *a.* Ⓔ is incorrect because it results in a sentence fragment. Ⓓ is an economical and clear choice that retains the meaning of the original.

24-5. Ⓔ The original sentence contains a subtle error in faulty parallelism. the items compared—*success in school* and *playing marbles*—become parallel if *success* is changed to *succeeding*. Ⓔ makes this necessary change and also brings the compared items closer together in order to further clarify their relationship.

25-1. Ⓓ The paragraph implies the importance of articulation disorders by mentioning how heavily they contribute to a clinician's caseload.

25-2. Ⓐ Bacon advocates retaining dignity without intruding upon liberty. The author implies that retaining dignity is impossible without intruding upon another's liberty by stating that not intruding upon liberty is impossible. Ⓑ, Ⓒ, and Ⓓ contradict the author's argument, and Ⓔ presents an irrelevant issue.

25-3. Ⓑ II only. The only reasonable completion of the argument would be that the alkalies in Lake Huron may be insufficient to support *Alpha splendes*.

25-4. Ⓒ I and II only. The author both relies on an interpretation of Bacon's statement and discusses liberty and dignity in absolute terms; I and II subvert such reliance. III supports, reiterates in fact, the author's argument.

25-5. Ⓑ III only. The same word may have more than one meaning, each of which may be completely different from the others. In this case, the word *ball* means two different things.

26-1. Ⓔ Flamo Lighters claim to be convenient (*in your pocket wherever you go*), have longevity (*ten-year guarantee*), be winter-proof (*all-weather*), and be dependable (*always reliable, always dependable*). They do not profess to be all-purpose, however.

26-2.   Ⓐ The final statement that elders believed to possess special powers are *sometimes treated with a deference based on fear rather than love* assumes that deference is normally accorded based on love.

26-3.   Ⓔ Choices Ⓐ and Ⓑ are not implied; they are explicitly stated. Ⓒ is vague; the meaning of *consequentiality* is not clear. Ⓓ is incorrect because the author is arguing that doing nothing has no consequences. Choice Ⓔ is correct. This author says that doing nothing keeps us safe from consequences; this could be true only in light of the implication that doing nothing is not an act.

26-4.   Ⓑ According to the author, the alternative to experiencing consequences is playing it *safe*. This can mean only that consequences are dangerous.

26-5.   Ⓓ *Evolution* is to *species* in the same way as *bush* is to *branches*. Just as the branches of a bush reach out every which way in varying lengths, the results of evolution (forms of life, species) have developed in irregular "branches." This is the main point of the paragraph.

27.   Ⓓ Shark study has been slowed because the sharks are so dangerous and live in murky waters.

28.   Ⓓ All organisms have a bioelectric field, so the male shark would be able to find many sharks more easily than one. They congregate to make it more difficult for the male to grasp one, not to make detection more difficult.

29.   Ⓒ The *third eye* is the light-gathering organ.

30.   Ⓑ The sharks' sensing the voltage created by currents moving through the earth's magnetic field is at least tangentially relevant to choice Ⓑ.

31-1. Ⓑ Choice Ⓑ eliminates the *irregardless* of the original wording. *Irregardless* is incorrect in standard written English. Choices Ⓒ and Ⓓ change the original meaning slightly and are therefore wrong. Choice Ⓔ is not idiomatic.

31-2. Ⓐ Choice Ⓑ is a dangling phrase. Choice Ⓒ is wordy and changes the meaning. Choice Ⓓ has a misplaced modifier (*complete*), and choice Ⓔ has no grammatical subject.

31-3. Ⓒ The verb in this sentence should be *is* (not *are*) to agree with the singular subject, *actor.* A parenthetical phrase enclosed by commas and beginning with words such as *along with, including,* and *as well as* changes the number of neither the subject nor the verb. Choice Ⓑ correctly uses *are* because the subject in this sentence has been made plural; however, the construction is awkward and wordy. Choice Ⓓ retains the incorrect *are* and changes the meaning of the sentence. Ⓔ leaves out the fact that the actor is on the train.

31-4. Ⓒ The original contains two errors: *principle* (fundamental truth) is incorrect usage, and *reason . . . was because* is a redundant phrase. Only choice Ⓒ corrects both of these errors and retains the full meaning of the original.

31-5. Ⓓ *Continually* is a squinting modifier, unclear because it may refer to either *reading* or *reminds.* Choice Ⓓ clarifies its reference. Choice Ⓔ is vague and wordy.

32-1. Ⓓ A misplaced modifier here makes it seem that liberal activists had *the power to destroy the world.* Choice Ⓓ logically links nuclear weapons with the power to destroy the world. Although choice Ⓑ is somewhat clearer than the original, it creates a clause incompatible with the rest of the sentence.

32-2. Ⓔ Choice Ⓔ corrects the "disjointed" wording of the original sentence.

478 ANSWERS AND EXPLANATIONS FOR THE PRACTICE TEST

32-3. Ⓑ When subjects are connected with *nor* or *or,* the verb is governed by the subject closest to it; in Ⓐ and Ⓓ, the closer subject does not agree with the verb. Ⓔ is awkward. In Ⓑ, the subject, *director,* agrees with the verb, *predicts.*

32-4. Ⓑ The introductory phrase is a dangling modifier and makes the sentence seem to say that the poetry is composing at the keyboard. Choice Ⓑ makes it clear that the poets do the composing and does so without significantly altering the meaning of the original.

32-5. Ⓔ Choice Ⓔ correctly states *his joining.* The possessive *his* is called for here before the *-ing* verb form *joining.* Choice Ⓓ, while grammatically correct, slightly alters the meaning of the original sentence.

33-1. Ⓐ All of the other choices are much less relevant than the issue of how efficiently and effectively the program helps students to achieve competency.

33-2. Ⓐ Only this choice necessarily introduces a contrasting statement, one which would probably take issue with the points of the argument. Ⓒ and Ⓓ might possibly begin critical, contrasting statements but may have other uses as well.

33-3. Ⓑ This suggests that exterior forces, such as advertising, influence consumer choices and undercuts the contention that consumers know what they want. Each of the other choices is either irrelevant or strengthens rather than weakens the argument.

33-4. Ⓒ Voltaire's statement shows the irony that the descriptive word used (*common*) may not, in reality, be so. Likewise, the adjective describing the shrimp (*jumbo*) indicates that the shrimp are large; this may not be the case.

33-5. Ⓔ Choices Ⓐ and Ⓑ are irrelevant to the argument, and Ⓓ is an illogical criticism. Ⓔ is a logical conclusion that poses a significant problem.

34-1. Ⓒ The student's qualification shows that he or she doubts whether the senator's statement is absolutely true, but the response is not so pronounced as to suggest any of the other choices.

34-2. Ⓑ The first speaker puts forth a "perfect" view of friendship (idealistic), and the second questions the endurance of friendship (cynicism).

34-3. Ⓓ I and III. Neither consumers nor legal loopholes are mentioned in the statement.

34-4. Ⓒ If no speech that presents one or more facts is uninformative, any and every uninformative speech must present no facts.

34-5. Ⓔ Since all speeches intended to persuade contain few or all facts, such a speech cannot be uninformative, since an uninformative speech is *factless*.

35. Ⓔ Though parts of the passage would support the ideas of Ⓐ, Ⓒ, or Ⓓ, the best answer here is Ⓔ. In questions about the "purpose" of a passage, the best answers apply to almost all of the excerpt, not to just one paragraph.

36. Ⓐ The rhetorical purpose is its function in the development of the argument. Though some feel the GNP ought to include the work described in the third paragraph, the author takes no stand. In any case, II is not a rhetorical purpose. III is inaccurate.

37. Ⓑ Choices Ⓐ, Ⓒ, Ⓓ, and Ⓔ are all listed or implied as growth factors in the passage (end of the last paragraph).

38. Ⓓ The GNP does not include *productive but unpaid work*. But a salaried stock broker would be paid for time spent doing research.

39-1. Ⓓ In the original, the subject, *shopper*, does not agree with the verb, *tend*. Choice Ⓓ corrects this error without making additional, unnecessary changes.

39-2. Ⓐ The original is perfectly clear and correct, and none of the other choices is an improvement.

39-3. Ⓓ Choice Ⓓ provides the parallel structure needed in this sentence for the three ideas stated in a series. The other choices are structurally wrong or alter the original meaning.

39-4. Ⓒ Choice Ⓒ clarifies the ambiguous wording of the original sentence. It is clear in Ⓒ who is arriving and who is doing the meeting.

39-5. Ⓐ Of the choices given, the original is the best phrasing. The commas in choice Ⓑ change the meaning of the original by making the phrase nonrestrictive. In Ⓒ, *graduated high school* is not acceptable standard written English. Choice Ⓓ is awkward, and Ⓔ changes the meaning of the sentence.

40-1. Ⓓ The verb *lying* (resting—lie, lay, lain) is correct here; *laying* (placing—lay, laid, laid) takes an object.

40-2. Ⓔ Choice Ⓔ is the most direct, concise wording of the original sentence. The verbs in these answer choices are the problem areas. Choice Ⓑ, for example, is incorrect because of the present tense *is* and *attracts*.

40-3. Ⓑ Choice Ⓑ corrects the verb problem in the original sentence. *Have and will continue to include* is better expressed as *have included and will continue to include*.

40-4. Ⓒ Choice Ⓒ supplies the correct verb for this sentence, *would*. The other choices either introduce additional errors or change the original meaning.

40-5. Ⓔ Choice Ⓔ eliminates the *but* in the original wording and supplies the correct punctuation for the *which* clause, needing commas to set it off from the rest of this sentence.

41-1. Ⓒ The passage establishes that the survivors were caught in a life and death "survival" situation. While Ⓑ may be a possible choice, answer Ⓒ logically follows the sense of their dilemma, clouded by uncertainty and the possibility of death.

41-2. Ⓔ This choice raises the question relevant to establishing the mural as art in Aristotelian terms.

41-3. Ⓑ The conclusion that highway deaths will be reduced with the advent of automatic restraints is necessarily based upon the assumption that such restraints reduce highway deaths. None of the other choices focuses on the conclusion; Ⓔ is an assumption which could motivate the passage as a whole, rather than just the conclusion.

41-4. Ⓒ Each of the other choices requires assumptions and conclusions not supported or implied by the argument. The stress in the argument on reduced funds leads logically to the conclusion that further spending is unwise.

41-5. Ⓔ This choice weakens the point made by the final observation. Each of the other choices either strengthen points made by the observation or are irrelevant.

FINAL PREPARATION: "THE FINAL TOUCHES"

Before the Exam

1. Spend the last week of preparation primarily on reviewing already completed problems, some basic skills, strategies, techniques, and directions for each area.

2. Carefully review the sections on taking the GMAT CAT and the general strategies.

3. Do a quick review of each of the question types and the specific strategies.

4. Don't cram the night before the exam. It's a waste of time.

5. Make sure that you are familiar with the testing center location and nearby parking facilities.

At the Exam

6. Arrive at the exam location and check in at least 30 minutes before your scheduled testing time.

7. Remember to bring a valid photo-bearing ID, your score recipient information, your authorization voucher (if you requested one from ETS), and a few pencils to the exam.

8. Guess if a problem is too difficult or takes too much time. If possible, try to eliminate one or more of the answer choices before guessing.

9. Take advantage of having the scratch paper. Do calculations, redraw diagrams, note eliminated choices, or simply make helpful notes.

10. Make sure that you are answering "what is being asked" and that your answer is reasonable.